The killer
they called
a god

By Ian Ward

MEDIA MASTERS
SINGAPORE

Published by Media Masters Publishers.
Cover & Design by O'Art Creative, Singapore.
Printed by C.O.S. Printers Pte Ltd, Singapore.

First published December 1992
1st reprint March 1993
2nd reprint October 1996

Media Masters Pte Ltd
Newton Road PO Box 272
Singapore 912210
Fax: (65) 484-2559

ISBN   981-00-3921-2

Acknowledgements

I wish to record my gratitude to Professor Michael Leifer, of the London School of Economics, Dr. John Pritchard, of Kings College, London, Mr John Taylor, of the Modern Military Branch, US National Archives, Washington D.C., Mr. Edward J. Boone, Jr., archivist at the MacArthur Memorial, Newport, Virginia, USA, and the staff of the Public Record Office, Kew, London, whose expertise, guidance and patience at various stages of the research for this book provided me such a wealth of leads and ideas to pursue.

To Mr Joseph Cusselle and Mr Richard Crewdson who travelled from London to Singapore and shared with me their personal recollections as witnesses to vital segments of these quite extraordinary events, my heartfelt thanks.

I am indebted to Hong Kong-based Mr. Kevin Sinclair, a fellow writer and friend of many years standing. When I drew blanks, Kevin, as is his style, came to the rescue with precise details of long-forgotten events.

I must also acknowledge the invaluable contribution made by my researcher in Japan, the Australian journalist, Mr Cameron Hay. His disciplined enthusiasm and tact in handling what were clearly delicate enquiries, together with his commitment to accuracy, have been important elements of our research effort.

And, finally, I salute my editor and wife, Norma Miraflor, who has been involved in every phase of this project.

Ian Ward
Singapore
October, 1992

About the author

Ian Ward was South East Asian correspondent for the Daily Telegraph, London, from 1962 to 1987. He spent a large part of these 25 years as a war correspondent covering regional conflicts. He resides with his wife in Singapore.

Photo credits:

Contents

To Mrs Elizabeth Choy,
who survived,
and to the thousands who didn't.

Chapter 1

A witness returns

———— ✦ ————

The early morning sun danced off the harbour waters and threw jagged shafts of light against the white walls of Sentosa Island's pristine arrival concourse. Somewhere in the bowels of the *Sea Emperor*, the rumbling diesel engine that had powered the ferry across the brief expanse of water from Singapore's Tanjong Pagar docklands growled into reverse. With the first run of the day sliding neatly into position beside Sentosa's berthing pontoon, lines snapped into place around bollards and the ferry's safety door slid open.

Normally, a surge of tourists, bedecked in a fruit-salad of colours and chattering in a dozen languages, would have disgorged across the pontoon, up the steel companionway and down the concourse proper to the entrance gate. But it was too early for the tourist traffic. It was even too early for the regular stream of Japanese expatriate businessmen who, with their state-of-the-art golf clubs and buggies, have become a feature of the Keppel Harbour ferry scene. Daily, they beat determined paths to expensive communions with nature on the resort island's manicured fairways.

A group of Sentosa Development Corporation cleaners — three Chinese, a couple of Indians and four or five Malays — was all that stepped from the *Sea Emperor* this trip. They sauntered off down the concourse to be swallowed up by the nearby mass of offices, nerve-centre of the pleasure-island's attractions.

The solitary figure in spotless white trousers, matching bush-jacket, and well polished leather shoes, waiting just inside the entrance gate, could have been mistaken for a Sentosa staffer at his official welcoming post. But a closer look at the slim man would have undermined such hasty assumption. His was a ruddy European skin, unbattered by the harsh equatorial sun. A shock of white hair neatly framed an open, friendly face.

"I'm Joe Cusselle," the stranger smiled, stepping forward. His handshake was strong; his voice, soft and modulated with just a hint of Cockney origins. He wore the effects of jet-lag rather well. It had been a tiring flight to Singapore the day before, made all the more arduous by a delayed departure from London's Heathrow Airport.

But tiredness was not an issue. Joe was anxious to get moving. The stride and purpose of the man belied his 71 years. It was as though he had resolved to let instinct direct him back half a century to that horror-filled corner on the island he had then known — far more appropriately, it seemed — by its Malay name, Blakang Mati. Translated: "Beyond Death."

As he walked, Joe explained that as long as he kept pressing in an easterly direction along the island, he would find the location. Once he was in the general area he would be able to pinpoint it exactly by the contours of the land. He could never forget those shapes. They were etched deeply in his consciousness; they visited him constantly. They were vivid among the tormenting images of his private hell.

Joe first chose a tourist path that wound through a heavily wooded section and ran towards the island's well signposted Maritime Museum. "I seem to recall this in my day," he said, looking up and focusing on the thick foliage blocking the sun. "It was always so much cooler here."

Joe's mind drifted back There was nothing of note about his early life. Born in the Lambeth area of London on May 30, 1920, he had received a typical working class upbringing. When Britain went to war with Germany, he volunteered for service in the army soon after his nineteenth birthday. A rush of volunteers swamped an already understaffed recruiting system and an interviewing officer had advised Joe it would be simpler for him to go home and await his call-up. This duly came a few months later and he was assigned to the 7th Coastal Artillery Regiment to train as a gunner.

Following a stint on twin six-pounders, Joe soon found himself aboard the merchant ship, *Capetown Castle*, as part of his unit's 11th Battery, bound for Singapore. In the hold of the ship, along with a mass of other military supplies being rushed to the Far East, were the 11th Battery's twin six-pounder guns and spare parts, a collection of search lights, generators and associated communications equipment that had all gone aboard in Glasgow.

Joe had joined up to fight a war for King and country. But as far as he could make out, he was being sent to a remote backwater that seemed blissfully at peace. It made little sense. Still, Joe's short time in the army had taught him the futility of ever applying a private's logic. Instead, he contented himself with deliberating whether his assignment to Singapore might, in the long run, work out to be a stroke of good fortune. After all, he was a young man. Single. Who could tell what surprises the exotic East might hold?

The *Capetown Castle* duly berthed at Tanjong Pagar docks on July 25, 1941. After disembarking, Joe and his fellow artillerymen were driven by military lorries the short distance to Jardine Steps, then the sole terminal for all Blakang Mati traffic. After four or five minutes in a military launch, the new arrivals were soon clambering ashore along Blakang Mati's main wooden jetty. Anxious to create a good first impression, the gunners reformed and marched as smartly as their six-week-old sea legs would allow to the island's main barrack square. There, they were briefly greeted by an officer and shown to their quarters in a long stone building overlooking a football field. In a cavernous room which today houses Sentosa's rare stone collection, Joe was allotted a bunk along with 47 others.

At this point, Joe paused with his recollections. His chosen path had run on past the Maritime Museum and suddenly broken into open ground. Through scattered trees on the left he glimpsed segments of the Singapore Navy's patrol boat base on nearby Pulau Brani. An open gateway in a fence led to a section of the Sentosa Golf Club's admired 18-hole Serapong course.

"If we cut across here to the shoreline, and follow this east, we'll find it," said Joe, looking down a stretch of empty fairway to a bunker position. A Malay groundsman had just begun raking the sand trap in preparation for the first group of early morning golfers. The hint of a breeze drifted across from Pulau Brani as Joe pressed on. He resumed his remembrances.

He recalled how the weapons were assembled and installed in various positions around Blakang Mati. The 9.2 inch guns were concentrated around Connaught Barracks itself, high on the island's commanding hill. The two twin six-pounders which he would help to man went to a specially constructed artillery position located on a small rocky islet off Blakang Mati's north-eastern extremity. The islet was marked on Admiralty charts as Berhala Reping.

From Berhala Reping, Joe and his fellow gunners commanded the eastern entrance to Keppel Harbour. North across a few hundred yards of water lay Singapore's docklands. Beyond this was the railway station and then the downtown business district concentrated around Raffles Place and Collyer Quay. Although he never had a chance to visit them, Joe learned that the cluster of islands he could see south-south-east of his artillery position comprised Kusu, Lazarus and St John's. In the distance to the south-east on a clear day he could also make out Pulau Batam in the Dutch-held Riau Islands group.

The British Army's Berhala Reping artillery post completely enveloped the tiny rocky outcrop on which it had been placed. Thick, reinforced concrete formed the base of the essentially circular position. The two twin six-pounders were embedded on the seaward side, their revolving turrets facing open water to the

Twenty-year-old Private Joseph Cusselle (on the right) poses with a fellow 7th Coastal Artillery Regiment gunner in front of their barrack block on Blakang Mati shortly after their arrival on the island from Britain in July, 1941.

Fifty years later, Joseph Cusselle, retiree, returns to Sentosa to recapture the past . . . . and exorcise its horrors.

east. Immediately behind the guns and driven deep in the bedrock was the thick iron and concrete walled magazine for ammunition storage.

In the centre of the fortification, and also dug into the bedrock was the machine room housing the all-important main generator. This supplied current for the emplacement's powerful searchlights. These, in turn, were manned by a crew of six Indian servicemen. Atop the machineroom was a three-storeyed concrete lookout tower. The lower level served as a general mess room for on-duty gun crews. Above this was the radio room and above this again, the look-out position. To the rear of the position was a guard house. To the right of this house a set of rail tracks ran across an 80-foot long reinforced concrete bridge that linked Berhala Reping to Blakang Mati proper. All stores and ammunition were pushed manually in small trucks across the bridge which, at high tide, spanned a stretch of water some four feet deep. At low water it became an exposed mudbank. From the point where the supply bridge joined the larger island, grubby shorelines of mud, sand and mangrove bushes stretched away at sharp angles on either side. When the tide was running, Berhala Reping seemed at the focal point of a surging water race with currents splitting on its rock face to swirl past into Keppel Harbour, on one side, and down along the southern coast of Blakang Mati, on the other.

Again, Joe's conversation reverted to the present as he crossed a short fairway running alongside the water's edge and saw, un-obstructed, Singapore's renowned container terminal rising against a backdrop of the island city's distinctive skyline.

"What an extraordinary difference 50 years makes," he remarked softly, pausing for a moment to take in the natural pastel seascape of merging blues, greys and greens to the right, and the concrete and glass pillars to progress etched out by the early morning sun on the left.

Then, as if moved by some sudden compulsion to see his mission quickly completed, Joe glanced over his shoulder towards the high ground in the centre of Sentosa. His eyes searched for bearings, his mind for recollections of five decades ago. Just ahead a clump of bunkers marked a point where the coastline swung away to the right, beyond a high point of land.

A note of urgency underscored Joe's observations. "It's four or five hundred yards beyond that hill," he said, adding, as if to convince himself, "I know it is. I can sense it."

Joe's pace quickened as he strode towards the pathway leading up the hill. The climb had him puffing heavily. The descent to the nearest green on the other side was easy. Joe walked around the smooth putting surface and looked east along the 540 metre, par four, 16th hole which hugged the coastline along its entire length.

All reminiscing ceased. Specks of dirt and lawn cuttings clung to his white trouser cuffs and blotches of perspiration stained his jacket as he set off briskly down the fairway.

Just beyond the 16th's tee-off position, Joe crossed a short causeway leading to the 15th green. There he abruptly halted. Immediately in front of him, on the other side of the putting surface and to the right of twin sand bunkers, a dense tropical foliage of trees, vines and palms smothered a hump of earth, sand and rock that projected 10 to 15 feet above the surrounding terrain. The freshly painted, camouflaged facade of a military tower, an unmistakeable World War 11 relic, rose incongruously among the trees, as if directly challenging the peaceful ambience within which it now nestled. Broad-leafed vines wound round the structure's lower stanchions in uncanny natural competition to the painter's art. Further to the rear, and almost completely obscured by the foliage, was the shell of a reinforced concrete building. Beyond a rock face to the left were the gun positions that had been built specially for the twin six pounders five decades earlier.

Joe remained silent, his eyes transfixed on the mound. Then he edged to the right to a point where a now rickety concrete bridge protruded from the mound over one end of a land-locked water hazard. Looking back towards the tower to check bearings once again, Joe began to count thirty paces roughly south from the western end of the bridge. There he paused. Head bowed, Joe Cusselle struggled to control his emotions. When finally he looked up, his eyes brimmed with tears.

"I personally buried 25 or 30 people just here, beneath my feet. All Chinese civilians. All males. All so young," he exclaimed. His voice shook. Walking back the way he had come, Joe paced out a further thirty steps in a general north-westerly direction from the end of the bridge. "And this is where I buried 20 or 30 more. Here, where I'm standing."

Again Joe paused, struggling for words.

"They were so young," he repeated. "Their wounds were so massive . . . . upper bodies and heads . . . . blown apart by machinegun fire."

Joe glanced along the bridge to the concrete ruins of the once small but proud British artillery outpost of Berhala Reping. Reclamation work had engulfed the rocky islet, fusing it within Sentosa's recreational landscape. He found it impossible to reconcile how the scene of such appalling slaughter by the Japanese military fifty years earlier could be relegated to the status of curiosity piece on a playground dominated by a contemporary Japanese business elite. No plaque. No in-scription. Did no one care?

"You know," he confided, quietly, "not a single night has passed for me since then without terrible nightmares . . . . the frightful things I saw here."

P rivate Joseph George Cusselle, of Heathfield Rise, Ruislip, Middlesex, one of the few surviving eye-witnesses to the Japanese massacre of thousands of civilian Chinese in Singapore between February 18 - March 4, 1942, had been compelled to return to the scene of his life-long torment. Perhaps, by confronting Berhala Reping once again, he could

*The British artillery base of Berhala Reping, off Blakang Mati's
north-eastern corner, as it was in 1941. Note the lookout tower
rising among the trees on the left and the bridge linking the rocky
outcrop to Blakang Mati. Beyond are the waters forming the eastern
entrance to Keppel Harbour — the killing waters.*

*Foliage-covered Berhala Reping today. A war relic curiosity piece
amid the tranquillity of Sentosa Island's Serapong golf course. The
tower still rises above the trees and the bridge still spans that short
stretch of water.*

15

exorcise the anguish and fear that always managed to shatter what should have been precious, reflective moments. If nothing else, he owed it to his wife of many years, whom he adored, who had stood by him in good times and bad, at least to try and lay these ghosts to rest.

Gazing across the channel marking the entrance to Keppel Harbour, Joe recalled how he first learned of the British capitulation to the invading Japanese 25th Army commanded by "Tiger of Malaya" General Tomoyuki Yamashita. In the late evening of Sunday, February 15, 1942, the city of Singapore across from Berhala Reping — for weeks the target of intensifying air attacks — went suddenly and eerily quiet. A radio message to the rocky outpost informed the artillery crew of Britain's surrender and commanded them to cease resistance and stand down all weapons. There was one further instruction: remain in place and await further orders, this time from the enemy High Command. As it happened, the Japanese, with so many other matters on their minds, promptly forgot about the lonely British artillery position. What was more, it would be three weeks before someone remembered. The oversight would have horrifying repercussions for Joe and his comrades.

The Berhala Reping soldiers were initially dumbfounded by the surrender. With the exception of low flying Zeros on strafing runs against their gun position, the artillerymen had yet to sight the enemy. Their remote location had kept them largely ignorant of the day-to-day battlefield developments. From routine contacts with Connaught Barracks they gathered the Japanese had made major advances. They had seen, of course, the expanded enemy bombing attacks across the water. Fires had been raging throughout the city. Then there was that pall of oily smoke blanketing the northern reaches of Singapore where the Royal Naval Base's fuel storage tanks, a key target for repeated Japanese air and artillery strikes, had been blazing for days. All these clearly pointed to a tough battlefield situation. But the thought of unconditional capitulation had never entered the artillerymen's minds!

Monday, February 16 was unnerving in its stillness. Tanjong Pagar and the port area across the harbour entrance remained deadly quiet. On Berhala Reping, there was little to do but speculate on the sort of treatment they might expect as prisoners of the Japanese. Stories of brutality by the army from the Land of the Rising Sun abounded. Then someone suggested the entire gunnery crew make a bid to escape that night in the two motorboats kept moored by the bridge for supply runs to Jardine Steps.

Stocks of tinned food and fuel were readied for rapid transfer to the boats when darkness fell. Timing their departure to the night's high tide became critical. The two motor boats, already deep drafted vessels for their size, were being pushed even deeper in the water with the combined weight of men, supplies, and personal weapons. The decision was taken to jettison all weapons in the water beside the Berhala Reping bridge. In the event, one boat made its getaway. The other, to which Joe had been assigned, remained stuck fast on the muddy bottom as the peak of the tide came and went.

Clambering back onto the artillery outpost in the pre-dawn darkness, Joe and the hapless gunners, whose luck had run out that night, resigned themselves to the unsavoury fate of becoming prisoners of war.

Tuesday slid into Wednesday, then Thursday as the remainder of the forgotten gun crew sat and waited. Peak tides were receding and there was never high enough water to float their boat off the bottom. Furthermore, each low tide uncovered the depressing sight of their weapons lying caked in mud beside the bridge where they had been ditched. All further thought of escape was abandoned.

Dawn on Friday broke slate grey, flecked with orange, across a lifeless sea. Joe was up early preparing breakfast from tinned rations stored on the lower level of the look-out tower when a long burst of rapid machingun fire demolished the morning calm. Then another . . . . and another . . . . and another. The artillerymen instinctively dived for cover. They were used to judging distances of weapons firing across open water. The machinegun was reckoned to be about 300 yards away.

Joe called to a gunner he knew to be at the look-out level: "What the hell's going on?"

The look-out peered hesitatingly over the parapet. "Buggered if I can see anything," he shouted back after a pause. "There's a tugboat steaming round in circles about 350 yards due east of here. There's another one leaving the Tanjong Pagar dockside and looks headed for the same area."

By the time Joe and two or three other gunners had climbed to the look-out level, the first tug had been replaced by the second and was now on course back to Tanjong Pagar.

As the British servicemen on Berhala Reping trained their eyes on the second vessel, they glimpsed what they assumed was a package being hurled into the water from its after deck. This was followed by a second package. Then a third. Churning foam at the stern of the tug signalled the vessel was backing up. As the tug became stationary in the water, the air reverberated once again with the growl of automatic fire.

"It's a machinegun in the bows," cried Gunnery Sergeant Quilter. "I can see the muzzle flashes."

The tug had swivelled around in the current so that the floating "packages" were on the far side of the hull and all but obscured from Berhala Reping. But Joe and the others could still clearly see the water spouts and spray as the rounds tore into the target area. "They're shooting at the packages," cried one of the gunners.

Someone suggested that the Japanese were trying to detonate boxes of faulty ammunition. But that didn't make sense. Not in the water.

Three short bursts of rapid fire momentarily set another patch of sea near the tug boiling like a cauldron. Then the vessel turned and headed back to the docks. Throughout the day, the

Close-up view of the Berhala Reping tower, now backdrop to the Serapong course's 15th green.

Oblivious to the history surrounding them, two Japanese women golfers stroll past the Berhala Reping tower and bridge in readiness to hit-off on the 16th tee.

extraordinary actions of the harbour craft became the topic of exhaustive conjecture on Berhala Reping. There seemed no credible explanations for such activity. When the two tugs repeated their curious early morning missions at dawn the next day, the mystery for the artillerymen only deepened . . . as did their personal fears.

The outgoing pre-dawn tide the following day, Sunday, February 22, provided the gunners with the grotesque answer. There in the mud, a few paces south from where the concrete supply bridge ran onto Blakang Mati, lay the bodies of four Chinese youths, bound back to back by their upper arms. Their heads, faces and upper torsos bore fearsome wounds.

Peering through the half-darkness, the artillerymen spotted a second group of bodies lying in the mud on the other side of the bridge. This comprised three youths bound back to back. Again, all had suffered massive wounds from the chest upwards. Another two similarly bound bodies lay a short distance from the second group.

"Good God!" gasped one of the gunners. "Those bastards aren't shooting at packages. They're shooting at people. They're massacring the Chinese!"

A blast of rapid machinegun fire jolted the stunned servicemen to their senses. Another tug was back at the eastern entrance to Keppel Harbour. They watched it, silhouetted against the dawn sky.

Splash . . . one group. Splash . . . .splash . . . . splash. Another three.

The gunners did some ghoulish, mental arithmetic. "Oh, Jesus, that could be anything from twelve to sixteen men," thought Joe as the next cruel snarl of machinegun fire rent the morning air. This time the tug was positioned closer to Berhala Reping. The hapless groups of men could be seen frantically struggling in the water, their heads bobbing up, then disappearing beneath the surface, then thrusting up once more.

Brrrrrrrrrr . . . . *Brrrrrrrrrr* . . . . *Brrrrrrrrrr*. More bursts

A closer view of the bridge from which the Berhala Reping artillerymen attempted their daring escape in two supply boats. It is the same bridge which, fifty years later, served as Joseph Cusselle's primary point of reference for locating where he buried some 50 massacre victims.

of machinegun fire.

Then silence. In the sea, stillness. With propeller blades abruptly churning into life, the tug completed one circle of the area as the executioners surveyed the waters for signs of life. Satisfied, they headed back to the docks. Enroute, the returning tug passed the second vessel steaming eastwards. Crews waved in recognition and in a few minutes the macabre, monstrous dawn ritual was being enacted yet again.

The sea executions continued for eight days. And every high tide brought new groups of dead Chinese men to the stretches of Blakang Mati shoreline running away on both sides of the island from Berhala Reping. And every low tide exposed more of the maniacal handywork of the conquering troops.

Some mornings, the tugs would return to Tanjong Pagar for two or three repeat boatloads comprising anything from three to ten "packages" a time. The surrendered British gunners, forgotten on their outpost by defeated and victorious High Commands alike, sat, members of a mute and petrified audience in their front row seats to the slaughter.

Theirs was an extraordinary predicament. The two twin six pounders on Berhala Reping, at some well chosen time, could easily have intervened and demolished both tugs as they transported their tragic cargo to the killing waters. The idea was agonized over repeatedly. But what was the point? Such intervention would have been suicidal, bringing overwhelming firepower rapidly onto the artillery position.

Moreover, it would have done nothing to help the Chinese. Those trussed up on the decks of the tugs when the bombardment began would either have been killed in the blasts or drowned. Those ashore awaiting their final boatrides would simply have been transferred to replacement vessels. Aside from the humanitarian impassé there were the capitulation orders to consider. The gunners had been instructed by Malaya Command to stand down their arms and surrender. Orders of such import could never be ignored.

In reality, if the forgotten gunners, could have known the extent of the operation being launched throughout Singapore by the Japanese High Command — of which the Keppel Harbour slaughter was but a part — they would have realised the utter hopelessness of Berhala Reping's moral dilemma.

Sgt Quilter, highest ranking soldier left on the outpost, organised burial parties the morning the bodies began coming ashore. He talked of the health hazard. Indian searchlight operators attached to the British unit refused to touch the corpses or have anything to do with their disposal. Joe Cusselle and his friends worked throughout daylight hours. Paramount in their minds was the need to bury the massacred men with as much dignity as possible.

As the bodies had suffered such damage, it was impossible to move them from the mudflats to higher ground. Cutting the restraining bonds, the soldiers buried the dead where they lay, side by side in beach graves 18 inches deep. Any deeper and subterranean water would fill the shallow trenches, making burial impossible.

Fifty years later, Joe shook his head slowly as his eyes followed the contours of the Berhala Reping bridge back to the remains of the concrete guardhouse and the look-out tower cradled in the greenery beyond. Land reclamation for the golf course had pushed back the sea. But the waters that had been his life's nightmare, there at the eastern entrance of the harbour, were just as they had always been for him, ghostly calm. This time there was no snarling machinegun to disturb the stillness.

Minutes passed. Then the frantic cackle of a blue kingfisher, perched nearby, heralded the approach of the day's first golfing party. A jaunty sextet of Japanese business executives, caddies and Louis Vuitton golf bags in tow, approached down the 15th fairway. Stopping opposite the tower, they looked quizzically at the curious structure, then at the nearby bridge. One ventured an observation in a grunted staccato, stabbing a golf club shaft towards the tower to enhance his punchline. His companions guffawed in appreciation and the game moved on.

"It's time to go," said Joe, gently, as he set off to retrace his steps back to Sentosa's ferry wharf, taking particular care to give the Japanese sportsmen a wide berth ■

Chapter 2

Slaughter at Changi Point

———— ◆ ————

A s the first boatload of doomed Chinese made the dawn run to Keppel Harbour's eastern entrance on Friday, February 20, 1942, Wong Sin Joon sat shivering on the floor of the Victoria School's assembly hall, some four miles to the north.

Armed Japanese military guards stood impassively on the hall's four doorways. The hall and school buildings remain intact today, little changed from half a century ago. But the occupancy has switched. What was once Victoria School is today Singapore's Christ Church Secondary campus.

Located on the second storey at the rear of the main school building overlooking Kitchener Road, the hall was large enough to accommodate a badminton court which was marked on the wooden floor boards in white paint. A three-foot high stage, normally used for school assemblies, was located between the two doors at the top end of the auditorium. From here, the guards had an elevated view of the 70 young Chinese men huddled in rows amid the court markings.

This had been Sin Joon's third night under detention. Although desperately tired, he had only managed to snatch fleeting moments of sleep the entire time.

Known more popularly as Leo among his fellows in the Straits Settlements Volunteer Force (SSVF), he wondered whether it was fear, exhaustion, or the cool of the early morning that was making him shake. He decided it was all three, aggravated by severe pangs of hunger as well. He had barely eaten since Tuesday when a number of rifle-toting Japanese troops, wearing armbands, burst into his home at 57 Owen Road, a few blocks away. They had ordered all occupants to report immediately to Jalan Besar between Maud and Syed Alwi Roads.

Heeding Japanese advice to take enough food to last a day or two, Sin Joon, his wife and their young daughter, walked the short distance down Kitchener Road, past the New World Amusement Park. By the time they turned right into normally bustling Jalan Besar, a mixed Chinese and Muslim trading thoroughfare lined with two-storeyed shophouses, it was four o'clock in the afternoon.

Though the street was packed with humanity, the atmosphere was anything but bustling. Thousands of men, women and children, young and old, sat elbow to elbow along the edges of the road, across the five-foot ways, in the doorways of the shophouses and in the lanes leading off on either side. The whole area had been partitioned at various points by lengths of coiled barbed wire. In each sub-divided section, Japanese military men, aided by interpreters and a number of local assistants, pored over sheaves of mimeographed name lists. As they worked, stoney-faced armed guards paced back and forth along the barricades in a calculated show of intimidation. The overwhelming atmosphere of cowed compliance attested to the success of the Japanese tactics.

More people were interned in the nearby Siong Lim Saw Mills and on the Victoria School playing field where hundreds of Chinese families had been forced to camp out in the open. Next door to the school, another contingent of Japanese troops had commandeered the Jalan Besar Football Stadium on Tyrwhitt Road in preparation for an expected overflow of detainees.

Sin Joon and his young family were placed in the already

crammed quarters of a tiny ground floor store in Syed Alwi Road. As darkness fell, cooking became impossible. Water was scarce and the overburdened toilet facilities soon blocked and overflowed. Whether under cover or in the open, conditions progressively worsened. By nightfall, detainees were forced to snatch what sleep they could, sitting cross-legged and leaning against one another for support.

What had triggered this extraordinarily inhuman Japanese operation against Singapore's local Chinese population? How much further would the humiliation go? Sin Joon felt certain the sinister name lists he had seen earlier held the key to Japanese intentions.

Throughout the following day, Saturday, alarming rumours ran back and forth among the desperate families. With every passing hour came heightened tensions. Previous Japanese military atrocities against mainland Chinese were already well documented. Every adult camped along Jalan Besar was fully aware of the invaders' record of brutality in Manchuria and China. Graphic reports of the Rape of Nanking and other atrocities had been widely disseminated by local Kuomintang and Communist organisations since the Japanese invasion of Malaya began 74 days earlier. The aim had been to galvanize anti-Japanese sentiments among the island's 450,000 ideologically divided Chinese. The propaganda effort achieved its purpose by raising the ogre of a frightening common enemy. But it also fuelled intense and widespread fears which were only compounded as Chinese refugees from the fighting in Malaya poured into Singapore, effectively doubling the island's overall population, in eight weeks.

Anxieties along Jalan Besar would ease a little on Saturday afternoon when the Japanese announced that all women and children could return to their homes early next morning.

True to their word, those policing the concentration areas were in place shortly after dawn on Sunday. Women and children were organised in long lines that snaked through the

Two of the very few photographs in existence showing the concentration of Singapore's Chinese population which preceded the massacres. Above: This photograph was taken in the early stages of the operation. Below: An exit gate through which all detainees had to pass. Behind this and other similar tables sat the Japanese soldiers empowered to make decisions on who, among those filing past, would live . . . . and who would die.

various cordoned-off sectors. Promptly at 8 am, segments of the barbed wire entanglements were pulled aside forming exit passages through which the promised release took place. Along with the women and children went the aged men.

But the sense of relief among those set free would be short-lived. The Japanese insisted that all men and boys above the age of 16 years would remain under detention. At this stage the confused public at large could never have foreseen the enormity of the crime about to be perpetrated.

The Japanese army was ready to put in motion a human screening programme prepared months in advance. It was the first stage of a horrifying broader plot to subjugate the island's Chinese. It was personally orchestrated by a mercurial ultranationalist occupying a key position on the 25th Army's High Command. His plot would culminate in one of the worst atrocities of the Pacific theatre. The scheme was so calculatingly devious that, despite its tragic consequences, the truth would remain concealed, and the identity of the real culprit cunningly protected, until today.

In essence, a handful of military thugs were empowered to decide who, among the Chinese males in Singapore, had the right to live or die. Those condemned became immediate targets for faceless firing squads at secret execution grounds specially chosen in remote sections of the island. As the screening began, hundreds of thousands of lives rested precariously on the whims of the obsessed arch-plotter, his small coterie of fanatical conspirators, and the pawns they had positioned to implement the killing orders.

Sin Joon farewelled his wife at the barbed wire barricade and returned to the Syed Alwi shophouse to await developments. Throughout the concentration areas, Japanese soldiers and their interpreters began asking questions. From time to time, references were made to the mimeographed name lists. Some of those detained were being released. Others were being formed into squads and marched away. Early in the afternoon, an SSVF colleague stopped by to inform Sin Joon that the Japanese wanted all volunteers to surrender. Sin Joon was suspicious. He decided to circulate and test the situation more closely for himself..

Near the corner of Syed Alwi Road and Jalan Basar, a local Chinese stood under a white banner. He was publicly requesting anyone who had seen Mr Tan Kah Kee to make himself known to the interrogators. This filled Sin Joon with apprehension.

If the Japanese had wanted to eliminate anyone, it would be Tan Kah Kee. For four years, Tan had headed the region's United China Relief Fund and during this time had been responsible for remitting millions of dollars to the Chungking regime's war coffers. Indeed, he had emerged one of the Kuomintang's prime sources of foreign exchange. In the dramatic days following the Japanese landing in Northern Malaya and Southern Thailand, some fifty leaders of Singapore's notoriously disparate Chinese groups had called on the Governor, Sir Shenton Thomas, pledging loyalty to Britain's prosecution of the war.

As the only one who enjoyed wide support across the local Chinese political spectrum, Tan Kah Kee, tin and rubber wheeler-dealer, a man who had won and lost several fortunes in his time, was seen as the island's only mutually acceptable anti-Japanese figurehead. Under heavy pressure, Tan ultimately accepted the role. Now Tan Kah Kee headed Japan's Singapore hit-list. But Japanese determination to seize Tan would be frustrated. Several days before the final siege of Singapore began, the businessman and his family had departed for Sumatra, spirited out by British military intelligence. Not even his closest friends knew his whereabouts.

Sin Joon mingled with the crowd and surreptitiously approached one or two of the locals working with what he now recognised as the organising unit, the infamous kempeitai or military police. He was trying to size up Japanese intentions.

Tan Kah Kee, businessman, prominent member of Singapore's Chinese community and collector of funds for Chungking. Tan was the man most wanted for elimination by the Japanese.

They wanted all Chinese members of volunteer services to come forward, identify themselves and surrender. In return, those who gave themselves up were assured they would have a pass to go home and, ultimately, a job. There was an urgent requirement for law and order, explained the interpreters, and as the volunteers had undergone training with the British, they were admirably qualified for police and related work.

The alternative was bluntly presented. Should volunteers fail to respond to the offer, they would, within three days, be rounded up and executed by firing squads. Sin Joon held deep reservations about the Japanese assurances. What did they mean by "volunteers?" His unit was but one of several that could be so classified. There was its Malayan counterpart, the Federated Malay States Volunteer Force (FMSVF). There was also the clandestine guerrilla unit codenamed Dalforce, comprising largely Singapore communists who had gained freedom from prison sentences in return for their services under arms against the Japanese. Then there were all the civil defence volunteer organisations; the Air Raid Protection (ARP) wardens, the volunteer fire fighters, the ambulance drivers, stretcher bearers and hospital orderlies. The list went on; all were volunteers. If the Japanese meant what they were saying, they were looking to recruit a huge police force. It didn't add up.

Sin Joon went in search of his volunteer friends, Corporal Chia Tiang Bee and Corporal Koh Jiak Yong. He located them later in the afternoon. Both warned Sin Joon against declaring himself and asked him to accompany them while they investigated the Japanese offer further.

Together the three men sought the views of other detained SSVF members. Nearing the exit gate of their Jalan Besar concentration centre, they saw a crowd of people, some of them volunteers, submitting names and addresses. Much to their surprise, they recognised the man taking down the particulars. He had been a member of the SSVF's E Company, their old unit. Furthermore, they also saw one of their officers, a Chinese lieutenant, supervising those who had already identified themselves.

As they continued to observe from the sidelines, a batch of civilians were released from detention with pass marks stamped on the palms of their right hands. Encouraged by this, the three friends decided to try their luck in the queue. As they progressed up the line and neared the gate, Sin Joon heard someone exclaim in Chinese : "There they are!"

Immediately, the three were brought before the kempeitai soldier in charge. Beside him stood the SSVF lieutenant. The lieutenant assured them in Chinese that they had nothing to fear and that he would take care of them. Together with a number of other volunteers, and a batch of civilians, they were formed into two lines and marched off to the nearby Victoria School compound. There they were directed down the side of the grey concrete and brick building to a pair of stairways at the rear leading up to the assembly hall. As he climbed the stairs, a cold chill of realisation gripped Sin Joon. Instinctively he knew he had made a terrible mistake by identifying himself. He thought of his wife and young daughter. He wondered how they were and, more pointedly, whether he would ever see them again. Before nightfall, the Chinese lieutenant walked into the hall and asked everyone to provide their names and addresses once more. He needed accurate records, or so he claimed. That was the last anyone saw of the lieutenant.

In the half light of the early Sunday morning, Sin Joon spotted his two friends, Tiang Bee and Jiak Yong, towards the back of the assembly hall. Both looked tired and frightened. Then he recognised Private John Peter Tan, also an SSVF member. There were several other volunteers and civilians he knew by sight. He was taken aback by the number of teenagers that had been singled out. What could the Japanese possibly gain by incarcerating so many children?

Around 3 pm, three lorries and a private car pulled up in the school's driveway. From one of the lorries tumbled a

The backstairs leading to the former Victoria School assembly hall. Today a library for pupils of Singapore's Christ Church Secondary School, the second storey hall in late February, 1942, was utilised by the Japanese kempeitai as an overnight holding area for Chinese men and youths selected for execution.

The field in front of the former Victoria School, commandeered as a central holding area by the kempeitai officer in charge of the Jalan Besar screening programme.

detachment of Japanese troops armed with light machineguns. The soldiers hustled the detainees into two rows of 35 men each. They then began tying the prisoners' hands behind their backs and leading them, one by one, to the empty lorries.

With the human cargo spread evenly across the three vehicles and with military guards posted, two at the front and four at the rear of each load, the tragic convoy, led by the private car, drove out of the school grounds. It turned into Lavender Street, then into Kallang Road and finally bumped and rattled its way along the main route to Changi at the north eastern corner of the island.

Perhaps they were being taken to Changi Jail, thought Sin Joon hopefully, as the lorries approached the forbidding high walls of the penitentiary. As the jail facade slid past on the right hand side of the convoy, then Selarang Barracks' main gate on the left, the bewildered prisoners finally realised their fate. They were being driven to their execution.

The road swung to the right through a wooded area, left across some undulating terrain and then set off on a final straight run to the jumble of rusty corrugated iron shops and attap kampong huts that comprised Changi Village. Before reaching the village, the convoy passed through a section that was obviously part of a prisoner of war camp. European soldiers in fatigues looked up as the lorries passed. The convoy veered to the right and lurched to a stop near the Customs House on the banks of Changi Creek. All prisoners were ordered down from the vehicles. Those in the first lorry-load were taken into the Customs House, searched and relieved of all possessions. Gold rings, cash, watches, pens and other personal articles were dumped on a table.

Pressed for time, the Japanese decided to dispense with searching the remaining two batches. Instead, they herded all prisoners together and, at gun point, ordered them to walk to the beach on the far side of the spit of land separating — as it still does today — Changi Creek from the sea.

As they neared the sand, the prisoners caught their first sight of the firing squad, lying prone in prepared positions, facing the water . . . . waiting.

Sin Joon went rigid. His legs felt as though they'd turned to blocks of ice. Others in the group began wailing. The younger ones were crying out for their mothers and fathers. Sin Joon found himself crying too but somehow couldn't shed tears. The column of prisoners jerked to a standstill, paralysed with fear. Japanese guards moved in wielding rifle butts, jabbing and swiping. Relentlessly, they drove the prisoners to the water's edge and re-arranged them into two lines, 35 in each, both facing the firing squad.

Sin Joon just had time for one last glance at the executioners. Machinegunners were positioned on the left and the right. In the middle were the bren-gunners. A small, burly Japanese officer barked an order. Instantly, the prone marksmen opened up, raking their weapons back and forth in deadly crossfire over the two pitiful human rows.

As the bullets tore into their targets, men and boys crumpled and fell. Some, spun by the velocity of the rounds, were hurled backwards. Within minutes the beach was littered with bloody corpses. Then the incoming tide began lapping around the bodies and the shallows turned crimson.

Two or three shots struck Sin Joon before he toppled, face downwards, onto the sand. Miraculously, he was still alive when the firing ceased. He dared not move. Holding his breath, he feigned death until his head was reeling. The water was seeping into his mouth and nose. Unable to hold any longer, he spluttered and gulped in several lungfuls of air.

Machineguns burst into action once again and bullets impacted all around him. Another two or three tore into his body and he cried out as searing pain shot up his left side. I'm finished, he thought. But he was wrong. Sin Joon, hit six times, was not only alive but he remained conscious. With extraordinary self control, he gathered his thoughts and resolved to lie absolutely still without breathing for just as long as he could. Once again, the firing ceased and then Sin Joon thought he heard the faint beating of a lone drum.

He waited. Silence. Gradually, he raised his head. Half-dazed and in terrible pain, he looked around. The executioners had left the beach. Only a foot or two from where he lay were the bullet-riddled bodies of his friends Tiang Bee and John Tan.

Sin Joon heard a low voice calling for help from just the other side of his two dead friends. Briefly, he puzzled over what to do next. He feared the Japanese might still be in the area and would resume firing at any movement. He decided that if he was to have a chance of survival, he must move on. He rolled over the corpses and came to rest beside the man who had cried out to him. In a now barely audible whisper the man urged that the two of them get away from the area, as quickly as possible.

"How can we escape with our hands tied behind our backs?" blurted Sin Joon, impatiently.

Sin Joon was instructed to manoeuvre his wrists until they were against the man's mouth. Then with his teeth the man proceeded to work at releasing the ropes. Within a few minutes the knots were untied.

"I've got a penknife in my trouser pocket," gasped the man, blood welling in his mouth. "Take it out and cut me free."

Sin Joon did as he was told and, as he was working, noticed movement to his left indicating three more likely survivors. After cutting through the first man's bonds, Sin Joon told him to wait while he released the other three. Two of the trio were volunteers he knew from E Company. One was Private Tan Cheng Cher, suffering from a gaping wound in his left shoulder. The other was a signalman who had been posted to Malaya Command Headquarters at Fort Canning. He had been shot through the thigh.

Ropes severed, the three started to move away. Sin Joon

Changi Beach, or Changi Spit as it was called 50 years ago. Today an idyllic seaside playground for leisure-seekers, this was the site of one of the first mass slaughters of civilians by Japanese forces in Singapore.

returned to the one who had fortuitously been carrying the penknife. Initially he thought the man had lapsed into unconsciousness. He shook him but there was no response. As the man's head lolled back, Sin Joon saw the massive wound in the centre of his throat. He was dead.

Unable to walk, Sin Joon crawled across the beach to a patch of lallang where he found the volunteers he had just released. Exhausted, the men agreed they must keep moving just as long as they could, following the coastline in a westerly direction. All were bleeding from serious internal wounds and dragging useless limbs with shattered bones. They were on the point of collapse when they reached another protective patch of lallang. There they lapsed into unconsciousness.

When Sin Joon revived it was dawn the following day. He could only locate the man with the leg wound. He prayed the other two had moved on safely and had avoided falling into the hands of the Japanese a second time.

Luck stayed with Sin Joon and his companion that morning. After crawling a further 200 hundred yards through foreshore scrubland, they were eventually located by British prisoners of war. The POWs had been detailed by their officers secretly to search the beach for wounded Chinese.

The remarkable sequence of events leading to the rescue of the Changi Point survivors is worth recalling. It was indeed a British forces POW camp through which the convoy of lorries had passed enroute to the Changi Spit execution point. From the moment the troops saw the convoy, they suspected the Chinese were to be shot. Their fears were confirmed a short while later when Japanese guards ordered all POWs out of the camp and onto the road that ran to Changi Village. From there they could no longer see the beach.

About a quarter of an hour later, the British prisoners heard bursts of automatic weapons' fire coming from the direction of the spit. These were followed by sounds of further intermittent firing that went on for about another twenty minutes.

As it happened, one of those ordered onto the roadway from the British quarters was Captain Alfred Roy, a doctor with the Royal Army Medical Corps. Some time after the shooting had stopped, Captain Roy and two of his orderlies were trying to establish the outcome when they noticed a squad of some 15 to 20 Japanese troops, under the command of an officer, walking from the beach and approaching three lorries in which they then drove away. Captain Roy made a mental note of the Japanese officer simply because he seemed so unusual. He was a small, rotund man and smoked a large Sherlock Holmes pipe.

The British were allowed back to their quarters around 6 pm that Sunday but were ordered to keep clear of the spit where, during the previous few evenings, they had gone swimming. Soon after dusk, a Malay fisherman stealthily approached Captain Roy outside the officers' mess to report that there were four survivors of the shooting hiding in the long grass back from the beach.

The doctor and two medical assistants returned to the beach track but could find no trace of any wounded. Next morning, a corporal from the 1st Battalion Leicestershire Regiment found a very badly wounded Chinese in a slit trench near the spit. The wounded man was brought to the British medical inspection room where Captain Roy dressed his wounds and covertly dispatched him to the 198 Field Ambulance Unit, located within the Changi POW complex.

Later in the morning, Captain Roy went back to the beach again; this time accompanied by his orderly, Sergeant B.W. Brown, of the 2nd Battalion, East Surrey Regiment. A large party of British prisoners were there burying the bodies. Captain Roy had in mind the Malay's remarks the previous evening about four survivors. Perhaps another three were lying somewhere near the beach. After a systematic search through the undergrowth, the doctor discovered a second and very badly wounded Chinese in long grass back from the sand line.

The wounded man, Captain Roy would later recall, was conscious and spoke English.

Along the beach the British prisoners were continuing with their gruesome task, burying the victims in shallow foreshore graves virtually where they lay. A Japanese officer supervised from the shade of a nearby coconut palm. Captain Roy was concerned by the Japanese officer's presence. He delayed moving the second wounded man until the burial party had gone a safer distance away. Then the second wounded Chinese, desperately weak from loss of blood, was taken by stretcher to join his fellow survivor at the 198 Field Ambulance Unit. Encouraged by the second rescue, the POWs extended their search further west along the beach and within a few hours had located Sin Joon and his companion.

O n the day following the Changi Spit burials, the British High Command had the opportunity to deliver the strongest possible verbal protest to the Japanese. It occurred during a tense meeting between 25th Army intelligence chief, Lt. Colonel. Ichiji Sugita, on the one side, and British staff officers, Brigadier T. H. Newbigging and Major Cyril Wild, on the other.

Exactly a week earlier, the same three men had faced each other across the surrender table when Britain's Malaya Command capitulated unconditionally to the invaders. Sugita, who spoke reasonable English, had been Yamashita's interpreter. Wild, who spoke fluent Japanese, had interpreted for Lt. General Arthur E. Percival, the British commander. Newbigging had assisted Percival.

Now the three were eyeball-to-eyeball in what was called the Changi Conference House, a small building in the British prison sector specially set aside for so-called "liaison sessions" between victor and vanquished during the immediate post-surrender weeks.

Newbigging, the senior officer, quickly took the initiative. Addressing Sugita in English, he berated the Japanese officer over the beach killings "just outside the wire of the Changi prisoner of war camp." He also complained that the British had been forced to supply burial teams.

Sugita replied abruptly in English: "These Chinese were bad men. That is why we have shot them. Have you anything else to ask?"

Newbigging shot back: "Yes, I have got something to ask. I ask that you should not shoot any more Chinese and that you should not ask our men to assist you by burying them."

Sugita, very agitated at this point, retorted: "We shall shoot them whenever we want to if we find bad men."

Neither British officer at this time had any clear idea of the extent of the killing going on in Singapore. Though, from Sugita's remarks, it seemed obvious that the Changi Spit slaughter was part of a much bigger and bloodier picture. Wild would not forget the words of the mustachioed, nattily dressed, Japanese intelligence chief. Indeed, he would live to see the day when fate would present him a golden opportunity to recall for history exactly what Sugita had said in that charged conference room. As such, Sugita's words, represented the first official Japanese comment on the Singapore massacres. That Sugita should respond so confidently and with such authority at this time is of some significance to our present investigation.

Sin Joon and the man with the thigh wound both responded well to treatment at the 198 Field Ambulance Unit and eventually rejoined their families. Records are not clear as to the fate of the other two survivors. But the chances seem strong that they, too, recovered from their wounds and returned safely to their homes.

As for the 66 Chinese men and boys killed at Changi Spit by the Japanese execution squad on the evening of Friday, February 20, 1942, their remains, presumably, still lie there beneath the sands of what has become one of Singapore's most beautiful outdoor recreational areas. Known as Changi Point Beach, it is now a weekend playground for the island's sunseekers, windsurfers, swimmers and picnickers. In the evenings, particularly when the steady north-east monsoon blows in from the South China Sea across the lower eastern corner of the Malaysian Peninsula, it becomes a haven for rod and reel sport fishermen.

There is no memorial, no plaque, not even an historical jotting to recall that evening fifty years ago. But it was here and in the waters at the eastern entrance of Keppel Harbour that the Japanese started their killing spree of Singapore Chinese civilians. The prime architect of the slaughter received regular progress reports through the special military channels he had carefully established. Initially he was delighted with the results. But it wasn't long before disillusionment set in. His original plans anticipated the execution of 50,000. At the rate the killings were taking place, the execution squads would be lucky to dispose of a fifth of their target number in the time allotted. This did not make him a happy man ■

Chapter 3

The real villain unmasked

————— ◆ —————

The Japanese orders resulting in the mass screening of Singapore's Chinese population and the subsequent massacre of thousands, stipulated two basic requirements. Firstly, the whole operation had to be carried out rapidly. Secondly, the executions must be accomplished with maximum secrecy.

Ironically enough, herein lies the very core of the evidence that debunks the long held theory that "Tiger of Malaya" Lt. General Tomoyuki Yamashita, commander of Japan's 25th Army, was the one responsible for issuing the orders to slaughter the Chinese in Singapore.

In the following chapters, it will become quite apparent that the 56-year-old general was not the villain. That the blame has rested on his shoulders all these years stems from a major legal blunder by the British in the immediate aftermath of the Pacific conflict. They either failed, or didn't want to understand the true role played by one of Yamashita's senior staff officers. When the British finally did recognise this man's monstrous activities for what they were, it was too late. The Americans were already protecting the evil genius in a classic "deal with the devil" arrangement.

Yamashita, following his blunt extraction of unconditional surrender from British Malaya Command's Lt. General Arthur E. Percival on the evening of February 15, was immediately consumed by an altogether different problem. Tokyo had ordered him to have his main force units reformed, resupplied and ready for redeployment by the end of the month. In short, after a bitter 70-day invasion against numerically superior defending forces, the "Tiger of Malaya" was then required to present his army fresh and ready for new offensives within 16 days!

It was a daunting task made more so by the fact that Yamashita knew the Imperial Army knives were drawn ready for the first opportunity to cut him back to size. His "folk-hero" public image, which burgeoned following the successes of the Malaya campaign and the spectacular fall of Singapore, had influential military quarters speculating he would soon be Japan's next War Minister. More powerful circles, however, including those involving Prime Minister Hideki Tojo himself, were clearly jealous of Yamashita's widespread popularity. Eagerly, they awaited their chance to move against him.

Yamashita's war diary reveals he was aware of his vulnerability. Furthermore, he was also aware that one of his senior staff officers, a man whom he instinctively disliked, was circumventing all normal military communication channels and making regular reports directly back to Premier Tojo's office.

It is against these circumstances that Yamashita's actions must be judged. For it was against this background that he grappled with Tokyo's insistence that the highest priority be given to bringing the Dutch East Indies, today Indonesia, quickly within Japan's Greater East Asian Co-prosperity Sphere.

Even if he had been harbouring personal ambitions to massacre large numbers of civilians in Singapore, which he wasn't, he simply had no time to attend to such matters. The demands of the Imperial Army Headquarters superseded all other matters and he worked at his desk, day and night, to meet them.

Local logistics problems alone were massive. The 35,000 strong Japanese invasion force deployed in the battle for Singapore had captured some 120,000 allied prisoners of war when the island fell. The sheer numbers of prisoners initially overwhelmed Yamashita who had been experiencing the greatest difficulties finding food and medical supplies for his own army, let alone an additional foreign force nearly four times its size. At the time he launched his attack on Singapore he was convinced he faced a defending army numbering no more than 40,000 men.

Broadly speaking, Yamashita's ground forces at the end of the campaign consisted of the Imperial Guards division (approximately 9,000 men), the 5th Division (13,000 men), the 18th Division (10,000) and ancillary troops (3,000 men).

The plans he drew up thereafter called in part for the Imperial Guards to move to Sumatra in early March. But there was also the vital matter of garrison forces for Malaya and Singapore to consider.

Some of the 5th Division would have to be sent back to Peninsular Malaya within a week for this purpose. The rest of the 5th would travel as reinforcements to the Philippines, while the 18th Division would be divided between Burma and the Andaman and Nicobar islands. At the end of this complex reshuffle of troops, the Japanese Army strength within Malaya and Singapore would total no more than a brigade, and a light one at that.

Immediately after the British surrender, both the intelligence and planning sections within Yamashita's High Command were reporting an urgent need to "mop-up" continuing elements of resistance in both Malaya and Singapore. Their advice seemed quite reasonable and valid given current field intelligence. This suggested significant numbers of British-trained local guerrillas, together with stay-behind British jungle warfare specialists, were in the process of going underground. Their ultimate aim was to launch hit and run attacks against Japanese garrison forces. The reports suggested, quite correctly as it happened, that the main force of the guerrilla units were hard-core communists recently released from prison sentences specially for the task.

Given the priority of Tokyo's demand for an immediately reorganised command, Yamashita stipulated three days were all that could be spared for such run-of-the-mill "mopping-up" measures. The three day time frame became a key component of the original killing orders and, as we will later discover, this became the focus of considerable concern for senior officers involved.

Post war British military investigators, determined to identify Yamashita as the source of the orders, never seemed even remotely puzzled by the extraordinary "time-limit" aspect of the case. The question the "time-limit" poses is this: Why would any commander, hell-bent on inflicting a policy of subjugation through widespread terror and massacres, begin by placing such impossible restrictions to its effective implementation?

Reality was that Yamashita had become totally absorbed by the "bigger picture" issues he was facing. He regarded the whole subject of mopping-up after a major campaign as normal, if not incidental. Consequently, he saw no reason to produce any special orders under his personal signature. The planning section head was reporting he had the matter under control. Why interfere? Yamashita's inaction at this stage was, of course, exactly what the real plotters of the massacres had been hoping and angling for all along. In effect, he played into their hands. It was a major error of judgement on his part with appalling consequences. Yamashita had become the target of a complex deception. He had been set up and failed to recognise it.

The originating directive was duly issued as a formal High Command document on February 18. Significantly, it did not bear Yamashita's signature.

Before outlining the tactics to be employed, the text dealt

with the High Command's reasons for taking action against the island's Chinese. It spoke of Singapore's threatening law and order situation that had to be controlled before any of the planned troop redeployments could get under way. It also referred to increasing anti-Japanese activities by Chinese guerrilla groups which, if unchecked, could have severe consequences on the overall operational readiness of Japan's garrisons in Malaya and Singapore. The directive made it clear that all anti-Japanese elements within the island's Chinese population were to be targeted and, once identified, eliminated.

It went on to define the five separate anti-Japanese categories against which action was to be taken:

1. Former members of volunteer forces.
2. Communists.
3. Looters.
4. Armed people or those found harbouring arms.
5. Anyone obstructing the Japanese operation or threatening law and order.

Dealing with the measures to be adopted, the directive ordered that military cordons be first thrown around Chinese residential areas to prevent anti-Japanese elements from escaping. The various screening areas were then to be divided into sectors, each with its own control centre. All Chinese — men, women and children — would be concentrated in these designated screening areas and the co-operation of local people would be sought to identify those belonging to the five specified categories.

Those determined to be harbouring anti-Japanese sentiments would be kept segregated. They would then be "disposed of" secretly at suitable sites around Singapore.

Working in parallel with the screening programme, said the directive, would be a major military search operation through private dwellings and any suspicious premises where fugitives could be hiding or weapons stored. Finally, the orders contained a most revealing footnote. The man in charge of the overall "mopping up" programme — within which the screening, searching and executing activities were to be the key components — would be one Lt. Colonel Masanobu Tsuji, the High Command's Chief of Planning and Operations.

Here was the real villain. At the same time brilliant and barbaric, ambitious and vindictive, the 39-year-old Tsuji had visualised a mass subjugation action against the Chinese of Singapore almost since the moment, 15 months earlier, when he was appointed chief planning officer for Tokyo's proposed campaign to drive colonial Britain from South East Asia. The sheer immorality of the methods he devised to instil Japan's authority on a vanquished island defies all reasoned explanation. He was a fanatic, a classic product of his country's arch-militarist era. Although never rising above colonel ranking, he wielded enormous powers through an elite soldiers' network of personal contacts linking him favourably to the highest offices of the land. Many a more senior officer quaked in his presence, terrified that the man's megalomaniacal whims might wreck their careers. Yamashita, for one, held Tsuji in particular contempt. He learned very early in the Malaya campaign that his Planning and Operations officer was the source of the special reports on the 25th Army High Command being fed back independently to Premier Tojo's office.

Tsuji plotted and orchestrated the Singapore massacres with consummate cunning and cruelty. The idea of conducting the killings under tight secrecy at isolated points on the island was as much intended to cover the tracks of his direct involvement as it was to enhance the effectiveness of the overall operation.

The British would wrongfully maintain that Yamashita was the instigator of the mass killings. Moreover, they would send for trial and convict war criminals with prosecution cases based on this erroneous assumption. Two senior Japanese officers would ultimately be executed and another six sentenced to life imprisonment under these circumstances. That Tsuji, the true culprit, should elude capture and blame and later publicly emerge as a prominent Japanese post-war politician are indications of the man's extraordinary talent for deceit and manipulation.

As we will discover, the Tsuji saga amounts to nothing short of the greatest case of international hoodwinking and criminal conniving in Asia this century. Duped at various times by the man and his machinations were the British, the Americans, the Thais, Generalissimo Chiang Kai-shek and the Nationalist Chinese, Communist China, a number of influential Australians and, of course, the Japanese themselves.

Tsuji was born in Ishikawa prefecture in 1902, the son of a poor farmer. With the support of a local benefactor, he enrolled at the age of 15 in the Nagoya Army Elementary School where his determination to rise above his humble origins and aggressively compete with the more privileged students was soon noted. He graduated top of his class, a feat which he repeated after entering the Officers' School Preparatory Course in Tokyo in 1920.

Throughout his youth, Tsuji showed scant interest in sports but developed an almost religious fervour for the Japanese art of swordfighting known as *kendo*. Although only 5 ft 2 ins in height, he possessed unusual physical strength for his size and was known to favour beating his opponents into submission with smashing blows. Those who knew him well saw a direct relationship between his attitude to *kendo* and his general approach to life.

After an attachment to the Kanazawa 7th Army in his home prefecture, Tsuji was promoted to 1st Lieutenant in 1927. A year later, he won a place at the Military Staff College where, in 1931, he once again graduated top of his year.

Tsuji's personal lifestyle was abstemious. He shunned

Above: A tyrant and fanatic in the making. As a 28-year-old lieutenant in the Imperial Japanese Army, Masanobu Tsuji stands proudly before a Japanese flag during a military ceremony in 1931.

Left: The complete tyrant and fanatic. Colonel Masanobu Tsuji displays the awards his butchery secured.

alcohol and seemed generally disinterested in women, spurning many a proffered introduction to daughters of Army top brass. Marriage into a well-placed military family was then considered an advisable career move for aspiring young officers. Eventually he wed a postmaster's daughter. Tsuji's wife bore him five children — two sons and three daughters.

Fellow officers who served with Tsuji regarded him as intrepid, scheming, high-handed and blessed with unbounded energy. Colonel Takeo Konishi, a contemporary, once described Tsuji as harbouring "extreme attitudes." He would completely shun those he disliked, yet show unabashed favouritism to those with whom he could work in harmony. He possessed a highly excitable temperament which would frequently give way to fits of violence "almost akin to madness."

Not surprisingly, very few officers enjoyed serving under him. He treated his subordinates abominably, and his personal relations with brother-officers were invariably strained. As a staff officer his life was austere and simple. He avoided socialising and never attended ceremonial dinners.

Singapore was but the beginning of Tsuji's evil trail. Although the killing of Chinese civilians on the island must, by virtue of the numbers involved, rank as his worst atrocity, he was destined to take his particular brand of satanic behaviour to virtually every major Pacific land-war battle zone before two atomic bombs extracted Japan's unconditional surrender on August 15, 1945. In all these places, he plotted and schemed with identical fanaticism and indifference to human suffering. His military career after Singapore would be shrouded in mystique, contradiction and deception. All were carefully calculated to camouflage his on-going activities.

As the mopping-up in Singapore got underway, Tsuji wheeled, dealed and manipulated a substantial relaxation of Yamashita's strict time-limit. He stretched it from three days to two weeks. But he was on dangerous grounds, and recognised it. He feared that contravening the Army Commander's instructions too brazenly might become a serious matter of contention within the hard-pressed High Command. He needed a month to six weeks to carry out the subjugation programme as he had originally devised it. But he knew he could never manipulate such a time frame.

Inevitably, Tsuji made mistakes and it was in Singapore that his self-spun protective web of trickery would begin to fray. Decades would pass before the web would unravel enough to reveal his treachery. Still, there is irony in the fact that Yamashita's insistence on limiting the military mopping up measures on the island would provide the first vital clues to Tsuji's activities. For all the elaborate secrecy precautions imposed by the crooked colonel, there were, — like Joe Cusselle, at Berhala Reping and Wong Sin Joon, at Changi Point — a limited number of eye-witnesses to the slaughter whose testimonies have been recorded. Forced to work against the clock, the executioners from time to time bungled their assignments. They were spotted at work. Some of their victims lived to tell the tale. And so the case against Lt. Colonel Masanobu Tsuji begins to shake loose ■

Chapter 4

The slaughter continues

———— ✦ ————

At about the time Sin Joon lay seriously wounded in the Changi Point lallang, Cheng Kwang Yu, a civil servant, was one of approximately four hundred Chinese prisoners being unloaded from a convoy of twenty lorries two miles further around the coastline at Tanah Merah Besar beach. Before they had departed the Victoria School compound that evening, the prisoners had been bound, hands behind their backs. At the beach, the Japanese divided them into groups of eight, ten and twelve men and lashed them this way with lengths of electric wire. With the light fading fast, the captives were made to shuffle to the water's edge.

Kwang Yu, a special examiner at the War Tax office prior to the fall of Singapore, lived at 729 Serangoon Road, and had been sent with his wife and children to the Syed Alwi Road concentration point. His wife and children had been released. He had been detained after identifying himself when government servants, bank clerks and commercial officers were ordered to form up separately from ordinary Chinese labourers.

As the prisoners reached the water's edge with their backs towards the road, Japanese machinegunners opened up from the rear. Several in Kwang Yu's group, struck in the first volley, fell, pulling him down with them. A fraction of a second before hitting the wet sand, Kwang Yu took a round on the side of the nose which spun him onto his back and caused blood to flow profusely across his face and head. Relying on instincts for survival in much the same way Sin Joon had done, Kwang Yu closed his eyes and feigned death. His shattered nose and blood-covered face helped the deception. The shooting stopped. But he soon heard the crunch-crunch of approaching boots in the sand. It was a second Japanese squad, altogether different from the machinegunners. This lot wandered among the fallen Chinese on Tanah Merah Besar Beach delivering bayonet thrusts into any form they felt still held life. One Japanese soldier stood flat on Kwang Yu's chest for the leverage necessary to stab to death the man lying beside him.

After some time, Kwang Yu heard the lorry engines starting up and the vehicles driving off. It was now dark and moonlight bathed the beach. He prepared to escape by first easing out of his bonds. Before departing, he took one last look along the foreshore. Asked to describe this scene some years later he said: "I noticed dead bodies were littered here and there just like fish in a market stall. The sound of groaning, wailing, crying and some cursing — just like hell on earth."

After four nights and three days in the beach undergrowth, Kwang Yu was eventually discovered by British POWs. They arranged for him to be taken clandestinely to Tan Tock Seng Hospital where he eventually recovered.

It is impossible to put an accurate figure on the numbers of Chinese massacred on Tanah Merah Besar Beach. Undoubtedly this stretch of foreshore, now reclaimed and buried beneath the Changi Airport runways, was one of the Japanese military's most heavily used Singapore killing grounds. Records indicate more people selected for death by firing squads were able to escape from here than from any other execution point around the island. This would suggest that the sheer numbers being handled by the executioners on the beach —definitely in the hundreds and probably well in excess of a thousand — created an element of confusion which alert and lucky individuals were sometimes able to exploit.

One such person was Chua Choon Guan, a taxi driver, who lived at 105 Koon Seng Road. He had been detained at the Jalan Besar Football Stadium concentration centre and selected for execution because of his physique. "They had a liking for those who were well built and they took us all out," Choon Guan would later recall.

Trussed up and pushed to the water's edge at Tanah Merah Besar, Choon Guan suffered machinegun wounds to the side and legs. He survived because he was knocked unconscious in the first salvo. Several of his fellow prisoners then collapsed dead on top of his prostrate body. In death they camouflaged him from the prying eyes of Japanese soldiers seeking to deliver final bayonet thrusts. It was dark when he regained consciousness. The incoming tide was washing over his face. He extricated himself from beneath the corpses, found a sharp rock on which to cut through his bonds, and then crawled to safety.

Those precious but scarce chances to cheat death came to the lucky few in a variety of circumstances. At one collection point along Jalan Besar a young man in his early twenties had been selected for execution. He was ordered to join a group that had been set aside and would later be taken away and ultimately driven to one of the selected beach killing sites. The young man instinctively felt he was in serious trouble. Before joining the group he asked to go back to the collection centre to retrieve his "other things." The Japanese consented.

In an interview with the Japanese *Nihon Keizai Shimbun* nearly fifty years later, he recalled how he had hidden for a few days before being released.

"I was lucky because those who were collected never came back. They were shot and massacred. So my good luck was to be allowed to go back to collect my things," he explained to his interviewer.

His name: Lee Kuan Yew, founder of modern Singapore. On such a slender thread once hung the island nation's political destiny.

Wong Peng Yin was in a group of 120 Chinese men and youths who were driven to Tanah Merah Besar Beach from Victoria School in the late evening. There they were roped together in groups of five, and ordered to march into the water. As the twenty-four separate bunches of men struggled across the sand, they noticed bodies from previously executed batches littering the foreshore.

Through shock and fear, the tragic little groups began reacting differently. Some moved straight ahead into the water. Some lagged behind. Some stumbled to the left; some wandered off to the right. For a while there was clearly confusion within the Japanese firing squad about the targets spreading so widely.

Peng Yin had waded two hundred yards across the shallows before the machinegun and rifle fire erupted. He and several others in different groups dropped into the water and were able to struggle free of their ropes.

They swam out to sea, protected by the oncoming darkness, then veered to the right in the direction of, a fishing village further along the coast. There Peng Yin came ashore and rested the night in a squatter's hut.

The next day, he was cautiously making his way back towards his home in Klang Road when he ran into a convoy of lorries in Siglap Village. In the backs of the lorries, just as he had been the day before, were a large number of Chinese men, their hands bound behind their backs.

Peng Yin hid in the village from about nine o'clock in the morning to two in the afternoon. More lorries arrived. He dared not move for fear of being spotted and dispatched to a firing squad a second time. Throughout the five hours he stayed concealed, Peng Yin heard frequent bursts of machinegun fire coming from a small hill alongside Woo Mon Chew Road, another of the execution grounds chosen by the Japanese.

Like Peng Yin at Siglap village, thousands of people must have heard the sounds of the firing squads at work around the island. But most massacre accounts have come directly from victims who escaped seaside execution lines.

There were, however, a limited number of eyewitness decriptions from bystanders. Some of these are contained in a forgotten file of statutory declarations from British troops on Blakang Mati. These men were occupying locations separate and isolated from Joe Cusselle and his Berhala Reping gunners. Their reports corroborate fully Joe's present day recollections. When coordinated with the Berhala Reping events, they reveal new dimensions to the killings at sea, which, like the rest of the Singapore massacres ordered by Tsuji, were intended to be hidden forever from history's prying eyes.

They detail, for instance, how British troops buried at least 300 massacre victims along the southern shorefront of what is now Singapore's acclaimed resort island. This is a figure far larger than the post-war official investigators conceded. The investigators placed the entire death toll from killings at sea off Blakang Mati at less than 300.

In one of the statutory declarations, Major Alfred C. Smith, who had been commanding officer of an FMSVF Machine Gun company, made the following observation: "At the time, we estimated that the total number executed was over 500 and this, based on the number of bodies which came ashore on our very narrow front, was almost certainly an underestimate."

The "front" Major Smith spoke about appears to have been a comparatively small central sector of Blakang Mati's south-eastern coast. Marine authorities confirm that the waters off Blakang Mati in the area that the massacres took place are subject to extremely swift tidal races. Therefore, the inescapable conclusion, given that the killings generally took place between 300 to 1,000 metres off shore, is that the overwhelming majority of bodies of those machinegunned in the water were swept out to sea by the currents. In short, the actual death toll in the waters off Blakang Mati was substantially more than 500; probably in the region of 1,500.

The affidavits placed the principal burial areas in the north-eastern reaches of the island, coinciding with descriptions given by Joe Cusselle, at a central point on the south-eastern coast and at certain points along the south-western coastline. These were the areas where the tide and currents tended to concentrate the corpses, which frequently became entangled on barbed wire barricades protruding into the water. The affidavits yielded another significant clue. Among the bodies buried by the servicemen were those of two or three women.

W hy did the British investigators underplay the extent of the killings off Blakang Mati? Part of the answer is that Tsuji's obsession with secrecy obscured their access to the facts. Then, after the war, the investigators became victims of the colonel's cohorts in Tokyo. Threatened by the possibility of being linked to the Singapore atrocities, several officers close to Tsuji worked on a most successful smoke screen to divert enquiries. We will look at this and related issues later as they form part of the sequence of events which allowed Tsuji to escape, free of all blame. Meanwhile, perhaps the British weren't the only ones fooled by Tsuji over the Blakang Mati killings.

On April 27, 1974, a workman laying pipes for a coralarium on then renamed Sentosa island, drove his changkol into a human skull some 18 inches below the sandy foreshore surface. Before the day was over, another skull and a collection of bones had been unearthed. Over the next four days a total of 12 more skulls and more bones were exhumed, all from shallow foreshore graves. These were graves just like the British soldiers had dug. What was more, they were in the same general area that the soliders had been digging 32 years earlier.

In the weeks and months that followed, Singapore's

investigating authorities worked on a variety of theories. These included suggestions the victims had been illegal immigrants from neighbouring Indonesia killed by pirates, members of a Chinese secret society wiped out in a mass execution by a rival tong and even a band of smugglers caught in a battle to the death over spoils. At one point, brief reference was made to the possibility that the skeletons might be those of war victims. But this theory was quickly dropped. Forensic tests at the time supposedly indicated the bones had been buried no more than eight years.

As time passed and no credible explanation for the graves emerged, pathologists released details of some of their findings. Most of the 14 skulls and skeletons had come from males between the ages of 20 - 40 years. The youngest was probably 16 years, the oldest 60. Two skulls were thought to have been those of females. One of the male skulls had been shot through the head. All this, of course, ties in closely with descriptions of the victims of the seaborne massacres as provided by Joe Cusselle and by the other British servicemen in their post-war affidavits.

On May 24, 1974, Singapore's morning daily newspaper, *The Straits Times*, quoted police sources as believing the mass killing on Sentosa had been the work of an expert crime syndicate. "Their identity and place of operation are as yet unknown," the newspaper reported. Eleven months later, on April 10, 1975, *The Straits Times* ran a story headlined: "Sentosa skulls keep their grim secret." It related how the skulls were then displayed on a wall shelf at the pathology department of the Singapore General Hospital in Outram Road.

A coroner's inquiry had recorded a finding of "murder by person or persons unknown" in the case of the bullet-damaged skull. Open findings had been recorded in the cases of another 13 skulls and broken up skeletons. Police had closed their files on the investigations, the paper said. The case had been classified "unsolved." ∎

Chapter 5

Stepping up the kill-rate

————— ✦ —————

By as early as February 21, the second day of the massacres, Tsuji realised the executions were running well behind schedule. Reports he was receiving at his Fort Canning headquarters, overlooking the island's business district, indicated both the screening and execution squads were functioning below operational capacities he considered effective. He resolved to adopt a higher profile and institute a series of on-the-spot inspections to ensure a substantial escalation of the kill-rate.

Word that Tsuji was dissatisfied and about to embark on personal tours spread quickly.

But the kempeitai officers were overwhelmed with the task they had been given. The three-day time-limit for processing such huge numbers was impossible to meet. Many more interpreters were needed. On top of it all, there was a general lack of comprehension of the subject matters involved in the screening process.

The pressure now being brought to bare by Tsuji forced the kempeitai into adopting even more outlandish short-cut solutions than they had devised thus far. Inevitably the key requirement for blanket secrecy was undermined. There was less time, for example, to reconnoitre isolated areas as possible massacre grounds. There was also less time to clear chosen execution areas of local population before the killings began.

Thus Lee Siew Kow became an eyewitness to a massacre on

February 23 and was subsequently able to record what he saw. While standing in front of his home at 23 Amber Road in the then seaside section of Katong, Siew Kow noticed three lorries, packed with Chinese men, motoring past. A short distance down the road, the three vehicles stopped and all occupants were ordered by Japanese military guards to climb down to the roadside. They were first bound individually with ropes, then in groups of three with wire.

As the guards led their prisoners to the beach down a lane by the side of the Chinese Swimming Club, Siew Kow followed, carefully avoiding detection. On the beach the guards ordered their prisoners to kneel in the sand facing the sea. From his position, little more than 30 paces away, Siew Kow saw one of the Japanese troops wave a red flag. Several of the Japanese then lunged at the kneeling men with bayonets. Others just opened fire at them. Siew Kow heard the terrible cries of anguish from those being slaughtered and was powerless to do anything.

The concentration point established on February 19 at the intersection of River Valley Road and Clemenceau Avenue reflected, in heightening chaos, Tsuji's demands for all-round increased efficiency. From the morning of the 21st to the afternoon of the 22nd, some 400 men and youths were detained on the strength of names, addresses and occupations given to Japanese screening officers in attendance. No form of systematic questioning or any interrogation procedures were applied. Some people were asked solely their names. Others just their occupations. Yeo Chee Hiam, who lived at 33 Devonshire Road, went to this screening centre with 18 members of his family. His brother was asked for his occupation by a Japanese working through a Malay interpreter. When the brother explained he worked as an assistant in his father's shop, the Japanese set him aside for execution. Chee Hiam's eldest son and several friends were similarly detained on the basis of their occupations. Pointedly, there were no hit lists in evidence at this camp.

Chee Hiam himself, as it happened, was released after providing his name, address and occupation. He left the compound to return home around 4 pm on the 22nd. It was the last time he ever sighted his son, his brother or his friends. Asked, five years later, on what he felt the Japanese based those life or-death decisions in River Valley Road during that 36-hour period, Chee Hiam suggested it was pure whim. Urged to be more explicit, he responded: "I can't give you a definition for that. Those people whose faces perhaps were displeasing to the Japanese were simply taken."

The kempeitai officer in charge of the Telok Kurau English School concentration point, off Telok Kurau Road, between Joo Chiat Place and Lorong J, developed perhaps the shortest of all screening short cuts. Based on a "show of hands" principle, it dispensed with the need for any form of personal questioning whatsoever.

The Japanese officer started by massing all Chinese from the Telok Kurau - Tanjong Katong locality onto the school field which is today part of the La Salle School campus. Males were quickly segregated from females and all females released. Elderly men were then allowed to leave. Those males remaining were all in the 15 to 50 year age group.

"Hands up," the officer commanded through an interpreter, "those with property worth $50,000 or more." The overwhelming mass of detainees gathered on the school playing field looked blank. The very few who owned up to possession of such wealth were immediately set aside in a guarded enclosure by themselves.

"Hands up all the volunteers," came the next command, followed by, "hands up the lawyers" . . . "doctors" . . . "school teachers and students" . . . "merchants" . . . "labourers and mechanics" . . . "Government servants" . . . "Hainanese" . . . "those who have lived in Malaya less than five years."

As each group was identified, its members were placed in

special roped-off enclosures on the school field. By late afternoon, the Japanese had set aside about ten lawyers and doctors, a hundred schoolteachers and students, a hundred merchants, three hundred labourers and mechanics and some two hundred government clerks. Not one personal question had been posed. Not a single answer recorded. Not a single name given, or taken.

Come nightfall, all those in the special enclosure were transferred to locked classrooms within the main school building or to guarded compound houses nearby in Telok Kurau Road. The following morning they were transferred, group by group at staggered intervals, to military lorries and driven to the 7 1/2 milestone, Siglap Road.

Khoo Ah Lim, a resident of Telok Kurau Road, detained because he was categorised as "educated", found himself in the back of one of these lorries. Ordered to the ground, he and his fellows were tied in pairs down a long length of rope. With a Japanese guard at the top end of the rope leading, another at other end bringing up the rear, and several on either side down the line for security, the detained Chinese were pushed, dragged and jolted through semi-jungle towards a small sandhill some way in from Siglap Road.

Their Japanese captors had told them nothing of their fate. But they knew, as they stumbled on, that this was to be their final walk. In fear and helplessness, one fell to the ground. Then another. . . and another. Suddenly all the prisoners in Ah Lim's line were on the ground crying and pleading. Callously, the Japanese guards began wielding rifle butts, jabbing and smashing, in an effort to get the line moving once more. It was the moment for which Ah Lim had been waiting. Trudging from the lorry, he had been working to loosen his bonds and the rope had begun to give. Quickly he slipped the knot over his wrists. He was free. With heart pounding, he took off into the jungle, away from that terrible hill, and ran and ran. Ah Lim avoided all built-up areas, seeking the cover of undergrowth on undeveloped hinterland. He didn't stop moving until he reached a friend's house in Changi in the early hours of the following morning. The convoy of lorries that had brought Ah Lim and his group from Telok Kurau School had been the same execution-bound procession that Peng Yin had encountered as he fled through Siglap westwards from the killing grounds at Tanah Merah Besar Beach.

U nder continuing pressure from Tsuji and his fellow organisers, the Japanese military relied increasingly on locals for screening assistance. It was an insidious process that frequently set friend against friend, neighbour against neighbour, colleague against colleague, and, in some cases, even family relatives against one another.

The original orders passed down to the kempeitai made it clear that help from local individuals would be important. But as the hours and days passed, the kempeitai section chiefs saw substantially increased local assistance as the only way out of their time-pressure dilemmas.

Sometimes it was relatively easy to persuade the gullible to help out as clerical assistants. After all, it was simply a matter of listing the names of those who had been chosen to become policemen, or whose previous training somehow qualified them for positions in Japanese occupied Malaya.

Those in command were not required to explain why, later in the day, the newly selected "recruits" were being driven off trussed-up in the backs of lorries.

More often than not, an element of persuasion was deemed necessary to secure local help in screening. This could vary from gentle coercion, to promises of special treatment, or open threats of execution for self or family. Without local assistance, the Japanese found themselves devoid of any means of identifying those among the detained belonging to the five wanted categories. Further simplifying matters, the Japanese, as the days went by, generally contracted the five categories to three: volunteers, communists and criminals. The simplification led to even great confusion and chaos.

Understandably, this period spawned intense emotions within Singapore's clan dominated Chinese community and backwards and forwards across the island's racial divisions. These emotions formed a broad spectrum from the deepest gratitudes to the most vehement hatreds. "Collaborator" accusations were too easily and too frequently levelled at a time when the mere act of survival strained wits, stamina and loyalties to breaking point.

Particularly delicate were the positions of police officers who were borderline cases as far as the Japanese were concerned. While the military authorities badly needed a police network to enforce law and order on the island, they also harboured grave suspicions as to the true loyalties of the entirely British-trained force.

Working from lists of Special Branch members, also prepared by Japan's resident intelligence network, kempeitai officers began making house calls on Special Branch detectives whose expertise had been clandestine political surveillance work. The kempeitai demanded, and at times certainly received, support for fingering suspected communists. Equally unnerving were the kempeitai's moves to divide and rule police ranks by pitting officer against officer within the screening programme

Detective Kang Thiam Huat, from the Criminal Investigation Department (C.I.D.), was a case in point. He found himself an inmate of the Syed Alwi Road concentration camp where he stayed for about seven days. As he attempted to leave in a line of detainees about to be released, he noticed a group of guards sitting by the exit gate along with a number of Chinese detectives. At the gate one of the detectives assisting the Japanese pulled Thiam Huat back by the coat. Eight other detectives were similarly identified and extracted from the crowd trying to exit Syed Alwi Road.

All the detained police were later moved to the Victoria School football field on Tyrwhitt Road where their details were taken down. Fearing the worst, Thiam Huat provided a false name. It was not long before he was singled out and given a fierce beating for misleading the authorities. The Japanese guards then pushed the battered but unbound detective into the back of a lorry with a number of other Chinese male prisoners. The drive to the sixth milestone, Changi Road, was fast and in convoy with other similarly loaded lorries carrying a total of some 300 to their executions.

It was late evening when they arrived at the beach. It was also high tide and the vehicles were able to manoeuvre fairly close to the water's edge. Thiam Huat watched as the first to alight were tied into groups of four. When it came his turn to get down, he dashed for the sea. As he dived beneath the surface he heard the sound of machineguns opening fire. There was agitation along the sand. His dive sent him bumping up against corpses of those shot earlier. Using the bodies as shields he edged his way into deeper water and eventually escaped by swimming down the coast into the darkness.

While the dreaded kempeitai enforced all screening programmes within the heavily populated areas of downtown Singapore, responsibility for these activities to the north and east of the island fell to units of the Konoye Imperial Guards under the command of Lt. General Takuma Nishimura. However, the Guards, heavily involved with reorganising their ranks prior to the planned early redeployment to Sumatra, were unable to begin their screening activities until the morning of Saturday, February 28 — nine days after the kempeitai.

Commandeering a large colonial bungalow known as Oehlers' Lodge, on Upper Serangoon Road, the Guards deployed sizable numbers of troops on house-to-house searches throughout the area. Here their tactics differed from those of the kempeitai. Elderly men, females, and all children below the age of fifteen years were not required to attend the concentration camp at the lodge. All males from 15 to 50 years certainly were. The Guards' job was to search out those males who had failed to report and to bring them in at bayonet point.

The lodge, a rambling home, built by a member of the Oehlers family, prominent in the island's Eurasian community, was located on the northern side of Upper Serangoon Road, several hundred yards before the Ponggol Road turn-off. A large bamboo fence fronted the road. Surrounded by substantial gardens, the house was approached along a U-shaped driveway. One side of the property was dominated by a tennis court, contained within a high, rectangular mesh-wire fence. Two gates led into the tennis enclosure at the top of the court, two at the bottom. The Guards decided this would be an ideal location for screening the entire Chinese community living along the length of Upper Serangoon Road to the eastern extremity at Kangkar where there resided an enclave of predominently Teochew fishermen and their families.

Troops detailed on search and arrest duties began operations well before dawn and were arriving at Oehlers' Lodge with the first suspects before 6 am. Three hours later, some 1,000 Chinese males found themselves incarcerated on the tennis court, armed sentries at all four gates. The Guards placed a high priority on detecting those with tattoos. Orders prepared at the divisional level indicated those with body markings were likely to be members of Chinese secret societies or other gangster elements. The first screening procedure was a thorough body search of all suspects. Every male sporting a tattoo was routinely set aside for execution.

Then began a question and answer interrogation of all detainees on the tennis court. This was carried out primarily through Taiwanese interpreters, operating with the Imperial Guards. But there were one or two Japanese soldiers who spoke Malay. The prisoners were asked about their attitudes towards the Japanese, whether they were communists, whether they were Government servants, merchants, students, employees of Japanese companies, working for British companies, or labourers. Probably more than any other screening of Singapore Chinese undertaken by the Japanese Army, this one adhered closest to the orders laid down by the High Command.

By early afternoon, approximately 400 of the original 1,000 suspects remained under detention on the court. The rest had been released. Gathered on the roadway outside the compound were several hundred deeply worried relatives and friends.

Around mid-afternoon, 12 military lorries pulled into the lodge driveway. Prisoners who had been discovered with tattoo marks — some forty in all — were loaded into the back of the first vehicle. With them went a number of Japanese troops armed with rifles and light machineguns. One by one the remaining eleven lorries were filled with Chinese men, youths and boys who were led across in groups from the tennis court.

The 12 vehicles drove off in convoy along Upper Serangoon Road, turned left into Ponggol Road and motored to the bus terminus located then, as it still is today, at the extreme end of the route where the road meets the Straits of Johore.

All prisoners were ordered to get down from the lorries. Then as evening approached, they were escorted to the Ponggol foreshore, group by group, and executed by firing squads. There were no eyewitnesses to this particular mass killing. Locals in the immediate vicinity had been driven away by the troops. But Puay Ah Boh, a fisherman who lived at 163 Ponggol Road, at the 11th milestone, certainly saw the convoy of lorries pass by that afternoon. In a while, he heard the "pop-pop" of the execution squad's weapons and the screams of the victims.

A day or two later, a complaint was lodged with the Health Department of the Singapore Rural Board. Many bodies were lying around the beachfront at the Ponggol Road terminus and were posing a health hazard. Here, the story of the Ponggol massacre takes a curious twist. The Japanese, as it happened, had temporarily delayed interning key Europeans attached to colonial Singapore's essential services. It was the invaders' only hope of ensuring such services continued functioning in the immediate traumatic aftermath of the battle for the island. Thus it became the official task of a group of defeated British expatriates, including a professor, two doctors, and a senior civil administrator, all attached to the Health Department, to carry out a formal inspection of the Ponggol massacre site. On them also fell the responsibility of handling the substantial health problems it posed.

A burial party was immediately organised which struck all the same grave-digging problems encountered by the British artillerymen at Berhala Reping. Solutions in both places, proved identical. The Ponggol grave-diggers abandoned efforts for burials on high ground. Instead, shallow graves were dug at low tide in wet sand near the water's edge. Over a three-day period, approximately 150 Chinese males were buried this way in the immediate bus terminus region

While burial work was still in progress on the fourth day, the grave-digging party was suddenly fired upon from concealed positions in the hilly terrain directly west of the terminus. The grave diggers ran for shelter and the firing stopped. As soon as the burial party resumed work, the firing also resumed. The foreman, a 45-year-old Indian, decided to abandon the task and return to the municipal offices for further instructions. Dr Ando, newly appointed Japanese chief of the Health Department, promised to determine the cause of the hostility. The following day, Dr Ando explained to his staff that the military had proclaimed the Ponggol foreshore a "restricted area." All civilians were prohibited from entering it. All burials, therefore, had to cease despite the fact, as the Indian foreman pointed out, the foreshore to the east and west of the bus

Ponggol Beach today. Some 300 - 400 Chinese youths and men were mowed down by Japanese execution squads on the foreshore of this little cove just west of the Ponggol bus terminus.

terminus remained littered with bodies as far as the eye could see.

The sudden "restricted area" proclamation was, of course, a somewhat delayed move on the part of the Imperial Guards to maintain execution site secrecy as stipulated under the original High Command orders. That the site had already been formally inspected by a group of expatriates, was a breach of security apparently regarded as insignificant by the responsible military authorities.

There is one other inexplicable aspect of the mass killings at Ponggol. This concerns a group of 22 condemned Chinese men and youths who travelled from Oehlers' Lodge in the convoy's second lorry that Saturday afternoon. Among this group was teenager Ng Kim Song, a student, who lived at 467 Upper Serangoon Road, Low Sze Thang, a fish and vegetable vendor, from 720 Upper Serangoon Road, and Sze Thang's second brother, of the same address.

Unlike the other eleven vehicles that carried on in the direction of the terminus, theirs stopped at the 9 1/2 milestone where the 22 were separated from the rest and ordered into a bungalow on the left hand side of the road. The newly constructed house, which was then deserted, belonged to the affluent Cashin family, well known in Singapore's Jewish community. At the Cashin bungalow, the Japanese once again searched for body tattoos and carried out a second interrogation to establish whether the prisoners were communists or whether they had donated war funds to China. These Japanese were unable to speak either Chinese or Malay But one, clearly the leader, communicated by scratching fundamental *kanji* characters — common to both the Chinese and Japanese languages — in the sandy ground with a stick.

The oldest of the prisoners was the sole member of the group able to understand written Chinese. Upon him fell the mantle of interpreter and official spokesman. He insisted to the Japanese that none of his fellows supported the Communist leader of the time, Wang Ching Wei, but were followers of Chiang Kai-shek. Moreover, he told the interrogators via reciprocal tracings on the ground, none of them could ever afford to send money to China as they were only poor hawkers of fish and vegetables. The Japanese thought for a while then hurried their captives back into the vehicle and drove them to join the rest of the convoy at the Ponggol terminus. When they arrived, most of the prisoners from the other lorries had alighted and were squatting at the side of the road with about 100 Japanese troops standing guard.

The 22 were ordered into another house, this time on the right hand side of the road, and were instructed to kneel. On the advice of the prisoner who could read Chinese they prayed for their lives. Some time later, the Japanese came and took away four of the group. The eighteen left behind soon heard rifle shots and knew their friends had been killed. The chances of their prayers being answered seemed very slim.

Then the Japanese soldier who communicated through signs on the ground returned. He ordered the 18 surviving prisoners into a nearby rubber plantation. When they had walked a hundred paces or so they stopped and the soldier again began scrawling in the sandy soil with a stick.

The one who could understand slowly translated: "He says . . . that he is . . . our saviour . . . and we should . . . run away."

Instantly the eighteen scattered into the plantation in different directions. After running four or five steps they heard the sound of weapons firing behind them. But none was hit, and all returned home safely.

Between three and four hundred died on the Ponggol foreshore that late afternoon and evening of February 28, 1942. Why those eighteen were allowed to escape the firing squad's bullets has never been explained, nor is it ever likely to be. The identity of that lone Japanese soldier who chose to display some mercy amid the butchery on the beach also remains a mystery. It is left to those who survived, and their descendants, to contemplate the reasons and their good fortune.

Late in organising the required screening procedure along Upper Serangoon Road, the Imperial Guards were similarly behind schedule in tackling the task in their other main area of responsibility — throughout the Chinese villages strung along the eastern sectors of Singapore's Changi and East Coast roads. It was not until Thursday, February 26, eight days after the Japanese High Command issued the order, that a Japanese pedalled his bicycle into Samba Ikat Village, at the 10th milestone, Changi Road, and displayed a number of posters in coffee shops there. These ordered all Chinese males above the age of 15 to report for "registration" at Changi Road's 8 1/2 milestone mark early the following Saturday morning, February 28. Similar posters were placed in nearby Mata Ikan Village and other smaller Chinese kampongs around this south eastern area of the island.

Before dawn on Saturday, the Imperial Guards began operating their 8 1/2 milestone concentration point and by mid-morning several thousand Chinese men and youths had gathered there. Those released after brief questioning received an identification paper listing their name, age, address and occupation together with a Japanese stamp and the signature of the issuing officer. By mid-afternoon, the Japanese authorities at this particular concentration camp had detained at least 300 men and youths from Samba Ikat Village alone. In the late afternoon, military lorries pulled up beside the camp and drove away crammed with prisoners.

Yeo Hung Chung, of 405 Samba Ikat Village, had earlier in the day reported to the 8 1/2 milestone screening operation. One of the fortunate ones, he had been issued an identification paper and had quickly returned home. Around 6 o'clock that evening he noticed three lorries driving slowly past his house. Each vehicle was loaded with people Hung Chung recognised had been with him earlier that morning. He particularly noticed his friend, Tay Cheng Kiang, a teacher from the village.

He also spotted two women among the prisoners in one of the lorries.

Twenty minutes later, Hung Chung heard the sound of machineguns firing. Not long after, the three lorries returned. Only this time they were empty.

At 7 pm, a second convoy of three lorries loaded with prisoners passed Hung Chung's house. Again, after a time, he heard machineguns. Again, the lorries drove by empty on their return journey.

Two days later, Tan Hai Suar, a farmer, was inside his Samba Ikat home, about to have his midday meal, when two cars carrying Japanese military officers drove by. One, flying a red flag, went past the front of the house. The other, with a blue flag, drove by the rear. Both vehicles stopped beside a nearby complex of air-raid shelters that had been constructed by the British as part of Singapore's southern defences prior to the outbreak of hostilities. After inspecting the shelters the Japanese returned to their vehicles and drove off.

Five hours later, Hai Suar spotted six lorries loaded with young Chinese men driving slowly towards his home. Also in the lorries was a contingent of Japanese troops. The six vehicles parked in a rear lane. Soon they were joined by the two cars that had driven up earlier that afternoon. Each still flew its identification flag. Hai Suar hid behind a mango tree and watched, horror-stricken. The Chinese in the backs of the lorries were ordered down and lined up along the open-topped air-raid shelters. Two Japanese officers who emerged from the cars proceeded to read aloud in the Japanese language from documents they had brought with them. The officers then departed.

Soon afterwards the firing squad began mowing down the Chinese prisoners with machineguns. The victims crumpled and fell conveniently into the shelters as the frightful shooting gallery continued. It lasted for about ten minutes, then abruptly stopped. A hideous chorus of wailing and crying, pleas and moans, rent the night air. Back came the shooting, but for a much shorter time . . . . followed by a few individual rifle shots. It was done.

Before leaving, the Japanese troops indifferently shovelled some earth into the shelters. But arms and legs and heads still protruded. Originally built to protect life, the shelters that evening were transformed into a grotesque montage of death, a grisly monument to vengeance and euphoric, post-battle madness. For several days Hai Suar and his fellow farmers in the area found it impossible to approach the area. Then the stench demanded action be taken and together they re-buried the dead.

T he agony of the condemned and executed was but part of the story. Equally monstrous was the agony of the condemned who, through miraculous good fortune, managed to escape. For them it would be a matter of learning to live with their anguish for years to come. But it was the widespread trauma of the bereaved — those countless thousands who lost loved ones during this brutal fortnight — that would have its lasting impact on Singapore society.

Lee Keng Jin, who lived at 94 Lorong N, Telok Kurau Road, was at the Telok Kurau English School on the afternoon of February 18, 1942 when his 18-year-old son, Chai Jiang, a clerk at the British Naval Base, was detained by the kempeitai. That night the frantic father, released from detention earlier that afternoon, traced his son to a compound house at 142 Telok Kurau Road, one of four similar houses where former government servants were being detained under armed military guard.

With the help of a small Eurasian boy, the father managed to pass some coffee and biscuits to his teenage son. On the following morning, the father again returned to the house with more coffee and biscuits. By now a large crowd of agitated relatives had gathered and the Japanese were prohibiting any contact with the prisoners. The distraught Keng Jin went off and returned again at 2 pm. But the house in which his son had been detained was now empty. So, too, were the other three houses. Desperate, the father made enquiries in the neighbourhood. While he had been away, all those held in the four houses had been driven in lorries to their executions.

Mrs Elizabeth Choy, at 82 years of age now one of the grand old ladies of Singapore, vividly recalls the day the Japanese began their mopping up operation in Singapore. As the artillery and aerial bombardment had intensified around her MacKenzie Road home during the final hours of the Singapore siege, it was decided the family should seek shelter in a safer area. Mrs Choy, her father, stepmother, three sisters, elder brother and his pregnant wife, and younger brother — a party with ages ranging from 5 to 70 years — moved in with a relative residing at the staff quarters of the Singapore General Hospital on Outram Road.

Reporting first to the Tanjong Pagar police station on February 18, Mrs Choy and her family were instructed to go to Jalan Besar for their "registration.". There all the women and children were released after an overnight stay. Her older brother also received his freedom early. When it came to the elderly father's turn to walk from the concentration camp he turned sadly to farewell his 17-year-old youngest and favourite son who remained under detention. Throughout the young man's short life he and his father had been inseparable.

"Father, Father, take me with you. Don't leave me behind. Why do you leave me behind?" pleaded the fresh-faced teenager. There was nothing the father could say, or do.

In the weeks that followed, recalls Mrs Choy, her father went nearly insane with despair over his missing son. For two months the family trudged the streets of Singapore hunting for clues of the youth's whereabouts. As they went, they heard rumour after rumour of the thousands taken away and shot.

Mrs Elizabeth Choy, OBE, OSS, PBS; at 82 one of Singapore's grand ladies. Mrs Choy was among the hundreds of thousands of Singapore Chinese caught in the Japanese screening programme. Afterwards she spent weeks searching vainly for her young brother. Her war was just beginning.

Clinging to the last strands of hope, they met hordes of fathers and mothers looking for sons, sisters looking for brothers and wives looking for husbands. Mrs Choy entered every Japanese office she could locate. Wherever there was a Japanese sentry posted she made enquiries. The answer was always the same: "We have no information."

At the end of two months, private enquiries suggested Mrs Choy's young brother had indeed been executed. But the information was vague and inconclusive and to this day all the family really knows is that the boy failed to return home from the concentration point at Jalan Besar.

Elizabeth Choy's war was just beginning. On November 15, 1943, she would be arrested by the Japanese. There would follow a harrowing 200 days of incarceration and torture at the kempeitai's infamous YMCA headquarters on Orchard Road, opposite the Cathay Building.

Mrs. Choy's extraordinary heroism and the awards bestowed on her by a grateful Britain have been the focus of numerous newspaper, magazine, radio and television interviews over the years. It is justly the stuff of local legend.

But an aspect of the Elizabeth Choy story never revealed until now is that the torturer she ultimately helped send to the gallows was the man who, faced with imminent death, would tell the British all he knew about Tsuji. His death row interrogation, as we will discover later in our story, would give the British their first real insight into the man directly responsible for the Singapore massacres ∎

Chapter 6

Tracing the origins

———— ✦ ————

November, 1941, was a busy month for General Tomoyuki Yamashita.

It began with a priority signal recalling him from his posting in Manchuria for meetings at the Imperial Military Headquarters in Tokyo. During these, he learned he was to be appointed commanding officer of Japan's 25th Army. His task was to drive Britain from Malaya and Singapore. Arrangements had been made for him to leave for his new command immediately.

Yamashita farewelled his wife Hisako during a brief evening meeting at the Japanese Officers' Club located behind the Emperor's palace, near the Yasukuni shrine. He told her nothing of his new appointment except that he was departing hurriedly for another extended overseas assignment. Within a few hours he was aboard a military flight bound for Formosa. There, he made an overnight stop and the following day, November 6, flew on to Saigon where, still attired in his Manchurian winter uniform, he first met his newly installed High Command.

Immediately, Yamashita encountered problems among fellow officers, some of whom had been involved in groundwork for the Malaya invasion for up to a year. They regarded his arrival as that of an outsider.

Colonel Masanobu Tsuji, for 12 months the Malaya campaign planning chief, had become mesmerised by his own importance during this preparatory period. He firmly believed destiny had decreed his personal role critical to victory. Tsuji was jealously protective of the knowledge he had accumulated and the network for which he had been the driving force up to that point. Ambitious, self-centred and short tempered, he was quick to recognise Yamashita's ignorance of tropical terrain and, from the very outset, viewed his commanding officer's appointment with disdain.

Yamashita noted, but initially ignored, all undercurrents and spent the next 18 days in Saigon immersing himself in the plans, strategy, and intelligence reports that had been meticulously compiled over the months. Tsuji and his immediate staff had drawn up what was known as "The 25th Army Operations Instruction Plan" — the invasion blueprint. It concentrated on battle tactics and strategy. At this stage, the planning chief held back any reference to the measures he had also prepared for subjugating Singapore's majority Chinese population once the island had fallen. He felt he needed further time to size up Yamashita's personality before suggesting anything quite so controversial.

At 9 pm on November 25, his 56th birthday, Yamashita flew from Saigon to Hainan Island, in Southern China where his army was assembling prior to boarding troop ships in the port of Samah. He joined his headquarters vessel, *Ryujo Maru*, and in a small stuffy cabin returned once more to studying maps, military assessments, and latest reports on the deployment of British defences.

On November 30, the 25th Army Commander received orders from Tokyo advising that the invasion of Malaya would begin on December 8 (local time). It had, indeed, been a busy month.

As the initial 20,000-strong invasion force transferred to the convoy that would sail them to the three projected invasion beaches, all soldiers — officers and other ranks alike — received copies of a pocket-sized booklet headed: "READ THIS

ALONE — AND THE WAR CAN BE WON."

The preparatory remarks explained that the booklet had been designed for easy reading in the cramped environs of a troop ship. Essentially it was a fighting man's guide to conquering Malaya and Singapore and explored a wide spectrum of subjects related to warfare in the tropics. There were instructions on what to do aboard ship while enroute to the beaches, tips on seaborne landing techniques, hints for marching through hot weather, camping in the jungles, tropical hygiene and the like.

But the booklet also endeavoured to present a simplified explanation of Tokyo's motivations for embarking on such an invasion. Sub-sections headed "A treasure-house of the Far East, seized by the British, Americans, French and the Dutch" and "A hundred million Asians tyrannized by three hundred thousand whites" were less than subtle exercises in last minute political indoctrination.

One sub-section dealt specifically with the subject of "Overseas Chinese." Its inclusion in the booklet clearly establishes that the perceived need to control the local Chinese, once Japan had seized Malaya and Singapore, had been under careful study for months.

The booklet purported to give a thumb-nail sketch of the background to the region's Overseas Chinese problems. Referring to the attempted attack on Japan by Mongol Emperor, Kublai Khan, which ended in storm-tossed disaster in Hakata Bay, some 650 years earlier, it related how the emperor had then swung his attentions south with an attack by 300,000 troops in a fleet of 1,000 ships on the north eastern coast of Java. The objective of this second attack, the booklet explained, had been to plunder rare South East Asian treasures.

Although the cunning local defenders had largely thwarted the invaders, there had, from this time onwards, been a continuing Chinese emigration to South East Asian territories. In these lands, the Chinese had risen from lowly positions, such as clerks and coolies, to become men of considerable fortune. Their successes had been largely achieved, the booklet claimed, by deceiving the gullible and lazy natives and colluding with the British, Americans, French and Dutch.

The economic power of the "Chinese colonists" had expanded dramatically over the years and their numerical strength throughout the whole area was now around five million. Specifically, the text drew the invading army's attention to the fact that Overseas Chinese in Malaya and Singapore contributed military funds to Chungking, then headquarters for Nationalist Chinese leader, Chiang Kai-shek, against whom the Imperial Japanese Army had been waging war since the mid 1930's.

The Japanese soldiers were advised to take note of three important facts about the Overseas Chinese in Malaya and Singapore. Firstly, they had engineered, in concert with the European administrators, a variety of clever economic and political schemes to extort money from the native population. Secondly, they had, for the most part, no racial or national consciousness. Finally, they harboured no outside interest other than making money.

It would therefore be difficult, the invading soldiers were warned, to win across Overseas Chinese to the idea of an Asian brotherhood, or enlist their co-operation in any scheme that did not promise personal wealth. For all intents and purposes the local Chinese were being portrayed as the invading army's second enemy.

The booklet was produced and published by the top secret Taiwan Army Research Unit which had begun operating in the Formosan capital of Taipeh in November the previous year. The unit had been set up on the personal orders of General Hideki Tojo, then Japan's War Minister, and was established as the intelligence and planning nerve-centre for the Malaya-Singapore campaign.

Pointedly, it was on the recommendations of Tojo himself

that the mercurial Tsuji had been sent from his staff posting at Tokyo's Imperial Military Headquarters to become a founder member of this important office. Tsuji's link to Tojo came through his close friendship with one Colonel Takushiro Hattori. Tsuji and Hattori had served together as fellow staff officers in Japan's Kwantung Army.

In the summer of 1939, both officers were on the operations and planning side of an infamous debacle on the Manchurian-Mongolian frontier which came to be known as the "Nomonhan Incident." Here the Russians inflicted some 30,000 casualties on the attacking Japanese force. Some historical accounts suggest Tsuji's involvement resulted in heightened Japanese casualties. To a lesser extent, Hattori was also held responsible. Tsuji was known to have covered up evidence pointing to accountability.

Nomonhan served as the catalyst for a bond of friendship between Tsuji and Hattori that would have devastating consequences in the years to follow.

Twelve months later, the two friends were rising stars on the Imperial Military Headquarters Staff in Tokyo. Hattori had the ear of Tojo and would ultimately become his secretary as well as Adjutant of the War Ministry. For the influence peddling Tsuji, Hattori was a trump card which he would unhesitatingly play throughout his World War 11 career. During his time in Taiwan, Tsuji reported regularly back to Hattori. His reports were fed direct to Tojo

In his personal account of the Japanese invasion of Malaya and Singapore, Tsuji boasted that, in six months, with a staff of 30, his Taiwan unit "planned the military operations of the whole Army which was to move south, and *also the administration of the territory to be occupied*." (Author's italics.)

In short, Tsuji and his fellow Taiwan unit colleagues, aside from their military planning activities, were directly concerned with all problems likely to be encountered while imposing

Japanese-led administrations in captured territories. From Tsuji's viewpoint, nothing was more critical in this area than the need to subjugate the Overseas Chinese.

Intelligence was the fuel of Tsuji's functions and copies of all reports from Japan's extensive pre-war spy networks operating in both Malaya and Singapore were destined to end up on his desk. Moreover, he had full authority to request any specific intelligence assignments from these networks in addition to establishing his own independent information gathering operations.

So it was that Tsuji, while working in Taiwan, ordered Japan's Singapore-centred espionage networks to collect name lists of all anti-Japanese Chinese residents on the island. Following the frustrations he had faced as a staff officer with the Kwantung Army, Tsuji was determined neither nationalist nor communist-leaning Chinese would be given the chance of undermining Japanese authority once Malaya and Singapore had fallen.

An important figure on the intelligence side of the Taiwan Army Research Unit was Major Tadahiko Hayashi. His operational skills on clandestine missions were greatly admired by Tsuji and, as the months went by, a close personal friendship developed between these two senior officers. Tsuji's fanatical militarist views were shared by the elitist Hayashi who soon found himself appointed to some of the Taiwan unit's most delicate planning projects.

Another close associate of Tsuji's at this time was Major Shigeharu Asaeda, a graduate of the Army Staff College, who departed a desk job at the Tokyo War Ministry under a cloud in late 1940 and pitched up at the Taiwan Army Research Unit offering his services for espionage work. Tsuji, quickly recognised a fellow ultranationalist. He regarded Asaeda as fearless, tough and dependable and employed him as one of his research officers.

With Hattori in Tokyo and Hayashi and Asaeda in Taiwan,

Tsuji had established the power nucleus he needed to propel his influence and ideas in the months ahead. In the latter part of 1941, as planning for the invasion entered its final stage, Tsuji dispatched Hayashi and Asaeda on related intelligence gathering missions to southern Thailand and northern Malaya. Both men went in disguise. Asaeda, in coolie dress, infiltrated as far south as the British military airstrips at Kota Bahru, Machang and Gong Kedah in the north-eastern Malayan state of Kelantan. The information both brought back after daring ground reconnaissance exploits proved critical to the invasion blueprint.

Later, Tsuji himself would make a dangerous photo reconnaissance flight from Saigon taking him first over the proposed invasion landing beaches at Singora and Patani in southern Siam. Crossing to the north-west corner of Malaya for an inspection of the British airbase at Alor Star, Tsuji would then track south to Sungei Patani, and even on to Taiping, before heading back to Saigon via an overflight of defence installations at Kota Bahru.

These and other exploits gained considerable kudos for Tsuji and his two cohorts.

As the time approached for phasing out the Taiwan Army Research Unit and incorporating its personnel within the 25th Army hierarchy, Tsuji and his team flew off to Saigon where they re-established their office on September 25. One by one, they received their new postings. Tsuji became chief of the 25th Army's Operations and Planning section. In an appointment over which Tsuji had considerable influence, Hayashi found himself installed as an intelligence staff officer within the new High Command structure. In a similarly manipulated appointment, Asaeda became assistant deputy of operations directly under his mentor. The very nature of their new jobs ensured that Tsuji, Hayashi and Asaeda, would all be working in close collaboration throughout the action to come. The old Taiwan unit was being dismantled, but the influence and elitism of its membership would prevail. No one would become more aware of this fact than Yamashita himself as the invasion he headed gathered momentum.

Coordinated seaborne landings on beaches at Kota Bahru in north eastern Malaya, and Patani and Singora in south eastern Siam were followed by rapid infantry thrusts south. The Japanese strategy was to keep defending forces continually off balance. Part of their plan involved maintaining simultaneous warfare on two fronts down the length of the peninsula. On the eastern side, Kota Bahru airport fell quickly, followed by the nearby Gong Kedah and Machang airfields. Within four days Japanese 18th Division units were in firm control of that region and the British north-eastern front defenders were locked into a perilous escape south down the single-gauge rail line linking Kuala Krai and Kuala Lipis.

But the main Japanese military punch would be delivered on British Malaya Command's north-western war front. While Japanese forces from the Patani landing drove across the lower reaches of Siam towards the hinterland Malayan border township of Kroh, those from Singora thrusted south down the main trunk route to engage Britain's 11th Indian Division defences at Jitra in northern Kedah.

Japanese 5th division infantrymen, spearheaded by tanks, hurled themselves against the inexperienced Indian troops on December 11. The highly mobile attacking forces employed swift out-flanking and encirclement movements. Tanks and tactics on land, and air support flown from the newly captured Siamese airfields at Singora and Patani, completely rattled the defenders and overnight Jitra became a rout. Maintaining their momentum, the Japanese invaders, without pause, advanced on their next target, the Kedah state capital of Alor Star. Here the British, unnerved by Jitra, decided to retreat and here, too, the old Taiwan hands began exerting strong influence on 25th Army strategy.

What amounted to a dramatically revised five-point

operational plan for the rest of the Malaya campaign was devised in Alor Star by the High Command's intelligence section headed by Lt. Colonel Ichiji Sugita but with major contributions by both Hayashi and Tsuji. Sugita and the Tsuji group worked well together and this close association would have an important bearing on events to take place in Singapore.

Given approval by Yamashita, the new operational plan from thereon became the primary reference point for all battlefield strategy and tactics. Not surprisingly, the plan was the source of further prestige for the Tsuji group. Years later, Tsuji would proudly boast that their plan 'worked perfectly, like the cogwheel of a watch.'

Using it as a basic reference document, he drew up a prospective campaign programme in his personal war diary:

December 15:	Crossing of the Perak River.
January 14/15:	Control of Kuala Lumpur.
January 31:	Seizure of Johore Bahru.
February 11:	Victory in Singapore.
	(The anniversary of the Emperor Jimmu's coronation in 660 B.C.)

Remarkably enough, the timetable was just four days short in predicting the fall of Singapore and Tsuji would later gloat: "The paper plan was realized almost as if the pages had been torn off a calendar."

Yamashita, for his part, had begun to sense the threat to his authority posed by the influence Tsuji was wielding through his network.

The Army Commander had also learned by this stage about his operations chief's regular reports, via Hattori, to War Minister Tojo. Among fellow staff officers, Tsuji frequently alluded to his special relationship with military headquarters in Tokyo. From Yamashita's point of view, Tsuji was not only undermining his authority on the spot in Malaya, but also exposing him to intra-War Ministry politics back home where he had no hope of defending himself.

The first open confrontation between Yamashita and Tsuji at a High Command conference occurred soon after the 5th Division's Kobayashi Battalion seized Penang island on December 17. Yamashita was angered by reports of widespread misbehaviour by Japanese soldiers on the island. He was particularly incensed that three of the invading troops had gone on a raping and pillaging rampage in the island's capital, Georgetown. Yamashita ordered that the three involved be executed. He also ordered the battalion's commanding officer, Major Kobayashi, be punished with one month's close arrest. This entailed the severe indignity of being removed from the battlefield in time of war, confined to quarters and reduced to half pay for the duration of the suspension.

Yamashita overlooked, or perhaps didn't know, that ten years earlier, Tsuji and Kobayashi had been classmates at the Ichigaya Military College. Tsuji vehemently argued that it would be wrong to punish Kobayashi during the campaign as it could affect the morale of other officers and units. Yamashita rejected this and instructed that Tsuji personally convey the order to Kobayashi and a regimental commander who was to receive a similar penalty.

A reluctant Tsuji complied and came away from his meeting with Kobayashi feeling his old classmate might well commit *hara-kiri*. Kobayashi avoided the ceremonial suicide option, but this did nothing to mollify Tsuji's bitterness towards his commander. Yamashita, for his part, went on to write in his diary: "I want my troops to behave with dignity, but most of them do not seem to have the ability to do so. This is very important now that Japan is taking her place in the world. These men must be educated up to their new role in foreign countries."

The Army commander was not content with letting the

problem lie there. He went to the extent of ordering the chief of the 25th Army's political section, Colonel Watanabe, to take strong measures against any soldier found ill-treating civilians during the campaign. Still, his instructions had little effect. The speed of the invasion south created more pressing problems and the majority of High Command officers seemed disinterested in such mundane matters as discipline after the battle. Defeat of the enemy was top priority. Everything else paled to insignificance beside it.

Tensions within the High Command were stretched even further with the mid-December arrival by train from Bangkok of the Japanese Imperial Guards Division This unit was led by Lt. General Takuma Nishimura, and his Chief of Staff, Major General Imaye. Immediately, animosity and suspicion erupted between Yamashita and the two Imperial Guards generals. The 25th Army commander found Nishimura arrogant and aloof and regarded Imaye, a former lecturer at the Tokyo War College, as an insufferable, intellectual snob.

"The Prince's Forces", as the elite Imperial Guards were known, had not seen action since the Russo-Japanese War in the early years of the century. Very conscious of this fact, Nishimura was anxious to have his troops notch up some quick battlefield successes to dispel widely held concerns over the Guards' lack of combat experience. Yamashita had his own plans for the newly arrived men.

With the British retreat to Kampar and obvious indications Malaya Command was preparing a major defensive stand at this tin mining town dominating the Kinta Valley, Yamashita decided on introducing new tactics. These involved sending boatloads of assault troops down the Malacca Straits to infiltrate eastwards from the coast. The infiltrating troops were to attack behind the defending lines and, if possible, cut off the British north-eastern war front from its only supply line — the main trunk route south to Kuala Lumpur and beyond to Singapore. On New Year's Eve, Yamashita confided to his diary: "On this first day of the New Year I breathe the air of the South. I was up at 5 am and it was already hot. I must put away recollections of the past. My duty is half done, although success is still a problem. The future of my country is now as safe as if we were based on a great mountain. However, I would like to achieve my plan without killing too many of the enemy."

Outflanking moves by sea were certainly not in the strategic campaign plan for Malaya revised by Hayashi and Tsuji in Alor Star. When raised by Yamashita during a staff conference at his Taiping headquarters, called to discuss strategy for the Kampar battle, the Army Commander ran into instant and determined opposition from senior officers. They argued that Japanese forces had been insufficiently trained in seaborne manoeuvres. Furthermore, they said, seaborne assaults down the west coast would be exposed to unacceptable risks from British naval patrols. Particularly vocal in his disapproval — and seemingly leader of the anti-Yamashita voices on this issue — was Tsuji.

Tsuji maintained that as infantry assaults down the main north-south trunk road had produced spectacular results, the formula for success should not be altered. More of the same outflanking and encirclement tactics on land was all that would be required to defeat the now demoralised British defenders. Furthermore, insisted Tsuji, the flotilla of motorized assault boats being shipped overland from the original invasion beaches should be preserved for the all important final crossing of the Straits of Johore and the attack on Singapore.

Yamashita ignored his critics, flatly overruled his planning and operations officer, and ordered 1,500 men from the 5th Division be dispatched in assault craft down the Straits of Malacca.

From an operational standpoint, the first Japanese attempt at infiltration by sea proved a disaster. By the time the boats began edging their way south along the coast, the concerns of High Command officers on the wisdom of the manoeuvre had filtered down to those directly involved. Confusion set in when the first British reconnaissance aircraft was spotted and the flotilla became split up. Only one of the assault's five separate units landed at its correct beachhead and then returned north to rejoin the main body of Japanese forces, its leader convinced the operation had been aborted.

Another unit suffered heavy casualties from British shore-based guns. It stumbled through mangrove swamps and got lost in nearby coastal jungle. Two others made it safely ashore — but in the wrong areas — and clashed briefly with British forces whose exaggerated reports on the coastal infiltrations resulted in an almost panic decision to abandon the defence of Kampar and withdraw further south. The seaborne infiltration attempt might have been a military fiasco, but from the psychological point of view its effect had been stunning. Yamashita was delighted. Tsuji was livid.

At the next staff conference, this time in Ipoh, Tsuji outlined the mistakes that had been made and urged all ideas of further seaborne operations be dropped. Once again Yamashita ignored Tsuji's advice and merely switched units in the boats; this time ordering Imperial Guards to infiltrate behind British lines. Recognising his views had been rejected a second time, Tsuji became so piqued that he refused to speak to Yamashita for 48 hours. Learning from the initial mistakes, Imperial Guards field officers quickly refined the seaborne manoeuvres. These resulted in accelerated withdrawals south by defending forces and have since become regarded by military historians as illustrative of Yamashita's genius when it came to devising unsettling combat improvisations.

These events are recorded, not so much to provide new insight on the course of Japan's Malaya campaign, but rather to demonstrate the extent of the running feud throughout this period between Yamashita and the influential clique of officers led by the petulant Tsuji, and to trace the animosity to its Taiwan unit origins. This aspect of the campaign has never been fully highlighted before because the overwhelming weight of historical research on the fighting has recorded events from the perspective of the British or Australian defenders. Within this context, rivalry and discord among the 25th Army's command hierarchy was of marginal interest. But herein, as we will see, lay the vital component, the very trigger mechanism for the Singapore massacres.

Before Yamashita moved his headquarters from Ipoh to follow the battles south, the first instalment of anti-Japanese Chinese names, requested by Tsuji back in Taiwan, was delivered to the High Command. Responsibility for its safe-keeping, ultimate preparation and publication fell to the intelligence section headed by Sugita and his deputy, Hayashi. There can be no question that Sugita by now knew as much about Tsuji's plans to instil control through terror in Singapore as Hayashi and Asaeda.

As the battles progressed down the Malayan peninsula to the final Singapore showdown, feuding within the Japanese High Command intensified. By late January, with his forces ranged against both Australian and British units across Johore state, Yamashita was now certain Tsuji was plotting his downfall in collaboration with Tojo and other key military figures in the Japanese capital.

Yamashita saw himself in a "win-but-no-win" situation. The more successful he became on the battlefield, the worse it seemed for him personally. Press reports from Japanese journalists covering the action gave star billing to the general they dubbed "Tiger of Malaya." As public acclaim heightened, certain senior officers at the Imperial Military Headquarters began the lobbying for Yamashita to become next War Minister. From Yamashita's viewpoint, newspaper accounts and the resulting adulation only fanned the fires of jealousy both at headquarters in Tokyo and within his battlefield High Command. Those close to the army commander recognised his torment and his Chief of Staff, Lt. General Sosaku Suzuki, noted

It is 5 pm on February 15, 1942. Britain's Malaya Command chief, Lt. General Arthur E. Percival (far right), walks dejectedly up the Ford Factory's sweeping driveway for his fateful surrender date with his Japanese opposite number, Lt. General Tomoyuki Yamashita. On the far left is Major Cyril Wild, Percival's interpreter. On Percival's immediate right is Brigadier Newbigging. The Japanese officer escorting the British party is Colonel Ichiji Sugita, Yamashita's chief of intelligence who also heads the enemy High Command's Information Bureau.

shortly before the battle for Singapore began: "Our general is near to mental explosion."

Viewed against this background, Yamashita's final invasion across the Straits of Johore with just 30,000 frontline infantrymen pitted against a combined defence force of some 120,000 men — an attack which ultimately delivered Britain her greatest ever military defeat — becomes all the more remarkable. Yamashita would later describe the gamble he took as "a bluff — a bluff that worked."

As he explained it: "I had 30,000 men and was outnumbered more than three to one. I knew if I had to fight long for Singapore I would be beaten. That is why the surrender had to be at once. I was very frightened all the time that the British would discover our numerical weakness and lack of supplies and force me into disastrous street fighting."

At 5.15 pm on February 15, Yamashita met his exhausted British counterpart, Lt. General Arthur E. Percival, in a cramped office in the Ford Factory at the 9th milestone Bukit Timah Road. There, in his final field headquarters for the campaign, Yamashita played out his bluff to its shattering conclusion. During those brief, one-sided negotiations, Percival conveyed his concern for the well-being of the shell and bomb blasted city's civilian population and the defeated troops wandering its cratered streets. He advised Yamashita there would be massive confusion throughout the town if the victorious army moved in that night. Percival asked his Japanese oppostite number to delay his entry to the city until the following morning.

Yamashita immediately agreed and, in fact, went a step further. One of his first orders after emerging from the surrender room was to place the Singapore city area strictly off limits to all Japanese main force units. Only selected kempeitai and auxiliary kempeitai troops would be allowed into the downtown area. They would form an integral part of a special garrison force created to ensure law and order. Yamashita's instructions on this occasion were a carbon copy of the

General Yamashita (far left facing camera) speaks to Major Cyril Wild (back to camera on left) during the surrender negotiations at the Ford factory. General Percival, the British commander, is back to camera on the right. The mustachioed Colonel Sugita is immediately to Yamashita's left.

Japan's 25th Army Commander-in-Chief, Lt. General Tomoyuki Yamashita — the "Tiger of Malaya."

measures introduced by the Japanese in China in an effort to avoid repetition of the horrendous Rape of Nanking in December, 1937.

This decision was consistent with the Japanese commander whose private war diary indicated he was continually troubled by the brutal excesses of his front line troops. It was consistent with the commander who had, against considerable opposition, insisted three of his infantrymen be executed and two senior officers severely punished following brutality against civilians in Penang.

It was consistent with the commander who had previously dispatched air-dropped letters to Percival seeking an early British surrender on the grounds that civilian lives could be saved if street fighting through downtown Singapore could be avoided. It would also be consistent with a commander who, within the next 48 hours would confide to his diary: "Some of our men don't know how to treat British officers and their behaviour seems impolite to me. I have given instructions that they must be more polite to surrendered officers."

Yet, 72 hours later, the Singapore massacres would begin ■

Chapter 7

Positioning the pawns

———— ◆ ————

A fter a crestfallen Percival had departed Yamashita's headquarters, the entire Japanese High Command staff gathered in an ante-room to celebrate their victory. Facing north-east towards the Emperor's palace and with *sake* glasses raised, they drank a silent toast.

That night, Yamashita retired to bed at 11 pm in his makeshift quarters at the side of the factory. Charged with emotion, the 56-year-old general found it impossible to sleep. Several times during the night, he left his room and wandered alone in the factory grounds. As the first grey smudges of dawn smeared an eastern sky on that Monday, February 16, Yamashita strolled to the edge of a tree-covered slope behind his headquarters' position, bowed low and ceremoniously to the north-east, and began praying.

In stark contrast to the tranquillity of that tree covered slope, the town area of Singapore six miles to the south had overnight witnessed widespread disorder. As word of the surrender spread, marauding groups of defeated, drunken soldiers, both Australian and British, lurched through war-wrecked buildings in search of more liquor to anaesthetize their shame. Emboldened by a paralysed police force, local looters descended on freshly vacated homes of wealthy expatriates who had fled the island in overloaded ships during the chaotic final days. They stripped houses bare while others concentrated on plundering department stores, warehouses, godowns and storerooms.

98

Unexploded ordinance, abandoned small arms, military equipment, rubble and bloated corpses littered the main thoroughfares. Most roads were heavily damaged after weeks of relentless Japanese air attacks and, more latterly, artillery bombardments. With a choice of firearms on hand for the picking, rival looting gangs shot it out with one another over left-behind spoils. The arrival of daylight did little to dilute the determination of the plunderers.

Tsuji and Hayashi had worked late into the night of February 15 preparing the plan for the victorious 25th Army's formal wresting of control of Singapore from the demoralised British. In fact it was a plan that Tsuji, as the responsible originating officer, had been brooding over for some days. He had been driven, more than ever, by the aberration that this was the decisive historical moment for which destiny had been preparing him. His intensifying discord with Yamashita throughout the Malaya campaign had only reinforced his resolve to continue manipulating matters to his own ends and he had proceeded with his tasks accordingly.

Tsuji had anticipated Yamashita's decision to adopt a cautious security approach and prohibit main force army units from entering downtown Singapore. He created, as Yamashita requested, a specially designated garrison force or keibitai, following the format established by the Japanese Army in China. It composed of kempeitai and what the Japanese Army classified as hojo kempei — auxiliary military police — extracted from main force units that had undergone some training in law enforcement duties.

An important ingredient was Tsuji's choice of Major General Saburo Kawamura as Singapore Garrison Commander. This was the man who would ostensibly be the high profile commander and from whom would appear to flow the entire programme of installing the new military regime and ensuring its authority. The 47-year-old Kawamura, a somewhat placid, ponderous man, more interested in debating political and military philosophies than formulating hard tactics, was ideal for what Tsuji had in mind. He was the perfect pawn, the convenient cover; easily manipulated, simple to dupe. Behind him Tsuji could operate his nefarious schemes with impunity.

The chief of operations had two more important moves up his sleeve. Firstly, to ensure direct control of the garrison command apparatus, Tsuji had his trusted Taiwan collaborator, Tadahiko Hayashi, temporarily seconded from the intelligence staff to become Kawamura's personal assistant. The secondment was strictly for the duration of the proposed "mopping-up" measures. Secondly, he made certain his reliable assistant, Shigeharu Asaeda, would remain on hand.

Tsuji was now positioned, protected and ready to introduce his solution to the local Chinese problem.

With typical flamboyance, he led the initial group of Japanese officers into Singapore city early on the morning of February 16 — the "first triumphal entry," he would later describe it. He drove from the Ford Factory with staff officers Okamura and Kawajima in a car bedecked with a Japanese flag. Tsuji recorded motoring past "shell craters, burnt-out cars and trucks, and other traces of the recent severe fighting" and described the town as a "whirlpool of chaos."

The three officers took group photographs of defeated Australian and British troops and were surprised to see a lack of hostility in the faces of the enemy. Tsuji would later write: "The English storehouses and dwellings were swallowed in waves of looting Chinese and Malays. Even the women and children were all mobilized like thieves at a fire. The inhabitants, who were to be pitied, were today giving vent to the feelings of hostility that more than a hundred years of coercion had aroused, and each was struggling to get to the front and take by force an indemnity several times the value of his losses during the war."

Tsuji drove on to the Malaya Headquarters at Fort Canning and, climbing to the roof of the building, noted the Japanese emblem fluttering atop Bukit Timah to the north. Concluding that the Fort Canning establishment was an unsuitable location for the 25th Army's initial administrative headquarters, Tsuji chose the school buildings and grounds of Raffles Institution as a temporary alternative. The classrooms had been used as an emergency hospital during the invasion and many were still blood-splattered. In addition, the complex had suffered several direct hits by artillery rounds.

The sequence of events as the Japanese now moved to assert their authority on the island is important to understanding how the Singapore massacres began.

Kawamura's captured diary, anonymously filed away and forgotten at the Government Public Record Office in Kew Gardens, London, provides a unique means of checking both the sequence and the degree of involvement of the Garrison Commander himself. The original diary, a small black book measuring 6 inches by 3 inches, filled with daily handwritten ink jottings, is accompanied by an extensive, if indifferent, typed translation in English.

The original document bears no formal identification linking it to an owner. Nor, for that matter, does the translation. Its file is merely headed "Jap War Diary." But by matching dates and appointments, it is simple to confirm that the little black book indeed belonged to Kawamura, the officer under whose apparent authority the Singapore massacres took place.

On February 15, Kawamura, then Commander of the 9th Infantry Brigade, recorded the appearance of white flags in British positions on the battlefield. The diary shows he shortly thereafter issued orders to his troops to cease all action as the enemy had surrendered. That evening, he emerged from his trench in a jungle treeline near MacRitchie Reservoir and ate with his officers and a press reporter from the *Chungoku Shimbun*.

Early the next morning, he called his men together and read them divisional instructions relating to the British capitulation. After paying homage to the Japanese Emperor, the unit listened to their commander's address on the subject of personal conduct

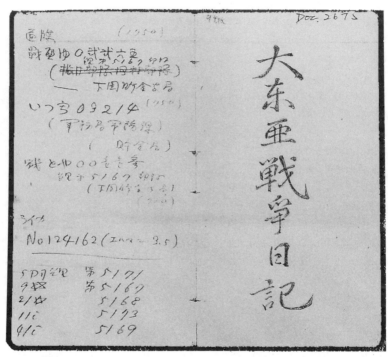

The inside front cover and first page of the private war diary belonging to Lt. General Saburo Kawamura, Japan's Singapore Garrison Commander at the time of the massacres.

now that hostilities were over. The diary goes on to reveal that the enemy directly in front of Kawamura's troops — that is, on the south side of Adam Road — were gradually disarmed throughout the day. As the numbers of prisoners began to accumulate, Kawamura formed a special unit commanded by Major Mitsushiba to handle POW problems.

First thing on the morning of February 17, Kawamura moved his brigade headquarters from the treeline to the nearby golf club building where the Singapore Island Country Club complex is now situated. He spent the remainder of the day re-organising his command and, in the early evening, received orders to assemble units further forward and begin sweeping the battlefields.

Late that night, according to the diary, Kawamura first learned he was to be Singapore's Garrison Commander. In other words two full days of Japanese presence in downtown Singapore had passed following the British surrender before the chosen Garrison Commander got to hear of his new assignment. Kempeitai officials would be in position more than 48 hours before Kawamura arrived at his post. Furthermore, as we will soon learn, killings bearing unmistakeable similarities to the required massacre format had begun long before Kawamura drove into town. The obvious question is posed: Kawamura — plotter or pawn?

At 10 am on February 18, the Garrison Commander was formally inducted by Yamashita himself at a brief ceremony in one of the Raffles Institution classrooms. Orders informed Kawamura that his garrison force would comprise the No 2 Field Kempeitai and auxiliary military police comprising the 1st Battalion, 11th Infantry Regiment and the 1st Battalion, 41st Infantry Regiment. His orders also informed him that Hayashi, from the headquarters' intelligence office, would be assigned to his command.

Following the conclusion of the formalities Yamashita, in the presence of the gathered officers, spoke to Kawamura in general terms about his first operational order as garrison chief. This concerned military "mopping -up" measures." The Army Commander referred to pressing requirements to move main force units to other theatres of combat. He pointed out the substantial law and order problem faced in Singapore. Furthermore, he drew attention to the expanding underground activities by anti-Japanese Chinese guerrillas and the security threat these developments imposed. His remarks were brief but he made one very significant final point. He said details of the methods to be employed carrying out the "mopping-up" operation would be issued separately by the office of the Army Chief of Staff, General Sosaku Suzuki. Yamashita wrapped up his session with Kawamura by urging him: "See that the work is duly carried out."

It was only later, when the written orders were given to Kawamura in Suzuki's office, that the newly appointed Garrison Commander realised the full extent of the "work" he would be required to accomplish. Here were defined the five categories of Chinese to be executed — former members of volunteer forces, communists, looters, those harbouring arms, and general trouble makers likely to disturb the peace. Here, too, were the extensive instructions to be followed for cordoning off areas of the island, concentrating the Chinese population under guard, screening out those to be eliminated, carrying out the executions, and conducting widespread searches for hidden arms and those trying to escape the screening process. The written orders also provided Kawamura with a most important piece of information. They notified him that Tsuji would be the officer-in-charge of the operation. He would be dispatched temporarily from his normal High Command activities to supervise this work and to handle any liaison function that might be required between involved units. In short, once the massacres got underway, Tsuji would be on hand to ensure nothing interfered with the smooth running of the mass killing programme.

The splitting up of orders in this way — very general remarks by Yamashita, on the one hand, followed by precise written commands, devoid of the Commander-in-Chief's signature and issued through Suzuki's office, on the other, raises immediate questions. Why, for one, should such an important and obviously controversial set of killing instructions be handed down through such convoluted channels?

The obvious conclusion is that an attempt was underway to obscure the issuing source's identity. But was this reflective of a commander who personally agonized over the behaviour of his front line troops down the length of the Malayan peninsula? Equally, could such underhand tactics be the stamp of a man renowned for directness in overriding opposition to his views?

The strong suggestion is that Yamashita, who only talked in terms of a military mopping-up operation, had nothing whatever to do with drafting the written orders to kill Chinese civilians. The unusual separation of Yamashita's verbal instructions and the formal written commands certainly indicates an opportunity for the perpetrator to shield his real intentions from an otherwise pre-occupied Army Commander.

Despite exhaustive official searches in the months following the end of the Pacific War, no copy of the killing orders were ever found bearing Yamashita's signature. Similarly, all research by war crimes investigators concurs that Yamashita's original verbal instructions were couched in very general terms and were essentially as I have stated above.

If one examines the implications of these verbal instructions dispassionately, it is difficult to conclude that Yamashita personally was calling for action that could, under conditions of the time, be construed as either illegal or excessive. Singapore, in the days immediately following the British surrender, unquestionably faced a crisis of law and order, with pockets of local resistance that had to be rapidly brought under control. Similarly, there was indeed a network of anti-Japanese Chinese guerrillas at large. Under the rules of war these were legitimate targets for a 25th Army regular mopping up operation. Thus, the terrible plot for mass killing civilians was contained, not in the verbal orders, but in the written ones.

Sceptics might argue that it would be simply impossible to hide the realities of such a large and violent operation from the attention of Yamashita and that ultimately he would surely have learned the truth. In pursuing this line I uncovered a document which, as far as I can determine, has never before been published, certainly not in terms of its relevance to the Singapore massacres. It is my belief that this document, taken in conjunction with other evidence, throws an entirely new light on the matter of Yamashita's involvement.

The document records details of an extraordinary interview with Yamashita carried out in Manila by a British war crimes investigator on the morning of October 28, 1945 — the day before the Japanese general was due to go on trial before an American war crimes court. The investigator was none other than Major Cyril H.D.Wild, the same officer who carried the white flag of surrender into the Ford Factory, who served as the British interpreter during the negotiations there, and who, two days after the Changi Point massacre, helped challenge intelligence chief Sugita on those killings.

Three years and eight months later, Wild, because of his exceptional fluency in Japanese, had been retained to track down war criminals. On the understanding the Americans would make Yamashita available to him, Wild flew from his Singapore base to Manila via Labuan and Morotai with a list of all known Japanese atrocities committed during and just after the 25th Army's Malaya campaign. His plan was to confront Yamashita with the list, point by point. In a three-page typed document on the Manila assignment, Wild recorded how he had been forewarned that Yamashita would be unlikely to talk as he had resisted previous interrogations, denying all knowledge of atrocities.

"I started, therefore, by reminding him of our previous meeting at the British surrender at Bukit Timah, Singapore," wrote the British investigator. "We then discussed the Malaya Campaign, and he expressed his admiration for the generalship of Lt. General Sir Lewis Heath, Commander 111 Indian Corps, and enquired after him and Lady Heath."

Wild then brought up the subject of the letter Yamashita had written to Percival five days before the capitulation in which he attempted to persuade the British commander to surrender early and avoid unnecessary slaughter of civilians. Japanese aircraft dropped copies of this communication close to known British field headquarters.

Yamashita insisted his letter had been written in all sincerity.

Preliminaries over, the investigator then explained to Yamashita how, on several occasions during his time as a POW, he had found the letter a useful document to quote when told by Japanese officers that owing to the unconditional nature of the surrender of Singapore, the British had forfeited all rights as prisoners.

To this, Yamashita responded: "Not officers, surely: you mean private soldiers." Wild repeated the word "officers" and Yamashita expressed his disapproval.

Wild went on: "I then said that immediately after the capitulation we had regarded ourselves as prisoners of an enemy who had fought fairly and from whom fair treatment could be expected.

"In both respects we had been quickly disillusioned. In particular we had soon heard from surviving witnesses of a number of atrocities perpetrated by the Japanese during or just after the action. Yamashita expressed his past ignorance and present disapproval of such things, and in proof of the latter he agreed to assist by naming those responsible."

Wild said that Yamashita disclaimed all previous knowledge of each of the atrocities as they were recounted for him in detail. "He took notes, including the names of some witnesses. He did not question any of the evidence. On several occasions he condemned the perpetrators in fairly strong terms," observed the

British officer.

During the conversation that followed, Yamashita provided names and locations of two high ranking Japanese officers whom he felt could help war crimes teams in their investigations. The final item on the atrocity list put to Yamashita was the matter of the Singapore massacres.

In this context, Wild reported:

"Yamashita said that after the fall of Singapore, the three Divisions were kept outside the city and none of them were allowed to enter it. He drew a map to illustrate their positions.

"The Divisions therefore could not be held responsible. Maintenance of order in the city was the responsibility of the kempeitai, who were entitled to kill bad characters, such as robbers and those in possession of weapons. I said that many hundreds, even thousands, of innocent civilians had been among those killed, and that the 'crime' of most of them was solely that they were young and Chinese.

"Yamashita said: 'Innocent? It should have been only the robbers and those with arms.' I asked who gave the orders to kill these people. He replied that the kempeitai did not need any orders but had full discretion and powers."

Wild then recorded the following question and answer segment between himself and Yamashita.

Interrogator: Was the commander of the kempeitai in Singapore in February, 1942, then solely responsible for killing these civilians?

Yamashita: Yes, he was responsible.

Interrogator: What was his name and that of the senior military officer responsible for the city?

Yamashita: I do not now remember.

Interrogator: Were you informed of these killings?

Yamashita: No. I was not informed.

Interrogator: Was that because you were too senior an officer to be troubled with such trifling matters?

Yamashita: That is correct.

Interrogator: How long did you stay in Singapore after the capitulation of February 15, 1942?

Yamashita: Until June.

Wild said he concluded his interview with Yamashita by asking if the Japanese general had any special statement to make which would be passed on the Supreme Allied Commander, South East Asia. Yamashita at first replied: "No, nothing special."

Then he added: "Until today I had truly never heard of any of these matters. Please tell Admiral Mountbatten that. Tell him, too, that on learning that Japanese soldiers did these things I have been astounded."

The report was signed "C.H.D.Wild", E Group, S.E.A.C.

It is, of course, easy to adopt the cynical approach and assume that Yamashita, given his predicament when he met Wild, would naturally have denied all knowledge of the atrocities. Still, if an argument is developed from the premise that all planning for the Singapore massacres was undertaken without reference to Yamashita — as it certainly was — then the rest of the statements in the Wild interview are not only plausible, but fall credibly into place.

Pointedly, Wild made no attempt in his report to give a direct personal judgement on the culpability of the man he had been sent to interrogate. But any reader of the entire document would have difficulty in avoiding the conclusion that the British officer was agreeably surprised by the extent of assistance Yamashita was prepared to offer. Similarly, it is difficult to avoid the impression that Wild felt Yamashita was genuinely appalled by what he had been told and that his explanations and observations were at least being made in good faith ■

Chapter 8

Kawamura and the kempeitai

———— ✦ ————

When Kawamura read his orders late in the morning of February 18, he was deeply troubled. He was being given just three days — the following Saturday, Sunday and Monday — to complete the so-called "mopping up" of Singapore. Alone, the hit lists called for the mass killing of tens of thousands if the job was to be done properly. Then on top of this were all the other candidates for execution determined by the five specified categories. Quite aside from any moral questions, three days was simply insufficient time.

The lists, Kawamura learned, had been supplied on request through the Army's intelligence network. From their size and scope, he correctly judged the lists had taken months to prepare. He assumed, again quite rightly, that as Tsuji had been designated officer-in-charge, the Tsuji network was the driving force behind the operation.

So it was a perplexed Garrison Commander who sought out Suzuki for a second time that day. As on the first occasion, they met at the Chief of Staff's temporary office in Raffles Institution. Suzuki cut Kawamura short, promising reasons and explanations at a later stage. However, the ubiquitous Tsuji was soon conveniently on hand and more than willing to fill in the details and provide clarifications.

"Volunteers and communists are preparing to wage guerrilla warfare and have gone underground for this purpose," he told Kawamura. "The Communists have been released from jails under special orders precisely for this reason."

Tsuji went on to explain that lists of anti-Japanese organisations had come into the Army's possession "in great numbers." These had already been sent to the kempeitai. Looting had become widespread and abandoned arms and ammunition littering the city were falling into the hands of the anti-Japanese Chinese.

"These people will be the object of this purge," Tsuji added. "If a search is made, many more Chinese will be arrested. There is the possibility of skirmishes occurring in various places, so see to it that necessary preparations are made,"

Kawamura would later recall that the operations chief then briefed him on secret re-deployments to be made by 25th Army units throughout South East Asia. Tough measures were needed against the local Chinese, Tsuji insisted, so that troop movements could proceed without interruption. As the joint security force to be retained for both Malaya and Singapore would only be in brigade strength, every effort had to be taken to eliminate the threat of guerrilla warfare in the two territories.

Tsuji told Kawamura that all orders for the "mopping up" operation had been fully drafted in advance. Only the garrison commander's signature was required before they could be passed to the operational units concerned. Perhaps sensing Kawamura's unease, Tsuji took the opportunity of giving assurances of his presence at all times to supervise the work.

He added: "Staff Officer Hayashi has been attached to your headquarters and he well understands the intentions of the Army. Please set your mind at rest."

Kawamura knew of Hayashi's temporary secondment from his orders. On the surface, there appeared no reason whatever for the Garrison Commander to doubt Hayashi's compre-hension of "the intentions." But herein lay the trap. They were, in reality, Tsuji's intentions; not the Army's.

In the days and weeks that followed, it became widely recognised throughout the 25th Army's High Command that the indecisive Kawamura had been given his assignment simply because Tsuji needed someone pliable in the post. It was also widely accepted that Tsuji had been feverishly manipulating his personal network of influence in Singapore, just as he had done in Taipei, just as he had done throughout the Malayan campaign. The Singapore massacres were the result; Tsuji's idea made possible by Tsuji's devious planning and ultimately supervised by Tsuji and his henchman, Hayashi. And on the sidelines was Asaeda.

Later in the afternoon of February 18, armed with a copy of the duly signed operational order, Kawamura drove to the kempeitai headquarters which had been temporarily installed in the Singapore Supreme Court building. He was accompanied by Hayashi. There the two men met the 46-year-old Commanding Officer of the No 2 Field Kempeitai, Lt. Colonel Masayuki Oishi. Kawamura handed Oishi the orders and asked the military police commander his opinion.

Sensing that Kawamura was worried about the moral implications, Oishi, a veteran officer of 25 years standing, replied: "Should it be the Army's operational order, there is nothing to do but carry it out." The Kempeitai Commander made no mention of the fact that he had seen the orders three nights earlier and as a result had drawn up the complicated subdivision of Singapore which his men immediately began implementing the next day — February 16.

Kawamura, whose concern was more focused on time-frames than moralities, thought for a moment and said: "But to accomplish this in three days is very difficult. Is there no way to ask for an extension?"

Leafing through the thick file which included the "hit lists", Oishi observed that the names provided the only real guide for the screening process. "It is absolutely necessary to have the cooperation of local police and influential Chinese," he told Kawamura.

Oishi further advised his Garrison Commander: "Elderly

people, women and children are not objects of this operation, so release them as soon as possible."

Kawamura seemed overwhelmed by the task he had been given and Oishi sensed he had better draw his superior's attention to some of the obvious pitfalls he was facing. The military police chief warned that the assembling and screening would take considerable time. It would therefore be necessary for all detainees to bring water, food and bedding with them to the concentration areas.

Oishi further suggested it might be wise to recruit certain local Chinese as agents for information gathering. Others, depending on their standing and influence in the community, could prove useful in posts associated with the restoration of law and order. Oishi then pointed out the acute manpower problems the Japanese were facing as they set about reorganising the civil police ranks.

Seemingly emboldened by the meeting, Kawamura finally requested Oishi to get together with Hayashi and ensure full instructions were passed down to the city's kempeitai units. In addition he ordered Hayashi to liaise closely with the High Command. Hayashi, only too anxious to comply, rushed off to report to Tsuji. The plot was working, and control was precisely where it was planned to be — in the hands of Tsuji.

The last entry in Kawamura's diary for February 18 were the words: "The able and very painstaking Staff Officer Hayashi was attached to my staff. I am glad to have obtained this addition of matchless power and intellect." The Singapore Garrison Commander would rue the moment he ever formed that opinion.

On the following day, February 19, Kawamura went on an inspection of downtown Singapore. Law and order was improving, he noted in his diary, but was still far below the mark. "I see small sun-flags fluttering. They cheer me a little amidst this desolation."

Also entered under this day were the words: "In order to

carry on a general arrest of law-flouting Chinese from the 21st, I gave necessary orders and urged the matter of collecting them into one place or sector." As far as Kawamura wanted the event recorded, this was the day on which the purge of the Chinese had been officially set in motion. But in fact the massacres had already begun by then. And, what was more, Kawamura knew it.

Before closing for the day, he wrote regretfully under his February 19 diary entry: "I feel keenly that the Japanese soldiers lack dignity to impress upon others. Especially such was the case with the air unit quartering at the Empire Docks."

Kawamura left out the bloody details, but what he had seen at the docks that triggered his disgust were the decapitated corpses of eight Chinese males. He had also seen for himself the eight heads that had been transported from the execution site and displayed at prominent points around the city as a warning to the public on the penalties for looting.

The air unit troops responsible for this had been allowed to enter the city on the day following the surrender. They were assigned as security for the Empire Docks and adjacent warehouse area, where Singapore's modern container terminal now stands. Soon after their arrival, the troops arrested 15 dock workers suspected of looting and bound their arms behind their backs with wire. The eight Chinese in the group were separated from the others and promptly beheaded by an executioner wielding a Samurai sword. The remaining seven, comprising Malays and Indians, were subsequently released with a warning to be on good behaviour. Witness to the entire incident was Malaya Command's Chief Engineer, Brigadier Ivan Simson, who had shortly before been taken prisoner. Mention of these killings is made in his book *Singapore, too little, too late.*

One very significant question is posed by this initial beheading incident. As the official order for the "mopping up" supposedly went into effect on February 19, what made this Japanese unit, 72 hours earlier, release the Malay and Indian looters and kill the Chinese in exact compliance with the spirit of the instructions yet to come? The answer is clear.

Kawamura's role in the massacre plot was purely a formality imparting a veneer of legitimacy to the killing procedure. From the moment Tsuji led the first triumphal entry into Singapore on the morning of February 16, all commanders of units assigned within the city limits knew precisely that he was the officer calling the shots at this time.

Within hours, these commanders had received, by word of mouth, very clear details of what they would be required to do and the methods they were to adopt. Tsuji's team had been hard at work and, as we will see, the process of mass-killing was well under way by the time the muddled Kawamura got round to appearing on the scene and formalising the orders.

The case of Kempeitai Commander Oishi further illustrates the superfluous position of Kawamura. Oishi was at the Ford Factory in Bukit Timah on February 15 when, soon after the British surrender, he received orders from Tsuji's operations section that he would be required to move his men into downtown Singapore at first light the next morning. Their immediate task would be two-fold. Firstly, they were to restore law and order. Secondly, they would ensure that the main force of the Japanese Army was kept out of the city.

Shortly thereafter, Oishi received a circular to say that lists of undesirable Chinese civilians were ready for collection at the Command's Information Bureau. This bureau came under intelligence chief Sugita's department where, of course, Hayashi worked. These name lists had been prepared and duplicated from those delivered in Ipoh six weeks earlier. Oishi promptly sent one of his staff round to collect enough for No 2 Kempeitai's requirements. In three days, a second batch of hit lists would be produced by Sugita's Information Bureau. Oishi would later recall: "The lists were very thick — like complete books filled with foolscap pages of names."

That evening, Oishi worked late. Using a captured map of

the island, he divided the downtown area into two main sections. He placed the lower section, stretching roughly from Keppel Harbour in the south to the Singapore River, under the control of 44-year-old Major Tomotatso Jyo. The upper section ran from the Singapore River across to the Kallang River in one direction, and from the waterfront to a line through Paterson, Scotts, Kampong Java, Norfolk and Balestier roads in the other This general area was assigned to 45-year-old Lt. Colonel Yoshitaka Yokota. Specifically, Oishi made provisions that Jyo and Yokota, as section commanders, would further subdivide their areas in order to effect greater control.

The lower section would be split into two sub-sectors down a dividing line running along Outram and Cantonment Roads. On the other hand, the upper section would be split into three sub-sectors by two dividing lines drawn from Newton Circus. One would run along Clemenceau Avenue, the other down the lower end of Bukit Timah Road, through Rochor Canal and Rochor Roads.

So, by late in the evening of February 15, before he had even taken his kempeitai troops into the city, Oishi was well aware that there would soon be an operation against the anti-Japanese Chinese. The detailed plans he had drawn up that night took into account requirements for concentrating and screening large sections of the population. That was precisely why he had subdivided the city so meticulously. Furthermore, he was required to ensure he had sufficient name lists to go round the various sub-sectors he had created.

Before dawn the next morning, Oishi called his two Singapore section commanders into conference at the Ford Factory. There he delivered the name lists and briefed the two officers on the details of his previous night's planning.

At this conference, it was decided that Jyo, in the lower section, would have 30-year-old Lieutenant Haruji Hisamatsu as one of his two sub-sector officers. A clerk in civilian life before entering the army as a cadet in 1935, Hisamatsu had served in

Manchuria before the Malayan campaign. He would be in charge of the critical Keppel Harbour wharf area, the biggest of the five city sub-sectors. His zone of responsibility would start at the wharves and extend north and west as far as Alexandra Road. The north-eastern and eastern extremities of Hisamatsu's sub-sector would be marked by Outram and Cantonment Roads.

At the same time, Yokota in the upper section would have 41-year-old Lieutenant Satorou Onishi as the officer-in-charge of the heavily populated northernmost sub-sector which had, running through it, the soon to become infamous Jalan Besar. Onishi, father of four and a regular army officer for some 18 years, had also served in Manchuria prior to the Malayan campaign. The remaining three kempeitai officers, chosen as sub-sector heads for the operation, would be Captain Uezono in the lower sub-section and Captains Goshi and Mizuno in the remaining two.

Each of the five sub-sector officers would have approximately 30 to 40 kempeitai placed under his command. He would also have a further 150 auxiliary military police. The auxiliary forces would undertake guard duty in the sub-sectors and assist in search and cordoning operations. They would also help in assembling the civilians at the various concentration points and, finally, undertake the execution of all Chinese categorized as undesirable and anti-Japanese. The regular kempeitai would be responsible for handling the screening procedure and deciding who would live and who would die.

Kempeitai chief Oishi, his two section commanders and the five chosen sub-sector officers, all travelled in the same convoy to downtown Singapore soon after dawn on February 16 to choose their respective operational headquarters. Oishi commandeered offices at the centrally located Supreme Court Building, opposite the Padang. Yokota moved into the Toyo Hotel in Queen Street near the corner of Middle Road, an establishment that had been Japanese-owned prior to the outbreak of hostilities and still employed Japanese-trained local cooks. Jyo took over offices in the old Central Police Station in South Bridge Road, on the junction of George Street where the Pidemco Building now stands.

Onishi went first to Kandang Kerbau police station but on the following day moved to the White House Hotel, a popular pre-war drinking spot for British servicemen which still stands on the corner of Jalan Besar and Mayo Street. There he established his personal headquarters. He made the nearby Victoria School building (now Christ Church Secondary School) and its adjacent playing field his operational centre. As the Jalan Besar Football Stadium next door offered such ideal enclosed premises for holding large numbers of detainees, Onishi absorbed this into his operational centre as well.

Hisamatsu decided to base himself at the Tanjong Pagar police station and, arriving there around noon on February 16, was well ahead of his fellow section officers in preparations for the mass-killing operation. Within 24 hours he had issued orders for assembling the entire Chinese civilian population throughout his zone and had designated three concentration camps: one at Neil Road, another at Tiong Bahru and the third at the Singapore Harbour Board compound.

The Neil Road camp was to cater for all those living in the area bounded by the General Hospital to the north, Kampong Bahru to the west, and Keong Saik and Bukit Pasoh Roads to the east. Tiong Bahru camp was for those inhabiting that part of the city demarcated by Henderson and Alexandra Roads to the north, Outram Road to the east, Silat Road to the west and the General Hospital to the south. The Harbour Board camp was exclusively to sort out those living in the Board's coolie lines, estimated at some 5,000 labourers and their families.

The round-up of Chinese in Hisamatsu's section began on Tuesday, February 17, following an early morning roll call parade in the courtyard at the rear of the Tanjong Pagar police station. All local police attached to the station were required to

The White House Hotel building, operational headquarters for Major Satorou Onishi, kempeitai sub-sector commander in charge of screening anti-Japanese Chinese males along Jalan Besar, still stands on the corner of Jalan Besar and Mayo Street.

attend the parade which was addressed by Hisamatsu. He spoke through an interpreter. The Kempeitai officer explained that the Chinese were to be concentrated at the three designated points in the Tanjong Pagar district. He ordered all local police to assist by going out and informing the public that the Japanese authorities expected full cooperation. Each individual was required to bring to the concentration areas enough food and drink to last three or four days.

Speaking slowly and deliberately, Hisamatsu made no attempt to hide the fact that a purge of Chinese males was underway. Carefully, he outlined the five categories the kempeitai were seeking to identify in the screening process. Copies of the hit lists were distributed and Hisamatsu went on to offer special rewards to local policemen for the arrest of prominent Chinese.

Around 11.00 am, Hayashi called on Hisamatsu to check on progress. The two officers discussed the problem of numerous fires raging in the wharf area and in the city itself. Widespread looting was continuing, particularly around the Railway Station and Empire Docks and Hisamatsu voiced his concern over the amount of opium that had been stolen from a drug storehouse located near the Pasir Panjang Power Station.

Hayashi indicated his displeasure over what he felt was a lukewarm effort at stamping out looting within Hisamatsu's sub-sector. He ordered the kempeitai officer to enforce stricter control and insisted he immediately round up all the Chinese men living in the Railway Station–Empire Docks vicinity. As Hisamatsu would later tell it, Hayashi became angry when the kempeitai officer indicated he had insufficient men to comply with these instructions and that, anyway, his orders must come through kempeitai channels.

"This is a Staff Office order and you must do this immediately," barked Hayashi. Hisamatsu agreed to comply and Hayashi left.

By the time Hayashi returned to Tanjong Pagar police station at 3 pm, the round up he had ordered had been completed. Hisamatsu asked what he should do next.

"As most of them are looters and as they will be back looting again if you released them, you should get rid of them all," replied Hayashi.

Again, according to Hisamatsu's account of the incident, he refused to obey the order claiming he was not prepared to undertake such instructions when they were only delivered verbally.

"I am not your direct subordinate. Commander Oishi and Commander Jyo are my direct superiors. If that is the order of the 25th Army HQ, please have it coursed through my superiors," requested the kempeitai lieutenant.

Hayashi reportedly replied: "I have never encountered such an officer. I will have you dealt with immediately." Hisamatsu insisted he ultimately released all those rounded up for Hayashi, was fully supported by his superiors and the matter went no further.

It is, of course, impossible to verify the accuracy of Hisamatsu's version of the incident. But there seems little doubt that Hayashi was at Tanjong Pagar on February 17 checking on progress and urging along the concentration and killing of Chinese males. Furthermore both Hayashi and Tsuji would make further personal inspections of the Tanjong Pagar operations in the coming days as they nurtured the plot to its ghastly conclusion.

Notwithstanding Hisamatsu's problems with Hayashi, the operational commands handed down to the five sub-sectors allowed each kempeitai officer-in-charge a degree of flexibility. As the operation unfolded at Tanjong Pagar, local police staff were able to watch Hisamatsu's particular interpretation of the instructions.

First, a cordon of troops was thrown around each chosen concentration area. Through these were established long, narrow passageways marked out by parallel ropes.

Down the length of the passageways, at intervals of approximately five paces, were stationed kempeitai troops with local assistants. Their function was to identify any of those walking through who might belong to one or more of the five wanted categories. Some of the informers were police acting under threats or promises. But the majority of locals thus employed were criminals released from their jail sentences in return for fingering others with prison records. One of the informers who functioned for the Japanese in the Tanjong Pagar area was a man who had been serving seven years for murder when Singapore fell. Each time an identification was effected the kempeitai quickly moved in, seized the suspect, tied his hands behind his back and led him to a special roped off area to be held under guard by the auxiliary police.

From time to time, when numbers warranted it, batches of detained men and youths were led away to the Tanjong Pagar police lock-up. There they were packed into the five available cells. Built to accommodate three prisoners each, the five cells and the small corridor onto which they opened held as many as 100 terrified Chinese at any one time. Here they awaited the processing of their execution arrangements.

Outside, in the police station's car park, were three lorries Hisamatsu had brought with him from the Ford Factory. When the cells became jammed to overflowing, the three vehicles backed up and lorry load by lorry load, 30 detainees at a time, were driven away in the direction of Pasir Panjang, never to be seen again.

Records suggest that as many as 700 Chinese males were held in the Tanjong Pagar police station between February 17-24 and were taken away from there to be shot. This 700 were almost certainly from the Neil Road and Tiong Bahru concentration centres.

Hisamatsu appears to have operated his Singapore Harbour Board concentration centre under separate arrangements. This is probably because the technique he devised for off-shore executions from the decks of Harbour Board vessels dispensed with any need to funnel the condemned through the holding cells at Tanjong Pagar. After the war, British Military investigation teams encountered great difficulties pinning down details as to where those executed off Blakang Mati were originally screened. At the same time the numbers of victims involved proved impossible to establish. The problem was that no one escaped the off-shore executions to return and reveal details.

Evidence suggests that all coolie labourers destined for the firing squads were incarcerated overnight in the wharf area near the Harbour Board compound. From there they were transferred each morning directly to the tugs for the grisly rituals off Keppel Harbour's eastern entrance. These were the executions witnessed eight dawns in a row by the British artillerymen on Berhala Reping.

At the other end of downtown Singapore, kempeitai officer Onishi, in the Jalan Besar area, also relied heavily on the services of locally recruited informers to identify those in the five classifications for extermination. But unlike Hisamatsu, who apparently made no secret of the fact that those picked out would be executed, Onishi kept such intentions to himself. He would later admit that a total of some twenty police volunteers and former convicts became involved in picking those to be massacred.

It is quite clear that Onishi knew on February 16 he would be required to complete the mop-up operation in his area within a three-day time frame. Indeed, he started making appropriate arrangements as soon as he took rooms in the White House Hotel on February 17.

Still, he would later maintain that he first learned of the intended purge when he saw Kempeitai Commander Yokota at the Toyo Hotel on the evening of February 18. According to this account, while waiting to be shown into Yokota's room, he was told by a non-commissioned officer that a "terrible thing" was about to happen as the result of a new order. Onishi was shown the order which he read through carefully before meeting Yokota.

During his conversation with Yokota, Onishi allegedly requested an extension of the three-day operation time frame, arguing that it was "difficult to execute any person who was not resisting." Yokota indicated he was of the same opinion but as it was an Army order, there was nothing to do but comply. Onishi duly received his written instructions together with the hit lists and returned to the White House Hotel to continue preparations.

These included calling in Warrant Officer Yamaguchi and Sgt. Major Kosai, passing them copies of the orders and making them familiar with the lists of names and their application. Onishi would claim that he neatly divided his organisation into four sections; the screening section — headed by Yamaguchi, an inspection section, an examination section and an arresting section.

But as we know from the accounts of those seized in the Jalan Besar area and who later managed to escape from execution squads, there was no order, only fearful chaos, within Onishi's sub-sector. One claim made by Onishi about this operation does, however, have a ring of truth. Tsuji, according to Onishi, dropped by the White House Hotel on Sunday, February 22. He arrived to enquire about the numbers screened thus far.

Onishi provided a figure of about 70 to which Tsuji angrily retorted: "Thousands should have been screened — what are you doing?"

As a result, a severely scolded Onishi "falsified" a report to the effect that 260 people had been taken away and executed in the Jalan Besar area, not 150. "I thought the intention of the Army was to kill as many people as possible. So I made such a report," Onishi would later insist.

Onishi was lying about the numbers. It is quite obvious from the stories recounted in Chapter 2 that well over 1,000 people were driven away in lorries from the Victoria School–Jalan Besar area to seaside execution grounds in the north-east of the island.

But the indication that Tsuji was active in the area, urging more intensive screening and larger numbers of executions, is fully consistent with other reports of his pattern of behaviour throughout Singapore during this period. As such, it is further strong evidence in the case against him ∎

Chapter 9

Laying the blame

———— ✦ ————

onsidering the Allied propaganda emphasis focused on Japanese military brutality throughout the Pacific conflict, Britain found herself remarkably unprepared for handling war crimes and criminals when Tokyo finally capitulated.

Emperor Hirohito's broadcast accepting defeat with the curious admission that the war situation had developed "not necessarily to Japan's advantage," came at 11 am, August 15, 1945. It was just 24 hours earlier that Britain's Allied Land Forces South East Asia (ALFSEA) High Command signalled the War Office in London for a decision on what should be done about war criminals and their trials.

Three weeks later, the command was still in the dark. Then, on September 7, the War Office finally issued instructions for commanders throughout the theatre to apprehend all war crimes suspects and collect evidence. They were to "seize and hold" as a matter of course all kempeitai personnel, members of Japanese intelligence agencies, whether military or civilian, and all guards of prisoner of war and Allied internee camps. The same instructions specifically ordered the commanders to refrain from setting up courts until they received further directions.

Here were the first legal grounds on which ALFSEA could take action. But the three weeks of indecision, as we will see, proved more than sufficient for Tsuji to make his getaway.

In due course, a separate War Crimes Section was established in Singapore. It acted as a registry with responsibility for collating information on alleged incidents involving British victims. It also kept case files on suspect identities and their locations. Britain fielded a total of 17 investigating teams throughout the theatre. These continually fed results of their work back to the registry.

For the first 15 months, this operation functioned largely within the Command's Adjutant General's branch. But the Deputy Judge Advocate General's office also assisted in an advisory capacity and provided prosecutors and judge advocates as the trials got underway. The split between the two departments proved less than satisfactory and, in 1947, the British registry came under the full control of the Deputy Judge Advocate General.

Similar operations were established in Singapore by the Americans, the Australians, the Dutch and the French. These, too, were attached to the British General Headquarters. They concentrated on investigating war crimes committed against their respective nationals but functioned in useful liaison capacities as well, enabling related intelligence information to flow freely between the various commands.

Quite apart from the critical three weeks lost immediately following the Japanese surrender, Britain's pursuit of war crimes justice in South East Asia ran into a spread of early problems.

An historical report by the High Command dated December, 1946, pointed out how a shortage of legally qualified officers was proving a severe administrative problem for the War Crimes Section. The granting of special emergency commissions to ex-Shanghai policemen helped. Several former prisoners of war, especially Japanese speaking officers, were persuaded to return to South East Asia to function as investigators. Still, there was always an extreme shortage of investigators competent in the Japanese language

There were other frustrations. Japanese defence lawyers, for one, rapidly devised an array of successful delaying tactics. The lawyers and their advisers within the Imperial Headquarters were confident America and Britain were both having second thoughts on the entire war crimes process. So together they played for time.

As a counter measure to the Japanese tactics, Britain's War Office issued instructions to all investigation and liaison teams to give the Tokyo-sourced rumours widest possible rebuttal. But the truth was that, whereas the British military were keen to prosecute, politicians in London were, indeed, losing interest. From the outset, His Majesty's Government had never harboured much enthusiasm for war crimes trials in the South East Asian theatre, especially those unconnected to British military personnel.

Adding to the confusion, merchant marine crews frequently refused to carry war crimes suspects bound for trials in Hong Kong and Singapore. At the same time, civilian police in Japan disliked working on war criminal location leads with the result that numerous wanted men were allowed to escape apprehension in their homeland.

Those investigators fired with a determination to see Japanese responsible for atrocities punished, hoped that publicity generated by the trials would eventually win over enthusiasm for their cause back in Britain. But, they were to be disappointed. As the December, 1946, report lamented: "With the exception of some of the Sunday papers and occasionally *The Times*, the press in the United Kingdom give no publicity to war crimes in South East Asia."

Efforts by the Command's public relations department to provide press releases of court reports proved fruitless. Foreign correspondents saw no point in accumulating large cable bills for stories which were never used. Concluded the report: "Consequently the War Crimes Section send handouts and yellow extracts from trials to AG3, War Office, who get these handouts into the papers from time to time and the short extracts into the *Daily Mirror* if they are sufficiently yellow."

Lack of political will in London, combined with the continual stonewalling tactics by Japanese lawyers and military officials of all ranks, sapped at the morale of British investigators endeavouring to come to grips with complicated cases. This, in turn, created a natural preference for concentrating on incidents where British military personnel had been victims. Understandably, there was dismay among the Singapore Chinese.

Amid the immediate post-war clamour for retribution, they feared the Japanese responsible for such barbarity on their island might never be brought to court. The island's Chinese language press entered the picture with lurid, often grossly distorted accounts of the various Japanese atrocities committed in Singapore. If nothing else, these ensured the massacres remained at the forefront of public concern. As the weeks slipped by without any apparent movement on the case, the returning colonial British realised they had the makings of a major political issue on their hands.

Three months after the Japanese surrender, the British devised a plan whereby the Yamashita trial, then underway in Manila, would be manipulated as a public relations exercise to the benefit of Britain's position with the Singapore Chinese.

A message was sent to the Americans in the Philippines on November 18, 1945, seeking facilities for a special visit to the trial by Mr Tan Kah Kee. Tan, the same businessman who had headed the Singapore Chinese anti-Japanese effort prior to the British surrender, whose name had been top of the kempeitai hit lists, wanted to travel to Manila with two companions named as Yap Twee and Hoy L.Chew.

The British request to the Americans made the motive behind the exercise very clear.

"CONSIDERED HERE THAT IT IS POLITICALLY MOST

DESIRABLE FOR THESE MODERATE AND INFLUENTIAL LEADERS TO ATTEND THIS IMPORTANT TRIAL WHICH IS FOCUSING ATTENTION UPON HORRORS OF JAPANESE REGIME."

The message assured that all expenses incurred in travel and accommodation by the trio would be met by London and that passage to Manila would be arranged via Hong Kong in a British aircraft.

Like almost everyone else, the Singapore Chinese were convinced Yamashita was the officer responsible for the massacres. The British therefore hoped the Tan Kah Kee delegation's visit would go towards placating feelings and demonstrating that Britain was indeed mindful of local Chinese sensitivities. The visit went ahead but failed as a PR exercise. The Chinese, understandably, wanted a major demonstration of justice being seen to be done on the Singapore homefront.

At this juncture, the speed with which the Americans were handling the Yamashita affair was viewed by Britain's war crimes investigators as the greatest threat of all to the successful prosecution of the Singapore case. Convinced Yamashita issued the killing orders, they regarded the Japanese general as their prime suspect. But at the rate the Americans were pushing matters in the Philippines, the celebrated "Tiger of Malaya" would likely be tried, convicted and executed long before the British had even a chance to talk to him, let alone charge him.

Yamashita, from the moment he walked out of the Luzon Island jungle on September 1, 1945, became the star attraction of a military judicial stage show personally choreographed by Allied Supremo, General Douglas MacArthur. Singapore could not have been further from the American general's mind as he wilfully manoeuvred proceedings for their maximum theatrical effect. He perceived this as his moment in history. He would allow no one and nothing to diminish its brilliance.

MacArthur wanted the world to remember him as the

warrior who made good his promise to return to the Philippines; as the soldier who delivered dramatic justice to a people subjected to so much wartime indignity. At the personal level he needed to salve, in some spectacular way, the humiliation he had suffered through the Japanese attack on the Philippines in December, 1941. The swift but well-publicised snuffing of Yamashita's life, from MacArthur's viewpoint, met all criteria.

Yamashita's trial was scheduled to open in Manila in a blaze of international publicity on October 29, just eight weeks and two days after his surrender. On October 18, Britain's Supreme Allied Commander, South East Asia (SACSEA), Admiral Lord Louis Mountbatten, cabled the following message to the US Commanding General in Manila:

FROM: SACSEA
TO: COMGEN AFWESPAC - MANILA
CONFIDENTIAL CITE 453
AM INFORMED THAT YOU ARE IN CHARGE OF ALL ARRANGEMENTS FOR TRIAL OF YAMASHITA IN CONNECTION WITH WAR CRIMES COMMITTED IN PHILIPPINES.

YOU WILL KNOW THIS OFFICER COMMANDED JAPANESE FORCES IN MALAYA BETWEEN DECEMBER 41 AND MAY 42. DURING THIS PERIOD A NUMBER OF SERIOUS ATROCITIES PARTICULARLY IN SINGAPORE WERE COMMITTED BY THESE FORCES.

AN INTERROGATION OF YAMASHITA WOULD PROBABLY YIELD VALUABLE INFORMATION AS HE MUST HAVE KNOWN OF MANY OF THE ATROCITIES AND SHOULD BE ABLE TO GIVE NAMES OF HIS SUBORDINATES CONCERNED.

WOULD YOU AGREE TO AN OFFICER BEING SENT FROM ALFSEA WITH NECESSARY INFORMATION OF ATROCITIES IN ORDER TO INTERROGATE YAMASHITA? IF SO PLEASE STATE DATE BY WHICH OFFICER SHOULD ARRIVE.

Here was an almost desperate attempt by the lagging British investigators to exploit Mountbatten's considerable personal influence and gain access, before it was too late, to the man they regarded as their prime suspect. Mountbatten's message, as it happened, paved the way for Major Cyril Wild to question Yamashita on October 28 and produce the important interrogation report we dealt with in Chapter 7.

On November 6, eight days after the Wild-Yamashita meeting, SACSEA was again cabling Manila:

FROM: HQ SACSEA

TO: COMGEN AFWESPAC

INFO: ALFSEA   FOURTEENTH ARMY

REFERENCE YOUR CITE 667696 GSGS TOO

APPRECIATE YOUR COOPERATION WHICH MADE SUCCESSFUL INTERROGATION POSSIBLE.   HAVE NOT YET SEEN FULL REPORT BUT IT WOULD APPEAR THAT TESTIMONY OF YAMASHITA MIGHT BE USEFUL AGAINST OTHER SENIOR JAPANESE OFFICERS BELIEVED TO BE IN JAPAN.

The information Wild had extracted from Yamashita was beginning to make an impact on the British. Official military correspondence from Singapore to London spoke of the results of the interrogation "exceeding expectations." On December 1, with the Yamashita trial clearly racing to its conclusion, the British Command in Singapore dispatched the following message to Manila:

FROM: HQ ALFSEA

TO: COMGEN AFWESPAC

INFO: SACSEA

CONFIDENTIAL

YOUR CITE 667696 OF 300539 OCT

YAMASHITA PROBABLY REQUIRED AS WITNESS TRIALS OF WAR CRIMINALS MALAYA.   ALSO FURTHER INTERROGATION

YAMASHITA DESIRABLE. UNDERSTAND IF DEATH SENTENCE PASSED EXECUTION WILL BE POSTPONED PENDING FULFILMENT REQUIREMENTS ABOVE CITED.

To say the least, it was an outlandish request. ALFSEA was asking the Americans to consider seriously a proposal for Yamashita's execution to be placed on temporary hold while the British got into the act. The British plan was, presumably, to shuttle the condemned man back across the South China Sea so he could give evidence against fellow Japanese officers in a Singapore war crimes court. Once the "Tiger of Malaya" had "shopped" his colleagues, a Royal Air Force transport would shuttle him back to Manila for his delayed date with the hangman.

If nothing else, the proposal underlined how little the British understood the motivations of the man who would one day become tagged the *American Caesar.* MacArthur's choreography for the Manila trial included arrangements whereby the court handed down Yamashita's death sentence on December 7, the fifth anniversary of Japan's attack on Pearl Harbour; a florid touch calculated to add a certain zip to headlines around the world.

At 5.59 am on February 23, 1946, Yamashita went to the gallows at Los Baños, Laguna, 35 miles south of Manila. The British had lost their principal witness, their eleventh hour request pointedly ignored by the Americans.

One final aspect of this episode bears close scrutiny. There appears to have been a perceptive switch in the British Command's evaluation of Yamashita's criminal culpability following the submission of Wild's report. This can be verified by comparing the choice of words and general substance of the October 18 cable to Manila with the November 6 and December 1 follow-up communications.

The October 18 cable, dispatched before Wild's trip to the Philippines, makes the point that Yamashita "must have known of many of the atrocities . . ." At very least this left open the possibility of the British charging the former 25th Army Commander on the grounds of "command responsibility." In this case, it would have been consistent for them to have pushed for Yamashita's Singapore arraignment. He would not have been the only senior Japanese officer tried on separate counts before military courts of different Allied nationalities.

However, the November 6 and December 1 messages, sent after Wild's return to Singapore, make it clear the British had now dropped any intentions of laying charges against Yamashita. He was wanted as a witness, not a defendant.

By this time, Wild had emerged as an almost legendary figure at the Singapore-based War Crimes Section. His credentials for the job were outstanding. He had joined the section two weeks after the cessation of hostilities. In February 1946, he became officer-in-charge of war crimes investigations throughout Singapore and Malaya and received promotion to full colonel. In terms of Japanese language skills no other British soldier could match him. Similarly unmatched were his unique historical connections with the 25th Army High Command. From the Ford Factory surrender negotiations, through his time as liaison officer between British prisoners and their Japanese captors, to the period he spent in the Siam labour camps, Wild had gained an exceptional insight into the Japanese military psyche. His final meeting with Yamashita in the Manila cell seemed to crown his remarkable wealth of experience.

There was one incident above all others Wild could recall which instilled in him a very personal determination to ensure the Japanese culprits were tried and punished for their atrocities against the Chinese in Singapore. It was that liaison meeting (see Chapter 2) with 25th Army intelligence chief, Colonel Ichiji Sugita, two days after the Changi Point massacre. Wild could never forget the utterly callous indifference of Sugita's "we will shoot them whenever we want to . . ." remark.

The Englishman was sure from the very outset of his investigations that if he got to Sugita he would be able to establish the full truth behind the Singapore massacres.

So it was on September 18, 1945, that Wild confidently submitted his first list of "wanted" Japanese war criminals. Sugita was No 2 on the list. Orders were dispatched to have all those named immediately arrested. It was a measure of the spoiling tactics practised by the Japanese, together with the lumbering Allied bureaucratic process, that it took Wild almost a year to get to interrogate Sugita. This he did in Tokyo's Sugamo Prison in the final week of October 1946. It represented the breakthrough for which he had been working from the very outset of his investigations. A handcuffed Sugita, was soon enroute to Singapore by military aircraft.

A few days after Sugita's departure, Wild, still in Tokyo, was called to give evidence at the International Military Tribunal for the Far East (IMTFE), where Japan's so-called "major" war criminals were on trial. The IMTFE, established under a special proclamation by General MacArthur in his capacity as Supreme Commander for the Allied Powers (SCAP), had begun its hearings on April 29.

Wild entered the witness box in the auditorium of the Japanese War Ministry on Tuesday, September 10, and provided a rundown on the main Japanese wartime atrocities in the Malaya-Singapore area. He placed particular emphasis on the Singapore massacres and described in detail the Changi Conference House confrontation he and Brigadier Newbigging had with Sugita.

Asked whether, in the light of his investigations, he could give an estimate of the numbers of Chinese slaughtered in Singapore immediately after the British surrender, Wild replied: "Yes, I can. The number was *definitely considerably in excess of 5,000 men*." (Author's italics)

Wild went on to relate how he had personally read the appeal from Yamashita for the British to surrender. It had been

September 11, 1946. Colonel Cyril Hew Dalrymple Wild gives evidence in Tokyo to the International Military Tribunal for the Far East (IMTFE). He is head of War Crimes Investigations in Malaya and Singapore and tells the Tribunal he is personally leading enquiries into the Singapore massacres.

airdropped into his Indian Corps area on February 10, 1945. "The grounds upon which General Yamashita asked for the surrender of Singapore were that the lives of the civilian population should be spared the horrors of an assault on a city . . .," Wild recounted. Although Wild did not say as much to the IMTFE, the document to which he referred amounted to further evidence suggesting Yamashita's concern for the welfare of Singapore's civilian population at the height of the battle for the island.

During the course of his Tokyo evidence, the British colonel revealed how interrogations he had carried out some days earlier in Sugamo Prison — almost certainly those with Sugita — had led him to uncover 26 highly incriminating secret documents within the Japanese War Ministry's files. These had been prepared soon after Tokyo's capitulation on instructions of the then acting War Minister, Lt. General Wakamatsu and had remained undetected by America's occupying authorities for over a year.

They represented studies undertaken by the War Ministry in expectation of Allied war crimes investigations. Devised to function as ministerial guidelines for defence presentations and rebuttals of charges in anticipated war crimes trials, they constituted a whitewash of Japanese atrocities throughout the Pacific theatre. Still, some of the information they contained was highly incriminating.

Once exposed by Wild, the Ministry's actions immediately backfired. The documents from then on served to underline the horrors that had taken place and, furthermore, to lay bare the duplicity employed in the Japanese cove-up operation.

The studies had been coordinated by the "Prisoners of War Investigation Committee", convened in early September, 1945, by Wakamatsu himself. Various sub-committees were ultimately assigned areas of investigation. One of these, comprising a chairman and four committee members, had been detailed to report on the Singapore killings which the Japanese themselves referred to as *"The Chinese Massacre Affair."*

The appointed sub-committee chairman was, incredibly enough, intelligence chief Sugita. Equally amazing was the appointment of Kempeitai Commander Oishi as one of the committee of investigators. The other three committee members — Lt. Colonel Isamu Hashizume, Lt. Colonel Kinotake, and Lt. Colonel Fujiwara — had all been in Singapore on Yamashita's staff at the time of the killings.

Sugita's sub-committee, known as the 4th Unit, produced their document under a "secret" classification on October 23, 1945. It was headed: *"A proces-verbal concerning the punishment of Chinese residents in Singapore."* Its opening passages argued that highly effective spoiling actions undertaken by anti-Japanese Chinese units during the invasion of Malaya had constituted a serious threat to the 25th Army. Come the British surrender, claimed the report, there had been a dangerous two to three-day gap between the British commander relinquishing control and the Japanese side assuming it. "During this interval," it continued, "implements of war such as rifles, ammunition, machineguns, revolvers, wireless equipment, light automobiles, etc. were moved away and concealed in the houses of Chinese and natives."

Wild was asked to give the Tribunal his opinion of this section of the document.

"It is quite untrue," he said. "There was no such gap. As I mentioned before, we got permission to retain five hundred British troops under arms until the Japanese took over control of Singapore. That was arranged on the evening of February 15 at our surrender. I left Fort Canning about eight o'clock in the morning of February 16 to go to Bukit Timah for another conference with the Japanese, and Japanese soldiers were already on duty in Singapore.".

The Sugita sub-committee report, read in its entirety to the Tribunal, went on to make some significant admissions. The Japanese High Command, it said, had indeed received lists of anti-Japanese Chinese names while stationed in Ipoh, weeks before its arrival in Singapore. The search for hostile Chinese, it also claimed, had begun as early as February 17.

Expanding these points, Wild told how his investigation had shown that a member of the Sugita sub-committee (presumably Oishi) had obtained from Singapore's main police station a list of Chinese detectives employed in the force. This list, said Wild, was handed to Sugita and 20 Chinese detectives were shot that night.

The report observed that it was clear the Singapore Garrison Commander (Kawamura) "did not issue orders based on his own personal view." It was also "very doubtful whether the mass execution of Chinese was due to the order of the Commander in Chief (Yamashita)."

Then who issued the order? The report was conveniently vague.

"As Lt. Colonel Hayashi, who was Chief of Staff in charge at the time, died on the field, it is impossible to establish the facts," was one of its observations.

It went on to concede that those "punished strictly" in Singapore totalled "about 5,000 up to the end of March."

Asked his interpretation of the phrase "punished strictly", Wild said: "We learned in captivity that that was the accepted Japanese euphemism for execution."

In an unusually frank admission, the Sugita sub-committee described the spread of what it termed the "subjugation operations" from Singapore up into the Malayan peninsula. Towards the end of February, elements of the 18th Division were dispatched to Johore while some of the 5th Division were sent further north to "carry out the subjugation operation against the anti-Japan Chinese."

The 5th and 18th Divisions commenced their subjugation operations on the Malayan peninsula in early March. These continued until late April. The breakdown of numbers of "wicked Chinese" caught during this period was given by the sub-committee as: Johore — 1,000, Seremban-Malacca — 1,500, Selangor — 300, Perak — 100, Pahang — 50, and Kedah-Penang — 200.

Maintaining that "most" of the detainees were released after investigation, the report added: "There were, however, many cases in which at the arrest the Chinese resisted by firing guns, which induced us to return fire and persons on both sides were injured and killed. Many people (leaders) were there who committed suicide, recognising their unfavourable circumstances."

Again, Wild was asked for his comments.

He told the Tribunal: "Among other things, I have been in charge of war crimes investigations in Malaya and Singapore since February, this year. I have some 30 files of evidence on the way in which this so-called subjugation was carried out. It can safely be stated that many thousands of Asiatic citizens of Malaya were killed by the Japanese shortly after the occupation."

Looking at the figures for Johore, Wild went on: "These include, no doubt, the whole of a peaceful Eurasian settlement near Johore Bahru city. All the Eurasians — men, women, and children — were murdered. On the evidence of witnesses, we exhumed their bodies shortly before I came up to Tokyo."

The Sugita sub-committee made two particularly significant observations at the close of its report. One was that preparations for "punishing the Chinese" had obviously been made in advance. This amounted to acceptance of the fact that the subjugation operation's scope was such that it could only have been undertaken after considerable planning.

The other observation was that as both Staff Officer Hayashi and Chief of Staff Suzuki of the 25th Army had died during the course of the war, more details could be gleaned by interrogating two officers named as Major General Iketani and Colonel Tsuji. It was an interesting throw away line, but nothing more than that. No member of the Sugita sub-committee had the slightest intention of following up such leads. Nor, for that matter, did anyone at the Ministry. They all knew Tsuji was on the run and, more importantly, why.

Asked by the Tribunal whether he had been able to find Iketani and Tsuji, Wild replied: "I know where they are."

This was true in the case of Iketani who had been identified under Russian custody in a Siberian holding camp. But as far as Tsuji was concerned, Wild only thought he knew.

As Wild packed his bags to leave Tokyo on the first available military aircraft following the completion of his IMTFE evidence, he realised time had become his biggest enemy. He was anxious to get back to Singapore as quickly as possible and begin a full interrogation of Sugita, the man he had been waiting to nail for over a year. Not that the intervening 12 months had been wasted. As he had told the IMTFE, his organisation had seen nearly 300 Japanese war criminal cases brought to trial during this period. Well over 100 of these had resulted in death sentences. There had also been about 150 terms of imprisonment handed down and approximately 50 acquittals. A further 100 cases were ready for trial.

But Wild and his colleagues well appreciated that political thinking in both London and Washington was fast swinging against their interests. The post-war emphasis now was for encouraging the rebirth of a democratic, anti-communist Japan. It was recognised in top military circles that a strong body of Allied opinion was working to have the entire war crimes programme in South East Asia terminated by June 30, 1947. Advisories were in the pipeline warning that a March 31, 1947, deadline was likely to be established for the completion of all investigations in the region. The one exception would be for those underway in Burma. Here the wind-up date would be April 30.

Of some embarrassment to London were the increasingly audible rumblings in Japan that British courts were vindictive, lacked justice and handed down a far greater percentage of death sentences than other Allied courts operating in the area. The British military argued that such results were due to the high standards maintained in the preparation of cases. Those regarded as less than certain convictions were invariably discarded as were those that the legal experts felt would fail to return death sentences or at least terms of imprisonment exceeding seven years. One suggested solution was to bring more minor offences to trial so as to "increase the number of sentences of imprisonment in relation to the number of death sentences."

While pro and anti-Allied war crimes factions battled it out, the British Command in Singapore circulated secret instructions to be followed until such time as London decided on a firm policy ruling. A War Crimes Liaison letter in late 1946 tried to steady the rocking boat. "No indication should be given to the Japanese," it said, "that War Crimes Trials will not continue indefinitely until all war criminals have been apprehended and brought to justice."

But for Wild, a highly experienced senior officer, the writing was on the wall. Just how truly formidable an enemy time had become for him, Wild could never have imagined.

He flew to Hong Kong via Taipeh, and held evening discussions on September 24 with the colony's senior war crimes investigators. During these he learned that the following morning's scheduled Royal Air Force Transport Command Dakota flight to Singapore, via Saigon, was fully booked.

Given the urgency of his mission, Wild sought priority for one of the flight's 14 passenger seats. That night the transport officer at RAF Kai Tak ran his finger down the Dakota's manifest and stopped opposite a booking in the name of a businessman from Melbourne. Within minutes a telephone call to the Peninsula Hotel informed Mr Norman Suchowolski that he had been bumped from the flight, despite his luggage having been transported already to the Hong Kong airport, weighed and checked-in.

The following morning Wild, clutching his precious satchel of files and notes, boarded the waiting Transport Command aircraft. It was 9. 30 am. Among his fellow passengers were Mr Rex Davies, a British prosecutor at the war crimes trials in Tokyo, and Mr R. Arch Gunnison, Far Eastern correspondent of the Mutual Broadcasting Corporation of America.

As the two-engined aircraft rumbled down the Kai Tak runway and slowly became airborne, a handful of well-wishers on the tarmac outside the RAF passenger terminal waved a final goodbye and watched the pilot track away over bustling Kowloon. Two minutes into the flight, the gentle ascent was suddenly shattered. The plane lurched. Its wings wobbled violently. Then it dived and slammed into the Kowloon Tong hillside, exploding into a fireball on impact. All 14 passengers and five crewmembers aboard died instantly. The colony's daily press called it Hong Kong's worst air disaster.

In Hong Kong, an unnerved Mr Suchowolski quickly donated $150 to the Society for the Protection of Children and a similar sum to the United Jewish Overseas Relief Fund. At the same time, a shocked military command began organising a large funeral for Wild and the nine other servicemen killed in the crash.

In Singapore, members of a stunned War Crimes Section pondered how they were to tackle future investigations with the driving force and intellectual core of their operation so abruptly removed. Of particular concern were the on-going investigations into the various massacres of civilian Chinese on the island. Wild had become so deeply involved with this case, and his expertise and language skills had proved so critical to it, that it would be impossible to find anyone equivalent to take his place. Not only was time running short; local Chinese political pressure was mounting. When were the British going to try Japanese for the Chinese massacres?

It would be several days before Colonel Ichiji Sugita, newly lodged in a Changi Jail cell, heard of Wild's death. One can only surmise what went through the intelligence officer's mind upon hearing the news. His chief accuser had perished. Undoubtedly destroyed with him were all the vital interrogation notes taken during their meeting in Sugamo Prison.

Within a matter of weeks, Sugita would switch roles. From No 2 suspect on Wild's "wanted" list he would emerge as a key prosecution witness. Thus, the sudden demise of Wild, Britain's most respected Far Eastern war crimes expert, resulted in a major change of course for both the investigation and prosecution of the Singapore massacres case. Who had it right? The expert who had headed the investigations for over 12 months, or those who tried to follow in his footsteps? ■

Chapter 10

Telling it the way it wasn't

———— ✦ ————

I t took 40 minutes on March 10, 1947, to drive the seven accused Japanese from Changi Jail to the Victoria Memorial Hall, in Singapore's Empress Place, for the opening day of the "Chinese Massacre" trial. Hundreds crammed the roadway at the back of the hall for a glimpse of the handcuffed men as the three-vehicle convoy of military trucks, guarded by armed British Seaforth Highlander troops, reversed onto the rear doors of the building.

It was 9.30 am when the guards led the prisoners, one by one, into a small waiting room behind the main auditorium where handcuffs were removed. Several guards remained with the Japanese as the door was locked from the outside. The public gallery of the converted auditorium opened at 9.45 am. Within three minutes all seats were filled. A huge crowd milled in front of the hall hoping more seating would be made available. However, in view of the bitter memories of the massacre period, military authorities organising the trial were determined to keep public numbers manageable.

The Seaforth Highlanders were assigned to positions on either side of the dock to guard the accused throughout the hearing. Numerous police officers were also stationed in the body of the hall. All were alerted to a possible assassination attempt against the Japanese prisoners from the public gallery.

Among the main concerns of the British authorities in the run up to the trial had been the likely reaction of the public at large

Within minutes Singapore's Victoria Memorial Hall was jammed with spectators eager to catch a first glimpse of the seven Japanese on trial for the "Chinese Massacre" affair. Outside the hall, hundreds more waited in hopes of gaining entry to the public gallery.

both to the proceedings themselves and, in particular, to the prosecution case. The local Chinese were demanding what they regarded as long overdue justice. But would the arraignment of the seven accused, the evidence given publicly against them, together with the punishments that would inevitably follow, be enough to satisfy the politics now involved?

In an exercise designed to defuse adverse post-trial Chinese reaction, the British military authorities contacted the press. A story in *The Straits Times* on March 8, two days before the opening of the trial, reported that, despite local estimates of 30,000 or more Chinese slaughtered by the Japanese, War Crimes investigators still counted the victims at approximately 5,000. Quoting a War Crimes official, the newspaper account said the discrepancy had occurred due to the number of Chinese killed in the shelling and bombing of Singapore, as well as in actual combat when the Japanese invaded. In other words, the British wanted to convey the impression that the local Chinese had grossly exaggerated the tragedy that had befallen their island and that no one should expect the trial to mirror death toll claims in the vernacular press.

The truth was, however, that the British, as a matter of expediency, had fallen back on the doubtful authority of the Japanese War Ministry's "Chinese Massacre Affair" report. It had become their primary reference document for understanding much of the case. And so the 5,000 death toll figure that had been part of the Japanese whitewash was rendered "official."

Five minutes before the trial was scheduled to begin, the seven accused, wearing military uniforms, were ushered under guard to positions in the dock. A hush descended on the hall, disturbed only by the rustle of papers as court officials and lawyers organised their files.

The Japanese officers sat in order of seniority. On the far right was Lt. General Takuma Nishimura, aged 59, beside him sat Lt. General Saburo Kawamura, 52, then Lt. Colonel Masayuki

Oishi, 50, Lt. Colonel Yoshitaka Yokota, 48, Major Tomotatsu Jyo, 47, Major Satorou Onishi, 45, and finally Captain Haruji Hisamatsu, 34. All wore distinguishing number cards on their chests. These ran in ascending order from one to seven, right to left, along the row.

Three barristers from the Tokyo Supreme Court — Mr Shozaburo Kurose, Mr Matsuro Fujiiwa, and Mr Kiyomasa Kakuda — represented the accused. Theirs was a thankless job. Quite apart from the generally one-sided legal fights they faced on behalf of their respective clients, regulations laid down by the British placed them in a decidedly second-class situation to the prosecution team.

A High Command circular dated September 20, 1946, set down the parameters for handling Japanese defence counsel involved in war crimes trials. They were to be treated as "surrendered personnel." They were to receive no pay, except from their own government. While performing their duties they were to be granted "reasonable freedom of movement and transport facilities." Finally, they were to receive prisoner of war scale of rations.

At precisely 10.00 am, the five uniformed officers appointed to hear the case entered the hall. The court president, Colonel P. A. Forsythe, from the King's Royal Rifle Corps, holder of the Military Medal, sat in the centre flanked by two colleagues on either side. The other four court members comprised Major P. Clague, Major A. A. Futcher and Major A.E. Dennis, all from the Royal Artillery, and Captain R. H. Tyson, from the Intelligence Corps.

Following the reading of the trial's convening order, the swearing in of the court, and the oath-taking by the interpreters and stenographers, the accused were formally arraigned.

All were jointly charged with having committed a single war crime. The charge sheet details, read to the court, specified that at Singapore Island, between February 18 and March 3, 1942, the seven named officers, all being responsible for the lives and safety of civilian inhabitants were, in violation of the laws and usages of war, together concerned in the massacre of Chinese civilian residents. The charge went on to refer to killings that took place at Ponggol, Changi Road, Amber Road, Singapore Docks, Mata Ikan, Changi Spit and Tanah Merah. In turn, all seven pleaded not guilty and an application by the defence to have the proceedings delayed was quickly overruled by the court.

The prosecutor, Major Frederick W. Ward, then rose to deliver his opening address. It was a critical moment. He was about to provide the first official account of the crime which had so shattered the island's population five years earlier. Although no senior British official in Singapore would have admitted it at the time, there was far more at stake in the trial days ahead than the fate of the seven Japanese officers sitting impassively behind their numbered cards.

Ward initially set out to establish the legal parameters of the case. The seven Japanese, he said, had been jointly charged with responsibility for a series of "close-set massacres" which had arisen from a "common plan." They had committed a crime against the laws and usages of war "which have grown through custom or convention to regulate the relationships which arise, or may arise, when opposing powers make war against each other."

Any relationship between one set in authority over another, he explained, carried with it certain duties and responsibilities. This was so whether the relationship was between master and servant, officer and ranker, jailer and prisoner, or father and son. Increased authority and power carried with them increases, in like measure, of duty and responsibility.

"In this case which opens today," said the prosecutor, "there exists just such a relationship — that between the members of an occupying power and the inhabitants of territory in the occupation of that power." That relationship had thrown upon the accused — members of the occupying power — the onus of

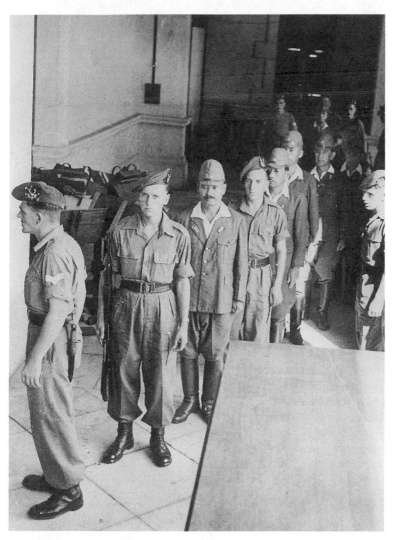

*On the trial's opening day, British Seaforth Highlander guards escort
the seven Japanese defendants, led by Lt. General Takuma
Nishimura, into the Victoria Memorial Hall.*

Shortly before taking their positions in the dock, the Japanese defendants answer a roll call and put on their numbered identification cards.

Lt. General Nishimura, former commmanding officer of the elite Konoye Imperial Guards, prepares to take his position in the dock.

The five military officers who will decide the fate of the seven defendants in the Chinese Massacre trial are sworn in. From left to right: Major P. Clague, Major A. A. Futcher, Colonel P. A. Forsythe (Court President), Major A. E. Dennis and Captain R. H. Tyson.

Defence and prosecution lawyers, together with the public gallery, stand as the Military Court's five-member panel enters the Victoria Memorial Hall's auditorium and takes its place.

The trial's crowded public gallery gets its first
glimpse of all seven defendants in the dock.
From right to left: Lt General Takuma Nishimura,
Lt. General Saburo Kawamura, Lt. Colonel
Masayuki Oishi, Lt. Colonel Yoshitaka Yokota,
Major Tomatatsu Jyo, Major Satorou Onishi,
Captain Haruji Hisamatsu.

complying with the associated rules and obligations.

He went on to draw the court's attention to the Hague Convention of 1907, which, although not formally crystalised into law, "still serves to reinforce existing conventions". Quoting from Article 46 of the Annexure, he argued that all belligerent powers had to respect "the family honour and rights, the individual life and property, as well as the religious convictions of the inhabitants of occupied territories."

Turning to the British War Office's Manual of Military Law, Major Ward read the following extract from chapter 4 which, he claimed, had a direct bearing on the prosecution case:

"It is the duty of the occupant to see that the lives of the inhabitants are respected, that their domestic peace and honour are not disturbed, that their religious convictions are not interfered with, and generally, that duress, unlawful and criminal attacks on their persons and felonious actions against their property, are just as punishable as in times of peace."

The prosecutor went on: "It can thus be said that nations have certain international obligations with which they are legally bound to comply, as well as a code of conduct which has gradually been built up."

Major Ward then moved to the charge sheet's allegation that an offence had been committed "jointly" by the seven accused. He quoted from a variety of legal reference books to substantiate the issue of admissibility of evidence in matters of common plans or conspiracies. Here was the linchpin of the prosecution case against the seven Japanese officers.

When several conspired to commit an offence, he said, each made the rest his agents to carry the plan to execution.

"We might well keep in mind the legal maxim: "Qui facit per alium facit per se — he who acts through another, acts through himself," Major Ward told the court.

In this case, the prosecution had to prove two factors. Firstly, the existence of an illegal course of action or common plan. Secondly, the participation of the accused in the furthering of that plan. Once these had been proved, contended Major Ward, the separate individuals involved in the conspiracy were responsible for all acts performed by any persons in execution of such a plan. In short, evidence against one could be considered as evidence against all.

The prosecution then reviewed the chain of command headed by Yamashita and the position of the various Japanese troop formations following the entry into downtown Singapore on February 16, 1942. To assist the court, the following diagram was submitted.

Gen. Yamashita

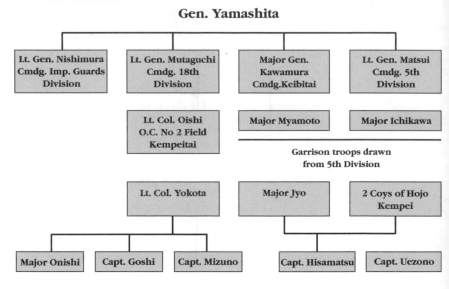

Major Ward explained that Nishimura's Imperial Guards Division had been given the task of garrisoning and administering the eastern half of the island. The area of Singapore town itself and the districts immediately adjacent to the perimeter of the town area, had all come under the jurisdiction of Kawamura who commanded the town garrison or keibitai. The northern part of the island had been given to General Matsui's 5th Division and the west to General Mutaguchi's 18th Division.

The prosecutor then went on to allege that once the military occupation of the island had been completed, Yamashita issued a general directive to his four area commanders — Nishimura, Kawamura, Matsui and Mutaguchi — to the effect that the Chinese population of Singapore was to be mustered in concentration areas. There the Chinese were to be screened. Undesirable elements, for example, those with anti-Japanese sentiments, ex-Government employees and the like, were to be taken away and killed.

"The original date set for the completion of the task was February 23 1942," said Major Ward, adding, "but the process of screening and killing alleged undesirables, a process which in fact resulted in the deaths of at least 5,000 innocent men and boys, continued until the early part of March, 1942,"

Here, for the first time, was the official death-toll for the massacres. It differed in both substance and impact from the *"definitely considerably in excess of 5,000 men"* description given by Wild to the IMTFE in Tokyo six months earlier. The prosecution figure would soon be roundly rejected by the local Chinese as being absurdly small.

Major Ward's contention was that a neat package of orders travelled from Yamashita down the 25th Army's recognised chain of command.

Major Ward continued: "These orders in amplified form were passed down by the Area Commanders — by General Nishimura to his Chief of Staff, by General Kawamura to his three sub-area commanders. One of these sub-area commanders was Lt. Colonel Oishi, from whom the orders were passed down through Lt. Colonel Yokota to Major Onishi and Captain Goshi on the one hand, and through Major Jyo to Captain Hisamatsu on the other."

Execution of the plan, originating from Yamashita, had been carried out by the sector commanders whose responsibility it had been for selecting the time, place and method of killing those Chinese coming under the various categories specified in the original instructions. Major Ward said the massacres had been carried out under the supervision of the kempeitai. The attached hojo kempei troops were often employed to do the actual shooting under the direct orders of a kempeitai officer. He claimed that the "field activity" had been left to the initiative of the individual sector commanders who had used their "discretion" rather than being forced by any "obligation."

Rounding off his remarks, Major Ward proclaimed: "Before the first prosecution witness is called, may I respectfully remind you, gentlemen, that — as in every criminal case — the onus of proof rests on the prosecution. If, at the conclusion of this case, there exists any reasonable doubt — not shred or shadow of doubt, but such a doubt as would influence a reasonable and prudent man in the conduct of his own affairs — if such reasonable doubt does exist, it should and must be given to the accused."

The prosecution had presented the basic arguments for its case against the accused. But in the light of what we now know, these were riddled with flaws.

The suggestion, for instance, that the massacres resulted when a single set of orders, originating from Yamashita, passed down the recognised chain of command was patently false. The mass killing plot was far more complex and devious. What is more, it evolved, not around Yamashita, but around Tsuji.

So, was Major Ward ignorant of the facts? Did he really believe Yamashita was the prime architect? Was there no evidence to suggest otherwise? Had he no knowledge of Tsuji's role? Or was the prosecution actually stuck on the horns of a dilemma? Under strong pressure from time and politics to deliver convictions, did the British investigators and their legal advisers err? Did they purposely overlook the role played by Tsuji? There is another possibility. Was the prosecution unable to pursue the case along legitimate lines because the real culprit — Tsuji — had vanished? If this was so, did someone in authority opt for the easy way out — a doctored prosecution case?

These are some of the questions that must be asked as the story continues to unfold. Several answers can be provided immediately.

Evidence certainly did exist indicating Yamashita's likely non-involvement. The texts of the cables to and from Manila, examined in the previous chapter, were a matter of High Command record. The clear preference of those in Singapore to use Yamashita as a witness, rather than place him on trial, was well recognised. Furthermore, British investigators and legal officers alike, who worked on the case, had all studied the report of Wild's Manila interview with Yamashita. It was, and remains, the only official record in existence of Yamashita's views on the massacres. This document included, of course, the 25th Army Commander's emphatic denial of involvement. Only two men could have given direct testimony on the Wild report: Wild himself and Yamashita. Both were dead. For whatever reasons, the Singapore prosecuting team at some point in the lead up to the trial, decided to ignore both the contents and implications of this very significant file.

Another document to which the prosecuting team had access was the transcript of evidence given to the IMTFE hearing in Tokyo. Even if all files and related notes collected by Wild in Japan were destroyed in the Hong Kong air crash, the original Sugita sub-committee report had been submitted as an exhibit at the Tokyo trial. Indeed, it had become a basic document for investigators and prosecutors alike.

It would seem impossible, therefore, for any British legal expert, preparing the Singapore case, to be ignorant of salient Japanese admissions within this report all pointing to the strong probability that someone other than Yamashita had been behind the slaughter. These included observations that plans for the killings had been laid well in advance, and that the main lists of anti-Japanese Chinese had been received in Ipoh, weeks before the invaders landed on Singapore. Yamashita simply could not have participated in the planning if only because he arrived so late to assume control of the invasion.

Likewise, the same Japanese report concluded that Kawamura had not issued orders *"on his own personal view"* and that it was also *"very doubtful whether the mass execution of Chinese was due to the order of the Commander in Chief (Yamashita)."* At very least, serious questions had been raised over the identity of the order's issuing authority. But the British decided to ignore these completely and press ahead with the court room portrayal of Yamashita as the arch-villain.

The degree to which investigators and the prosecution at the outset of the trial understood Tsuji's involvement is a moot point. Wild certainly appeared to appreciate that the man was critical to the plot . How much this view sustained in Singapore beyond his death in the air crash is difficult to establish.

What research can verify, however, is that while obtaining pre-trial sworn statements from the seven defendants, investigating officers were repeatedly confronted with very clear references to Tsuji's activities. None of these appears to have triggered the slightest interest among the team of sleuths assigned to the case after Wild's demise. And, as we'll soon see, whenever Tsuji's name was mentioned in evidence during the course of the trial, the prosecution either flatly ignored it, or vigorously played down its importance ■

Chapter 11

Getting too close to the truth

———— ♦ ————

When Colonel Ichiji Sugita was called as the trial's first witness, a murmur of recognition rippled through the crowded public gallery. His pre-trial suicide attempt had been widely reported in the Singapore papers and he entered the witness box with his neck heavily bandaged.

He had plunged a stainless steel table knife into his throat in an attempt to cut the carotid arteries. On his bed lay a hand written note saying: "I cannot bear to give evidence against my senior officer. I prefer to kill myself than be a witness for the prosecution. Best regards to our British friends."

A fellow Japanese trial witness discovered Sugita in the middle of his ritualistic death bid and wrenched the knife from his trembling hands. With breath whistling through a gaping neck wound, Sugita was rushed to the Alexandra Military Hospital by jeep. In three days, he was out of danger.

Viewed in retrospect, Sugita's presence on the Victoria Memorial Hall witness stand mirrored the highly confused state into which the investigation had fallen following Wild's death. Sugita had been Britain's second most "wanted" man in the region. This was well appreciated by investigators and military legal experts alike, as was the fact that he had been the issuing authority for the 25th Army's operational hit lists, the basic massacre documents. Added to this, his remarks to Wild after the Changi Point massacre were well documented. Finally, it was widely recognised among war crimes experts that Sugita had headed the Tokyo War Ministry's massacre cover-up. Now he was a key prosecution witness.

Assisted through his evidence by Major Ward, the witness provided details on Japanese troop dispositions throughout Singapore from February 16 onwards. He confirmed there had been two purges against Chinese civilians; the first from February 21 - 22, the second in the final days of February and the first few days of March.

Prosecutor: This first purge, on 21st and 22nd February, how many people, approximately, were killed?

Sugita: It is said about 5,000.

Prosecutor: And the second purge that occurred during the end of February and early March, approximately how many?

Sugita: About 300.

The prosecution at this time was holding in its files the pre-trial statement by Kempeitai Commander Oishi identifying Sugita's Information Bureau as the distributing point for the Chinese hit lists on the evening of the surrender. Yet Major Ward never once queried Sugita on this very significant aspect. Nor was he questioned on the role played in the affair by Tsuji. Nor, for that matter, did Major Ward seek to pin down a frequently waffling Sugita on the precise source of the orders for concentrating, screening and killing Chinese civilians.

Mr Shozaburo Kurose, counsel for Oishi, Yokota and Jyo, asked Sugita: "Do you know what policy Commander-in-Chief Yamashita took towards the Chinese on the whole before entering Singapore?

Sugita: I do.

Counsel: What was the policy?

Sugita: The policy was — No 1, to look after the Chinese with love. It was not an order towards the Chinese only. It was for the Malays and the Indians and other inhabitants of the island.

Counsel: Then, if they decided to massacre the Chinese after the surrender, the policy must have changed?

Sugita: Yes.

Counsel: Why did they have to change this policy?

Sugita: I do not know the details.

At this point, Sugita had to be lying. He knew exactly how the policy had been changed through the machinations of the intervening Tsuji. Indeed, he had been part of those machinations. He knew Tsuji was on the run and, more likely than not, his general whereabouts. Mr Kurose had come very close to tapping part of the truth behind the Singapore massacres. But here his line of questioning swung away to explore the degree of Chinese guerrilla activities encountered by the 25th Army both in Malaya during the campaign, and in Singapore after the surrender. This was to support the defence's general contention that action against anti-Japanese Chinese guerrillas had been justified, given the expanding threat they posed at the time.

Assisting the prosecution during the trial was local barrister, Mr Richard Lim Chuan Hoe, legal adviser to the Chinese Consul General in Singapore. He rose to re-examine Sugita on the vital matter of the alleged massacre order from Yamashita. Mr Lim said he understood the order given to Kawamura was of a very general nature and sought Sugita's views.

The prosecution team confers during a lull in trial proceedings. From left to right: Major M. G. Watson (chief war crimes investigator), Mr Richard Lim Chuan Hoe (prosecuting lawyer), and Major Frederick W. Ward (chief prosecutor).

Japanese defence counsel, Shozaburo Kurose, representing Oishi and Yokota, cross examines a witness.

Sugita: I have never seen this order, but the information we got during the investigation in Tokyo was that this order was a general order.

Mr Lim: And the details had to be worked out either by Major General Kawamura or his subordinate officers, is that correct?

Sugita: As I have stated this morning, the order was detailed as it went down the channels.

Once more, questions seemed headed in the right direction. There was obviously an awareness of a lack of continuity between the order "of a very general nature" directly traceable to Yamashita, and the one subsequently issued calling for mass killings of civilians. But this was still a long way from establishing the reality of two sets of instructions from separate sources. Again, ambiguity masked details and another opportunity to get at the truth was lost.

The second prosecution witness was former Japanese diplomat, Mr Mamoru Shinozaki, whose evidence had been eagerly awaited by the local Chinese community. During the occupation years, Shinozaki became one of the best known Japanese figures in Singapore and without question the most widely and genuinely respected. It was felt that if anyone knew the true story about the massacres, it was Shinozaki. Furthermore, he was just the sort of man who would tell it like it was. Shinozaki would not be one to disappoint his fans.

Under questioning from Major Ward, he described how he had been released from Changi Jail immediately after the British surrender, and how he came to learn about the concentration areas and the screenings. He related how he had manipulated senior military figures into giving him the power to issue passes that, in turn, had probably saved the lives of thousands of detained Chinese.

Shinozaki told the court he had sought permission from Kawamura to use "powerful type" on these passes. The Garrison Commander had also given him special arm band identification as a Foreign Office official attached to the High Command. "Then the soldiers who saw my pass, respected my title from the High Command although they did not know my name. Therefore many people came to me and I gave them protection passes and working passes," he said.

Shinozaki was clearly anxious to tell the court the full story about his passes. But the prosecution was more interested in using him to identify the prisoners in the dock and to establish their various functions during the massacre period. He was asked to name as many of the concentration camps as he could. "They were Ord Road, off River Valley Road, Arab Street, Jalan Besar, Tiong Bahru, and others I don't know," he replied.

Prosecutor: You mentioned visiting three concentration areas. Can you say whether or not there appeared to be any uniform method of screening?

Shinozaki: I received the impression that it differed according to the different places.

Prosecutor: Can you give any illustrations of that difference?

Shinozaki: At Ord Road, they had all the Chinese men there and ropes were around the place, and they had a desk at the entrance and the kempeitai people were interrogating there. At Upper Serangoon Road all the people were merely concentrated. A French bishop by the name of De Vales came to me and told me that the women might be in danger, and so I went with him and tried to help the women. At that time there was a second lieutenant at the place and that was how I knew he belonged to the Imperial Guards Division.

It was not until defence counsel Kurose began cross-examining Shinozaki that the court began to appreciate the witness' extraordinary story.

Shinozaki estimated that he had arranged for the printing of between 20,000 and 30,000 passes and had given them all out. On them were the Japanese words: *"The bearer is a good citizen. Please look after him and protect him."*

Defence: When did you issue the greatest number of these passes? Was it during the period February 19th to the 25th?

Shinozaki: At first the civilians did not know about these passes and until the 20th there were very few issued. Gradually the rumours went round and after the 20th a great number were issued. I gave several hundred to one person without even having names printed on them.

Defence: To whom did you give these passes mostly? What class of people received them?

Shinozaki: I did not care whether the person was good or bad, or whether he was a communist. Anybody who came and asked for a pass I gave it to him.

The witness also explained how, on numerous occasions when the passes failed to work, he had personally intervened to save lives. "In that case I went to the concentration camp personally, and with the sector commander's permission had the people released. In case the sector commander did not give me his permission, then I would go and contact Lt. Colonel Yokota or Major Jyo."

Defence: How many people were saved by you going directly to the concentration camp and having them released?

Shinozaki: I can give you a definite answer to this question. Through Yokota and through Jyo — and afterwards there was a Chinese society made — I am sure about 2,000 people were released. This is the actual number of people I had released. But the number that were released by passes I could not give you.

Now into his second day on the witness stand, Shinozaki, still under defence cross examination, was about to drop a bombshell. Kurose had been exploring the degrees of assistance provided to the kempeitai by influential citizens and local police, conditions in Singapore in the immediate aftermath of the British surrender and the position of Kawamura.

He then switched the line of questioning completely. "Do you know a person by the name of Staff Officer Tsuji, belonging to the 25th Army? And do you know a person by the name of Hayashi, a staff officer who belonged to the Keibitai Headquarters?

Shinozaki: Yes, I do. I have not met Colonel Tsuji, but I have heard of his name several times. Major Hayashi, I have met him several times, two or three times.

Defence: Do you know what part Hayashi and Tsuji took in this case?

Shinozaki: Tsuji belonged to the Staff Office and received orders of the Commander-in-Chief, and he was a man who was chief of the Operations Staff. He was a very strong willed and a very sharp man. He is the person who framed up the operational orders.

Defence: I am not asking you about personal character. I want only facts.

Shinozaki: I have heard afterwards that Staff Officer Tsuji is the person who made the plan of this massacre.

Defence: What about Hayashi?

Shinozaki: I have not heard directly, but I have heard that he was a good co-operator of Tsuji.

Defence: Do you know that Staff Officer Hayashi was transferred from the 25th Army to the Keibitai Headquarters?

Shinozaki: Yes, I know.

Defence: For what reason was he transferred?

Shinozaki: Major General Kawamura was a very quiet person and could not fulfil his work. So, in order to have somebody to do the actual work, he had Hayashi transferred.

We now know from Kawamura's diary and other sources that the Garrison Commander in fact had nothing to do with Hayashi's temporary transfer. This was all part of Tsuji's manoeuvrings to secure the framework for handling his mass-killing plans. Still, the defence questioning had on this occasion pushed the prosecution witness to the very brink of revealing the real mastermind behind the massacres.

Kurose's next question halted Shinozaki's review of the roles of Tsuji and Hayashi just as abruptly as the two names had been introduced. "When was the water police organised?" asked the defence counsel, and the prosecution witness veered off on another theme altogether.

Was Kurose at this stage privy to the truth? Did he have his own reasons for not wanting to pursue the line of questioning? Could he have been genuinely ignorant of the power-play within the 25th Army's High Command leading directly to the massacres? Or was there now in existence a conspiracy to protect the fugitive Tsuji? Particularly puzzling was the complete lack of reaction from the prosecution side to the quite extraordinary claims Shinozaki was making about Tsuji and Hayashi.

The questioning of Shinozaki continued and the Japanese defence counsel framed a broad query which produced a most unusual response.

Defence: You have said that you issued many passes and saved thousands of people. I don't think this could be done without the Army's help and I understand there must have been several political reasons. Would you explain the situation because this is very important as far as this case is concerned?

Shinozaki: I wish to state the meaning of my name first. My name is Shinozaki. 'Shino' means China and 'Zaki' means cape. So my name would mean 'Cape of China.' My name Mamoru in Japanese means 'protection' in English. This I have heard from my father when I was a child.

Shinozaki wanted the court to appreciate what he regarded as an important symbolic relationship between his name and the Singapore massacres. From his viewpoint, Shinozaki, the "Protecting Cape of the Chinese," had long been destined to undertake such a role. When the Singapore massacres occurred, and he was on the spot, it was as if destiny had finally beckoned and he simply had to answer.

Kurose was indifferent to such lyricism. "Instead of going into personal details I wish you would give me the details of the question I am asking," he retorted.

Little fazed by the defence's brusque reaction, Shinozaki went on to relate how the "Chinese problem " had been very serious just after the British surrender and that he "could not foresee what would happen if it was left alone." He then explained to the court how the arrest of prominent local medical practitioner, Dr Lim Boon Keng, had led to the formation of the society known as the Overseas Chinese Association, and how this, in turn, had served to aid many detained Chinese.

Shinozaki said he had been called by Yokota and informed that Dr Lim had been arrested at River Valley Road. Yokota had said: "This Dr Lim Boon Keng is like my father. Please handle him very politely." Shinozaki and Dr Lim had dined together to explore ways of helping the Chinese and defusing tensions. This had taken place between February 23 - 25.

From the dinner meeting had grown the idea of forming the association. Shinozaki told the court that the plan from the outset was for the association to co-operate with the Japanese Army. But its fundamental purpose was to protect the Chinese community and to rescue powerful leaders detained by the kempeitai.

Shinozaki explained it would have been impossible to form the association without the permission and understanding of "high Japanese Army officials." Yokota, a sympathetic man, had helped arrange the correct approaches. These were made to Kawamura and Major General Manaki, head of the Military Administration Department. Ultimately, the Association was given the go-ahead.

Mr. S. Q. Wong had to be released from detention before he could become vice president. "Then Mr. Chan Kay Tan, Mr Chan Kay San, Mr Lee Chong Sian, and Mr Lee Tian Pah became founder members of the committee and a name list was made of all the people that were going to be released," Shinozaki told the court

He continued: "I asked for all the names of the influential Chinese people who were detained to be written down on the list. I think there were several hundred names and this list was forwarded to Yokota and to Commander Manaki. All those people were finally released."

Mamoru Shinozaki whose decision to issue vast numbers of special passes saved thousands of Chinese from the execution squads in Singapore.
"I did not care whether the person was good or bad, or whether he was a communist. Anybody who came and asked for a pass, I gave it to him."
— Shinozaki.

Dr. Lim Boon Keng, founder of the Overseas Chinese Association.
"This Dr Lim Boon Keng is like my father. Please handle him very politely."
— Kempeitai officer Yokota to Shinozaki.

Dato S.Q.Wong became Vice-President of the Overseas Chinese Association, but had to be released from Japanese detention first.

During the Japanese occupation, the Overseas Chinese Association had two main departments, explained Shinozaki. One carried out the functions of the Chinese Consul General in Singapore. The other operated as the Chinese Chamber of Commerce.

"Due to the absence of a Chinese consul general here, Dr Lim Boon Keng acted as consul general in Singapore and also as the Chairman of the Chinese Chamber of Commerce, for the purpose of protecting all the Chinese people. The person who understood this was Lt. Colonel Yokota," Shinozaki recalled.

From the defence standpoint, there was advantage in trying to prove that a substantial level of collaboration had existed in the Association's relationship with the Japanese Military Administration. Kurose's questions tried to corner the witness into admitting as much. But Shinozaki recognised the trap. His own version of the delicate position of the Overseas Chinese Association during the occupation years amounted to a poignant comment on prevailing public opinion in early post-war Singapore.

Shinozaki explained: "The Chinese Association was set up in order to have the people released — the influential Chinese released. But it actually protected the Chinese people and it was like a brother looking after his younger brother.

"The British, for instance, was the father. The British left and the sons, the Chinese, were left, so the older Chinese people had to look after the younger brothers. Afterwards, this Association began to be called collaborators. I think it was unfair for them to use this name. . . . . . I am very sorry to hear this word. They are not collaborators. That is unfair.

"They looked after the younger brothers and younger sisters during the time when the real father had gone away and under the strong father — the Japanese stepfather. By this situation of community leadership, it is unfair to call them collaborators. It is not collaboration. They were protectors of their younger brothers and sisters," he concluded.

The conviction with which Shinozaki delivered his views more than compensated for the jumble of his words and nobody in court that day confused the meaning.

There followed a string of local witnesses — mostly Chinese, but with some Indians and Eurasians as well — providing harrowing first person accounts of the Singapore massacres. They described what went on at the concentration points, during the screening sessions and at the actual killing sites across the island. Some had miraculously escaped as the execution squads opened fire. Others had watched their loved ones taken away. One or two recounted how they had been involved in the screenings; how they had assisted the kempeitai make identifications and take down names. Some, whose names they had documented, had been friends and they had never seen them again.

On March 18, the seventh day of the trial, the prosecution case entered its final phase. With formal "live" evidence from the witness box completed, Major Ward began tendering original affidavits sworn in various parts of the world. These included eye-witness accounts by British servicemen, former volunteers, planters and businessmen who all described different aspects of particular massacres. Some gave details of the killings at sea off Keppel Harbour's eastern entrance. Others described what they had witnessed on the beaches in the Changi area.

Then the prosecution tendered affidavits sworn in Tokyo by a number of Japanese witnesses. One came from Colonel Isamu Hashizume, the 25th Army staff officer who had been one of the four sub-committee members helping Sugita prepare his massacre whitewash. He explained how the operations and planning department was grouped with the intelligence department in the same High Command section. Colonel Tsuji headed operations and planning assisted by Majors Teruto Kunitake and Shigeharu Asaeda.

It will be recalled that Kunitake was also one of the Sugita sub-committee members. Asaeda, of course, had been Tsuji's close cohort since Taipeh days. The inter-related intelligence department was headed by Sugita, assisted by Hayashi. Here, for the record, was the overall grouping within which Tsuji operated. But it would not be identified as such in the court.

What Hashizume's evidence did reveal, however, was just how closely linked the operations and intelligence departments were when it came to the mass killing of Chinese in Singapore.

According to Hashizume's affidavit: "Colonel Tsuji of the First Section of Army Headquarters, explained the Army Commander's intention in some detail to Major Hayashi who was then with Defence Force Headquarters as a 'Detached Staff Officer.' In the opinion of the investigation committee Colonel Tsuji's manner gave an impression of even greater strength of determination than General Yamashita's own." The "investigation committee" referred to by Hashizume was, of course, the Sugita sub-committee.

But the most fascinating of the Japanese affidavits read to the court that morning was the testimony of then 36-year-old Domei News Agency reporter, Mr Takafumi Hishikari, who was with the 25th Army High Command from December 31, 1941 until April, 1943. Most of this time he had spent in Singapore. He had been attached to the Intelligence Section at Army Headquarters and thus had regularly come in contact with both Sugita and Hayashi.

According to Hishikari, Sugita had told him two or three days after his arrival in Singapore that 50,000 Chinese were to be killed. These Chinese consisted of anti-Japanese elements, in particular communists and people suspected of guerrilla activities.

The journalist's statement went on: "Colonel Sugita told me that the order for the killing had come from the Operations Section of the 25th Army Staff and that he thought it had been planned by Colonel Tsuji or Major Hayashi. He said that he was not in agreement with this order.

"Later Colonel Sugita told me that it had not been found possible to kill the whole of the 50,000 but that almost half had been dealt with. Colonel Sugita did not give me any further information about this matter at any time."

Here, for the record, was Sugita's wartime estimate for the death toll — almost 25,000.

Hishikari recalled that when he spoke to Hayashi about the massacres a month later, the intelligence officer confirmed the original plan to kill 50,000 Chinese. Hayashi told him that after about half that number had been eliminated, an order was received to stop the killing. Hayashi did not disclose who issued the order for the massacres in the first place. Nor did he identify who called a halt to the killings. Hayashi admitted, however, he had been directly connected with the incident but did not specify in what way.

"From this conversation I formed the impression that the order had originally been issued by the staff without the Army Commander's knowledge and that when the Commander found out about it he ordered it stopped. But Hayashi never said so in so many words," asserted Hishikari.

By this point in the trial, four Japanese prosecution witnesses — Sugita, Shinozaki, Hashizume and Hishikari — were, with varying interpretations, all pointing to Tsuji's key role in the massacres. Grave doubts had also been raised about Yamashita's involvement and this in turn was seriously undermining the fundamental "joint plot" theme the court was being asked to accept.

There was more to come before the prosecution wound up its case.

Interpreters and investigators attached to the War Crimes No 7 team then began identifying a collection of statements taken from the seven accused after they had been returned to Singapore by the British military authorities and incarcerated in Changi Jail. They amounted to an amazing set of documents in that each accused appeared quite prepared to admit full complicity in the atrocities and most provided very full details of their individual involvement.

If there was an odd man out, it was Nishimura. Not that he denied involvement. Rather, he tended to emphasise that the matter had really been handled by others within his command. Nishimura admitted he had received orders on his arrival in Singapore calling for the Chinese inhabitants to be screened. "The orders stated that inhabitants who were considered to be anti-Japanese were to be disposed of, at my discretion," he said.

The Imperial Guards' commander conceded he had passed on these orders to his staff officers who formally issued them to the unit commanders assigned to the screening process. "The only reports passed to me personally of the activities of my units on the island stated that my orders regarding the disposal of the Chinese had been carried out," he said

Nishimura concluded his statement: "I have no conception of the place chosen for the shootings or of the unit or units who carried this out. I was too busy even to visit the units under my command at that time."

Far more typical of the voluntary statements read to the court that day was that made by Kempeitai Commander Oishi on November 9, 1946.

It stated:

Instructions came down to me from Army HQ through Kawamura that anti-Japanese Chinese elements were to be purged in three days and in carrying out the purge the killing of these Chinese was to be so conducted to avoid all publicity. Chinese picked out as undesirable in my five sectors were killed on 22nd, 23rd, 24th, and 25th. About 18th February, 1942, I passed these orders to my five sector commanders through Jyo and Yokota. I have no idea whether Hisamatsu was responsible for the shooting of Chinese at sea near Blakang Mati island. If such a massacre did take place it must be the idea of Jyo or Hisamatsu himself. I had no reports back from Jyo where undesirable Chinese of Hisamatsu were massacred. My daily reports from Jyo only stated the numbers of Chinese massacred and the method of execution, which was rifle fire.

I do not remember providing any kempeitai men on loan to General Nishimura to assist in checking Chinese in his area, but I heard from Kawamura's HQ staff members saying between 700 to 800 Chinese were massacred in the Imperial Guards Division area under Gen. Nishimura. On 17th February, 1942, I was ordered by Kawamura, then Keibitai or Singapore Garrison Commander, to transfer from 6 to 9 experienced NCO's and other ranks of the kempeitai to the area of Myamoto, Ichikawa and one other to help in searching out undesirable Chinese.

I detailed both Yokota and Jyo to fulfil this commitment. I have no knowledge what duties they performed besides helping in picking out anti-Japanese elements. I know Myamoto established muster centres in his area and Chinese were picked out as "bad hats" and shot. I cannot give any figures of numbers massacred.

I drew five companies of troops from the 25th Army HQ as auxiliary kempeitai to aid my sector commanders. Regarding the disposal of undesirable Chinese, I gave instructions on my own authority to my unit commanders to hand the Chinese picked out as such to the hojo K.T. attached to them and that the hojo kempei were to select the execution sites.

It is quite likely the sector commanders may have sent kempeitai NCO's on their own to accompany each execution and may have gone themselves as well. I do not know this for a fact.

The unit commander, if he was superior in rank to the hojo company commander attached to him, could give him orders off his own bat, and if lower in rank still had a "say" in deciding what was to be done in matters regarding details of shooting.

Kawamura told me that a 2nd and 3rd purge was necessary

as many Chinese from the outskirts of the city had avoided the general rounding up. Colonel Tsuji went to Onishi's collection centre to urge the K.T on to greater efforts to obtain more Chinese for massacre. I heard this directly from Onishi. I did not give any instructions to Hisamatsu and Goshi to increase their Chinese massacre totals.

During the period of massacres I had no contact with Colonel Tsuji and knew he was dissatisfied with the total of Chinese massacred only from Onishi.

After Hisamatsu's unit left the Tanjong Pagar Police Station for Sumatra on the 5th or 6th of March, 1942, Uezono took over the control of his area in addition to his own. The kempeitai unit which moved into Tanjong Pagar Police Station to take charge of it must have been a sub-unit of Uezono as there were no other kempeitai units in the area.

If, as you say, 96 Malay Regiment regulars were massacred at Pasir Panjang Gap by the kempeitai unit that occupied Tanjong Pagar Police Station on the day following the departure of Hizamatsu-Tai from there, then it must be Uezono kempeitai that carried out the massacre.

The   three-page statement was signed by Oishi on each page in Japanese.

There were eleven of these statements in all — two each from Nishimura, Oishi, Onishi and Hisamatsu, and one each from Kawamura, Yokota and Jyo. Not one of them reflected even the vaguest element of remorse.

But buried in the statement by Yokota, kempeitai section commander for the upper half of Singapore city, was the first indication of what would become the backbone of the defence case.

Said Yokota: "The order for the massacre of undesirable Chinese came from Army HQ and I merely relayed this on to my sector commanders. Since it came from the C-in-C of the Japanese Imperial Army, it was absolute and, as such, it had to be carried out."

It would be an argument that would be greatly expanded and explored as defence witnesses gave their testimonies in the remaining days of the trial.

For the moment, however, Oishi's sworn statement had, for the fifth time during the course of the prosecution's case, raised the spectre of Tsuji's involvement. But, as with the previous four occasions, the spectre just came and went ■

Chapter 12

The accused tell their stories

————— ◆ —————

The degree of damage to the defence case inflicted by the various sworn statements of the seven accused only became apparent to the three Japanese counsel after the documents had been read in court and tendered as evidence.

It was a bad slip on their part. They should have realised the incriminating nature of the statements long before that. Indeed, their court strategy from the outset should have been geared to discrediting the whole process leading to the formal introduction of such evidence.

Prior to the statements, very little in the prosecution testimony actually tied the seven Japanese officers directly to the crime from a legal standpoint. All the court had heard were emotive accounts of screenings and executions by eyewitnesses.

From the outset, Major Ward, infinitely more adroit in British law than the Tokyo barristers, realised the strongest evidence he possessed were the words of the defendants themselves. He constructed his presentation accordingly, introducing the sworn statements as a neat final act. This way, he felt, there was a good probability they would go unchallenged.

He was right. By 1 pm on Tuesday, March 18, the seventh day of the proceedings, Major Ward formally closed the prosecution evidence. The court president then duly adjourned the hearing until 10 am on Thursday, March 20, giving both sides a day and a half to review their situations before the defence took centre stage.

The Tokyo trio realised the full gravity of their procedural blunder during the 35-hour break. When the eighth day of the hearing commenced, defence counsel Shozaburo Kurose immediately applied for the prosecution case to be re-opened as "important, unforeseen facts" had come to light.

Kurose explained he wanted to examine the admissibility and credibility of certain statements made by the accused. Specifically he referred to a statement made by Kawamura on November 6, 1946, one by Oishi on June 1, 1946, another by Oishi on July 22, 1946, and a final one by Hisamatsu on May 14, 1946.

Replying to the application, the prosecution argued that under the Rules of Procedure, witnesses should not be called or recalled in order to supplement a negligence on the part of either the prosecution or the defence.

"I do submit that this has been negligence of conduct. These facts, such as they are, have come from the accused themselves — not from any fresh witnesses. The defence counsel have been preparing this case for five weeks before we came to court ten days ago. They have had every opportunity to question each of the accused, they have been served with copies of each of the accused's statement," said Major Ward.

He maintained that, six weeks earlier, all accused had received copies of the abstract showing that statements previously made by them would be tendered by the prosecution. "And now, after the prosecution case is closed, after every facility has been given to the defence for eliciting those facts, such as they are, now at the beginning of their own case, they come and ask for a recall. This is an unprecedented procedure on their part. I put it to you, sir, — and I say it in all seriousness — that this request is just another part of the series of obstructive applications made by the defence throughout this trial for adjournment after adjournment. I must oppose it on behalf of the prosecution."

In the event, the court rejected the application and ordered the defence counsel to proceed with their case. It was a bad start for the Japanese, and they knew it.

The joint opening address for the defence, delivered by Kiyomasa Kakuda, began by deploring how "beautiful Singapore, of all places, should have been harrowed by war" and in this place "where every prospect pleases" only man should have been vile!

"How 'vile' the prosecution has spared no pains to prove — while the press has expatiated on the subject. The defence, too, would be brutes, indeed, if they did not voice their hearty regret and lament, with the mourners, the many victims of an unrelenting militarism; quite apart from the fact that there will have been many mourned here this morning who laid down their lives in cheerful loyalty to the British Raj during those dark days."

The "British Raj" reference was a strange one that left many in the Victoria Memorial Hall puzzled that morning.

Kakuda continued: "Having said this, the defence desires nothing more than, having made their case as clear as that of the prosecution, justice be done and thereby this trial and its verdict contribute to the thorough cleansing of the residue of militarism from the world and result in furthering, ad infinitum, the friendly relationships that exist between the British Empire and China and restoring those that have always existed between your great countries and the fundamentally peaceful Japanese nation."

The defence explained it proposed arguing its case along three main lines.

Firstly, the acts allegedly committed jointly by the seven accused had been in the nature of a military operation. They were rendered necessary by the extreme emergency of the hour.

Secondly, whatever the seven accused had done during the course of the Singapore massacres amounted to nothing more than doing their duty as officers of the Japanese Imperial Army.

And, finally, craving the patience and indulgence of the court, the defence sought a verdict that took into account the precise significance of an order to a Japanese military man. Unquestioningly and naturally, argued Kakuda, the Japanese Army worked according to its own native law. In the Japanese Army, it was not permissible for a soldier, receiving an order, to decide for himself whether or not it was legal. Orders were absolute. That they could never be debated was part of the age-old Japanese system of Samurai law derived from centuries of absolutism. This was not only ingrained in every Japanese soldier's moral make-up, it was actually enshrined in black and white in the military Statute Book.

Kakuda asked: "Have these accused, by holding to their own domestic law, thereby broken international law?

He replied to his own question with an answer that left the public gallery momentarily stunned. "The point is not that those executions were the extreme penalty — that is, punishment — for some misdeed or other; but that anyone or anything hindering the operation of the Army could not be tolerated but must of necessity automatically be eliminated."

Kakuda continued: "By way of illustration, is it not like the deluded devotees in Indian processions who, flinging themselves in religious ecstasy before the juggernaut idol car, are crushed beneath its wheels in the relentless onward progress of the Juggernaut? The defence contends that, he who either got on the late juggernaut car of 'co-prosperity', or got out of the way — right out of Malaya or into POW camps — was safe!

"But it was not punishment if those who deliberately got in the way came to grief, or worse. It was just their fate. And does not character decide destiny? Even the scripture says, 'He who falls on this stone will be severely hurt, but he on whom it falls will be utterly crushed'."

For most in the courtroom that day, the parallel drawn between the hapless victims of Japanese butchery in Singapore, and Indian devotees, engulfed in ecstasy, flinging themselves beneath the wheels of a religious procession, seemed insultingly inappropriate and inaccurate. Seemingly oblivious to the impact of his words, Kakuda confidently wound up his opening address with the statement: "So, along these forthright lines the defence begs leave, sir, to carry their case."

F irst defence witness to give evidence was Nishimura who marked out on a court map the northern and eastern regions of Singapore island for which his Imperial Guards had been responsible.

Nishimura claimed that on February 17, 1942, Yamashita's 25th Army headquarters issued orders to the Imperial Guards to move on to Sumatra by March 6. So, from the outset, Nishimura's time in Singapore had been dominated by preparations for the division's new battle mission. His concentration on that task had paid off. The Imperial Guards had met their very tight departure deadline. While he was fully engaged in redeployment planning, another High Command operational order, this time calling for the screening of Singapore's Chinese population, was received by his divisional Chief-of-Staff, Colonel Shinryo Obata. The second order required the Imperial Guards to dispose of all anti-Japanese elements among Chinese living within the division's area of control. This was to be done by the end of February. Nishimura related how he had complained to his Chief-of-Staff that it would be impossible, within the given time frame, to carry out a proper investigation as to who were and who were not anti-Japanese.

Obata had confided to Nishimura that he shared the same view and had, in fact, mentioned as much to 25th Army Chief of Staff Suzuki, from whom he had received the order at Fort Canning. Suzuki had merely urged Obata to accept the instructions as they were, adding that Staff Officer Tsuji would be handling the matter and that the division should provide a number of soldiers to do the work.

"So I agreed to send my men to the 25th Army to the extent that it would not interfere with my operation, and appointed

Major General Kobayashi, the head of the infantry, as commander of this group. The carrying out of the plan was left in the hands of Staff Officer Tsuji and Major General Kobayashi," Nishimura told the court.

Having established his claim to being involved in other matters and his argument that the massacres had been the responsibility of Tsuji and the 25th Army HQ to which he had merely seconded troops, Nishimura was then closely questioned by his counsel as to his personal knowledge of the killings.

Counsel: Do you know that on February 28, 300 Chinese people were massacred at Ponggol, a district which was under the control of the Imperial Guards Division?

Nishimura: I do not know.

Counsel: Do you know that about 200 to 300 Chinese were shot at Changi 10th mile stone?

Nishimura: I don't.

Counsel: In fulfilling the 25th Army order, that is the screening of the Chinese people, did you receive the help of the kempeitai?

Nishimura: That I don't know. I do not even know what operational steps Staff Officer Tsuji took.

Counsel: Was the number of Chinese to be buried stated in this operational order?

Nishimura: No it wasn't.

Counsel: Did you give any figures of the Chinese to be buried to Major General Kobayashi?

Nishimura: No.

Later in the questioning, Kakuda asked Nishimura whether, at about the same time, or soon after he received the order, he had met Staff Officer Tsuji.

Nishimura: I was very busy planning the Sumatra campaign and as I had already appointed Major General Kobayashi for this work, there was no necessity for seeing Staff Officer Tsuji; so I did not see him.

Counsel: Do you know Staff Officer Hayashi of the Army headquarters?

Nishimura: I know him, because just before we left for Sumatra, he was attached to the Konoye Division as Staff Officer. I wish to state a fact that I remember occurring at this time. At the time when we were having a conversation at random, the subject turned to the Chinese massacre and I heard Staff Officer Hayashi boasting that the massacre case was not done by Kawamura. He said, 'It was done by Tsuji and myself.'

Counsel: Do you think you have responsibility for this act?

Nishimura: I myself do not think so.

Counsel: Why don't you think so?

Nishimura: I have only obeyed orders and should these army orders be illegal, the Commander-in-Chief who issued them must be responsible. Outwardly, the order came to the division. But, actually, the division loaned these soldiers and the actual work was done under the supervision of Staff Officer Tsuji. And even if the orders were illegal, I think I do not have any responsibility.

The defence counsel posed one final question to his witness.

Counsel: Supposing you disobeyed this operational order, what would have happened to you?

Nishimura: I have not for a moment thought of obeying or disobeying an order. It is a decided matter to obey orders. If supposing I disobeyed orders, I would be charged with insubordination and, being on a battlefield, I would be shot. To have a Japanese soldier charged with insubordination means losing the honour of a soldier and to a soldier death is preferable to dishonour. The soul of Bushido is only in the obeying of orders. The suicide planes of the Japanese in the air battles of this war, the human bullets of the Japanese, are all founded on obeying orders. The Japanese soldiers are human as well as any other people and they do not make light of life. To obey an order is, to the Japanese soldier, greater than life and this is the resolution held by we Japanese soldiers. The order issued by the Imperial Emperor to surrender unconditionally was carried out throughout the entire army without any bloodshed or resistance and this was all due to the absoluteness of an order.

In cross examining Nishimura, Major Ward was quick to pick up his reference to Bushido.

Prosecutor: Is courage and bravery part of the call of Bushido?

Nishimura: Yes, it is bravery that comes out from Bushido.

Prosecutor: Would it be courageous, would it be brave, would it be in accordance with the spirit of Bushido for you as a general to attempt to shelter behind Colonel Tsuji to save yourself?

Nishimura: According to criminal responsibility, it cannot be helped.

Prosecutor: So then, it is part of your defence that the murders carried out by troops of yours were being handled by Tsuji. It is part of your defence that the killings were Tsuji's responsibility and not yours.

Nishimura: As a fact, I think it is so.

Again and again, the name of Tsuji was regurgitated in the prosecution's cross examination of Nishimura.

Prosecutor: When the original orders were passed to you, did these orders state that anti-Japanese inhabitants were to be disposed of at your discretion?

Nishimura: It was an order to dispose anti-Japanese Chinese.

Prosecutor: At your discretion?

Nishimura: I think Staff Officer Tsuji supervised the whole matter and I think he did it according to communications of the Japanese Army.

After a luncheon adjournment, Major Ward returned to try a new tack with the seemingly immovable Nishimura.

Prosecutor: Can you quote me, General Nishimura, any Japanese Military Law or Military Enactment which authorises a member of the Imperial Japanese Army to kill an unarmed civilian?

Nishimura: I don't know the details, but in an emergency a thing like that could happen.

Another dead end. The prosecution switched tack again.

Prosecutor: You said that death was preferable to dishonour, is that right?

Nishimura: Yes, I consider dishonour more disgraceful than death.

Prosecutor: So in carrying out these massacres, was it death you wished to avoid or dishonour?

Nishimura: At the time I did not think either of these. I only concentrated on obeying orders.

Prosecutor: Now, as a rational being and one imbued with the spirit of Bushido, which would you rate more highly, your own life or the lives of countless unarmed civilians?

Nishimura: To obey an order is more important than my life and I merely obeyed my orders.

Another dead end. Again the prosecution came back to the role played by Tsuji and again Nishimura insisted Tsuji had been the man behind the massacres.

Prosecutor: What powers had Tsuji? I want a precise definition of his powers.

Nishimura: Staff Officer Tsuji was a staff officer of the 25th Army under the direct control of General Yamashita.

During a brief final re-examination by the defence, Nishimura was asked to explain what he had meant when, under cross examination, he had said the "work was left in the hands of Tsuji" and that he had "loaned soldiers to Tsuji."

"It means that the Konoye Division loaned soldiers to the 25th Army, and the 25th Army Headquarters had Tsuji do the work," concluded Nishimura. His evidence over, the former commanding officer of the Imperial Guards stepped from the witness box and walked to the dock to join his fellow accused.

Nishimura's evidence had been peppered with deviousness. But at the same time, the former Guards general had proven unshakeable on several important questions. From the prosecution's viewpoint, it had been important to pin down his personal assessment of the moral and legal aspects of the killing order itself and the massacres that followed. Frustratingly, they had failed on both scores. Time and again, Nishimura had fallen back to the basic argument that an order's morality or legality were immaterial to a Japanese soldier. An order was absolute. It had to be obeyed.

T he defence's next witness was perceived by Singapore's Chinese population at large to be the "big fish" among the seven defendants. It was widely recognised that Kawamura had been the Singapore Garrison Commander at the time. With Yamashita dead on the gallows at Los Baños, in the Philippines, Kawamura had become the logical focal point for a public seeking a replacement arch-villain.

Kawamura began his evidence by describing how he had received his appointment as Garrison Commander from Yamashita himself on February 18, 1942, at a classroom in Raffles Institution. At the same time he had received his formal garrison order. The substance of this was that as garrison chief, he would command two infantry battalions from the 5th Division, the No 2 Field Kempeitai, and some hojo kempei or auxiliary military police provided from the ranks of the Imperial Guards, the 5th and the 18th Divisions. The garrison force would be responsible for guarding key installations and roads within the city of Singapore and its eastern approaches. At the same time, it would enforce regulations restricting Japanese main force units entering the downtown area. It would also assist in establishing the island's new Military Administration by dispatching chosen troops to the required areas. Kawamura also noted how Hayashi had been seconded to the Garrison Command.

With the aid of a map, Kawamura explained to the court how his No 1 Infantry Battalion, led by Major Miyamoto, was positioned along the city's eastern approaches and, specifically, in the Geylang and Katong districts. His No 2 Infantry Battalion, under the command of Major Tadashi Ichikawa, was made responsible for the largely expatriate residential area north and east of Orchard Road, while the No 2 Kempeitai was placed in control of downtown Singapore itself.

Kawamura said he had been in the presence of Chief-of-Staff Suzuki, Tsuji and Hayashi when, directly after his formal induction as Garrison Commander, he received a verbal operational order from Yamashita to mop up anti-Japanese elements within the Chinese population of his command area. Yamashita had claimed the Army would soon have to be redeployed to new theatres and the security situation in Singapore remained very serious. Chinese guerrillas were moving underground with the aim of disrupting the Japanese military presence.

Kawamura, during the course of his evidence, emphasised the verbal nature of Yamashita's order and made it clear the Army Commander had spoken in very general terms. Yamashita had informed him that details of the "means and methods" to be employed would be issued separately by Chief-of-Staff Suzuki.

As this particular segment of Kawamura's evidence indicates very clearly the dual nature of the critical order, it is perhaps prudent at this point to explore whether he may have been intentionally lying to the court.

To have been lying, there would surely have needed to be advantage gained. For Kawamura, however, there was no value whatever in concocting such a story. The fact that there had been two separate massacre orders was never essential to the defence line he and his counsel had chosen.

Kawamura was telling the truth as far as he knew it. Yamashita verbally called for a crackdown on anti-Japanese elements. This had been portrayed as necessary within the context of the serious law and order situation compounded by the armed Chinese guerrillas moving underground. But then came the presentation of the operational blueprint which demanded a totally different approach. Instead of having a military target, the operation was to be directed generally against the male Chinese civilian population.

Kawamura and his counsel failed to recognise the importance of the separate orders. Though it is doubtful, given the overall conduct of the trial, whether accentuation of this flaw in the prosecution case would have helped the former Garrison Commander's defence.

As it happened, Kawamura went on to describe to the court how he followed up Yamashita's advice and went to see Suzuki. Tsuji and Hayashi were conveniently present for this meeting. Kawamura maintained this was when he first learned of the screening intentions, the five target categories for detention and the requirement for mass killing of unarmed civilians. The entire operation, he was told, was set for completion within the three-day period, February 21 - 23.

Kawamura described how he immediately doubted the operation could be accomplished within the specified time frame. In addition, the order to kill anti-Japanese elements was, he said, contrary to the usual methods adopted in such situations.

Kawamura said Suzuki had cut him short when he first sought clarification of the orders. Tsuji, on the other hand, had been most willing to provide the necessary explanations. Tsuji

Under suspicion, Lt. General Saburo Kawamura, former Singapore Garrison Commander (left), and Lt General Renya Mutaguchi, former commanding officer of the 18th Division, arrive at Changi Jail to be interrogated in connection with the Singapore massacres. Mutaguchi, who was also there for questioning on the Alexandra Hospital Massacre, was subsequently released.

The man appointed Singapore's Garrison Commander soon after the British surrender, Lt. General Saburo Kawamura. "In order to kill, I think every sector commander had the responsibility to pick out the people," he told the court.

Lt. General Takuma Nishimura: "Yes, I consider dishonour more disgraceful than death."

had concluded these with assurances that as he and Hayashi would be handling matters, the Garrison Commander could "set his mind at ease."

Kawamura told how he transferred his headquarters to Fort Canning on the evening of February 18 and there held a meeting with his three principal commanders — Miyamoto and Ichikawa from the two Infantry Battalions, and the No 2 Kempeitai's Oishi. It was at this meeting that the formal operational order for screening and killing Chinese civilians was passed down.

During his second day in the witness box, Kawamura recalled reports he had received from Miyamoto, Ichikawa and Oishi late on the afternoon of February 23 indicating between 4,000 and 5,000 Chinese had been executed or were still under detention thus far. He claimed he submitted these figures personally to Yamashita who told him: "Thank you for your efforts, but I do not think that all the anti-Japanese elements have been cleared up. You must watch their movements carefully. Arrest them when necessary, and continue the purge." Kawamura then added: "He said this very emphatically."

The emphasis Kawamura chose to put on this meeting with Yamashita is interesting. He and the six other accused had adopted the common line of defence that they were not part of a conspiracy or plot. They were merely doing their duty as officers in the Japanese Army and obeying an order from the top. If responsibility lay anywhere it lay at the top, with Yamashita.

The defence argument thus drew strikingly parallel to the main thrust of the prosecution case which maintained that the existence of a line of command from Yamashita downwards constituted a joint plot or conspiracy. The irony was that both prosecution and defence had become, for quite opposing reasons, firmly locked into establishing as fact the falsehood of Yamashita being the source of the killing orders.

Kawamura's version of the conversation he had with Yamashita on February 23 certainly supported the theory that the order had come from the 25th Army Commander. But it is also fair comment that as Yamashita was then dead, it may have been a convenient, if not desperate, defence ploy to lay the blame squarely on his grave. Dead men don't tell tales, much less contradict evidence. Kawamura went on to tell the court that after he had reported to Yamashita, he met Suzuki. "I told him that a certain number of people were detained for restoration work, and he was very much pleased."

Asked by Kakuda whether he thought the massacre operational order was "adequate" or "unlawful", Kawamura replied: "At the time I was only a brigade commander, and didn't know the general situation of the Army. When I was told by the Chief-of-Staff that this order was an order that could not have been helped, I understood him. I thought likewise." This response notably conformed with Nishimura's earlier reaction to the same general line of questioning.

Kawamura went on to explain: "For us to obey orders has been a long custom, and to obey is final; and I have never given a thought to not obeying an order. The concept of the Japanese soldier is exactly as General Nishimura said in this court yesterday. Under the circumstances, not only myself but all the other accused feel if somebody else had done the work it would not have been better. Such being the case, the fact that I stand in front of a War Crimes Court today is nothing but fate."

As if prompted by an important afterthought, he added: "I, however, regret the victims of this incident; not only do I condole with the bereaved relatives of the victims, but I also condole with the victims of Hiroshima — the victims of war — though such condolence amounts to nothing. I pray from the bottom of my heart for the peaceful repose of the souls of the victimised Chinese, although this was carried out by the operational order of the Army."

Kawamura concluded his evidence-in-chief by complaining of irregularities in the sworn statements purportedly made by him and tendered by the prosecution. One of the statements which the investigators claimed had been on oath was not so, he said. Amendments he had requested were entered wrongly. Hypothetical matters had been introduced with which he dissociated himself completely.

Under cross examination by Major Ward, Kawamura displayed little of the deviousness of Nishimura. Asked whether the massacre order he had pursued was one with which he was in agreement and considered justified, Kawamura replied: "After receiving the explanation, I thought the order was just and executed it according to the order."

The prosecutor asked Kawamura whether the order entitled troops under his command to kill civilian doctors, lawyers, students and teachers who were not under the five specified categories.

Kawamura: No, but outwardly they may be school teachers, lawyers, and so forth, but they must have connection with one of these five items.

Prosecutor: And if they hadn't, as many hundreds, if not thousands, hadn't, then those people were killed outside the scope of the orders, it that right?

Kawamura: Yes, that would be so, but I don't think there were such cases.

The prosecution then began exploring how the screening had been accomplished in the various areas.

Prosecutor: So the position is that you had such confidence in your junior commanders that you left the methods to them?

Kawamura: After speaking to the Chief-of-Staff, the screening of anti-Japanese elements became very easy, so I left them in the hands of my subordinates.

Prosecutor: By 'easy' you mean if you just suspected someone you would say "righto, shoot him.'?

Kawamura: No.

Prosecutor: If a person's name appeared on the list, did that mean he was shot?

Kawamura: Yes, it was such an order.

Prosecutor: So really you shot on mere suspicion?

Kawamura: The Army order was these words 'anti-Japanese elements, so dispose them.'

Prosecutor: Does that mean he was shot on mere suspicion because his name was in a book?

Kawamura: Yes, I have received an order to shoot such people from the Army, so they have been disposed.

Prosecutor: Now, I have got a book here, General Kawamura, and your name is in it. Do you call it justice if I took you outside and shot you on mere suspicion?

Kawamura: The Army ordered it so.

Prosecutor: I said would you call it justice?

Kawamura: It was shown to me at the time from the Army that these were the hostile Chinese.

Prosecutor: Do you call it justice?

Kawamura: It was a justified act according to the Army.

Prosecutor: But is it justice to your mind?

Kawamura: To obey the Army order is justice.

Towards the end of the cross examination, the prosecution once again returned to the involvement of Tsuji. Where had this High Command staff officer been working at the time of the massacres? Had he not been "just a sort of liaison officer" carrying information to Gen Yamashita?

Kawamura agreed with the liaison role but insisted Tsuji had also been there to "guide the purging."

About to wrap-up his cross examination, Major Ward asked Kawamura whether the individual sector commanders like Hisamatsu and Onishi had the "power of life and death" over the inhabitants of Singapore involved in the screening. Kawamura quickly became evasive, suggesting that the sector commanders executed people only in accordance with the Army order.

Prosecutor: I am asking; would the power of life and death in the Jalan Besar concentration area be in the hands of Onishi or not? The answer is yes or no.

Kawamura: No. He did not have the power of life and death. He had the duty to purge the people. They were listed by the Army HQ.

Prosecutor: And was it not his decision as to who should be killed?

Kawamura: He had the duty to pick out the people that were on the list and the names were given by the Army HQ.

Prosecutor: I'll put it this way, General Kawamura. Who was it that said 'take Wong Peng Yin and 120 Chinese to Changi and kill them'? You are not suggesting General Yamashita did so, because General Yamashita would not know of Wong Peng Yin. And Colonel Tsuji and Colonel Hayashi would not. And you only went there for 10 minutes. And the commander at Jalan Besar was Onishi. He was in complete charge there. Now, answer my question, yes or no. Was it, or was it not, within Onishi's power to take these men to Changi and kill them?

Kawamura: To execute them, I think, was Onishi's order.

Prosecutor: It was at his discretion, was it not?

Kawamura: It was not at his discretion. It was according to the Army order.

Prosecutor: Did he refer back to the Army Commander in every instance when a man was to be killed?

Kawamura: No. We received the execution report.

Prosecutor: After the execution had been carried out?

Kawamura: Yes.

Prosecutor: And who was it that decided that that particular man was to be killed?

Kawamura: In order to kill, I think every sector commander had the responsibility to pick out the people.

Prosecutor: And the responsibility, that power, came through Onishi from you, did it not?

Kawamura: Yes.

Major Ward had finally broken the witness on the important

question of line of command. This was the admission the prosecution needed. The major resumed his seat satisfied that where he had missed with the former Imperial Guards Commander, he had scored impressively against the former Keibitai chief. And, after all, Kawamura was the "big fish." ■

Chapter 13
Oishi calls foul

———— ✦ ————

With evidence completed as far as the two top ranking Japanese officers were concerned, the defence case now turned to concentrate on the activities of the No 2 Kempeitai to which the remaining five accused had all belonged. All five were scheduled to give evidence on their own behalf.

By this point in the trial, the tactics of both defence and prosecution had become readily identifiable. Major Ward, for his part, was holding rigidly to the course outlined in his opening address where he argued the need to prove only two factors: the existence of an illegal course of action or common plan, and the active participation of the accused in that plan.

The sworn statements, provided their legal acceptability could be maintained, amounted to extraordinarily convincing proof of participation. Establishing the actual illegality of the plan had become the more difficult task confronting Major Ward. It called for deft cross examination of all defence witnesses as inevitably they retreated to the safe-haven response — "I was just obeying orders and orders in the Japanese Army are absolute."

Sophisticated legal argument demonstrating that contingencies of war could never justify the mass killing of unarmed civilians was being retained for the prosecution's final summation.

As far as the defence was concerned, there were few

alternatives open. The sworn statements had assured this. Above all other considerations was the requirement to undermine the credibility of these damaging documents. But the question was, how? At the same time it was clearly vital to continue demonstrating uniformity of opinion among the seven accused. Specifically, they had obeyed an order which was absolute. They had been deprived, by the very nature of that order, of any right to evaluate, morally or legally, the actions they had been commanded to undertake. To have done so would have incurred swift death penalties under Japanese military law.

The first of the five accused military police to give evidence on oath was former No 2 Kempeitai Commander, Oishi, highest ranking of the group. Like Kawamura before him, Oishi made no attempt to deny his involvement in the massacres. He explained to the court in considerable detail how his men had established their points of control throughout the downtown Singapore area. He said he had received the order to screen and execute anti-Japanese Chinese from Kawamura on February 18.

Oishi also recalled receiving the lists of names of wanted Chinese from the 25th Army's Intelligence Office when the headquarters were located in the Ford Factory at Bukit Timah. The lists had comprised memberships of approximately 100 Chinese associations. The kempeitai commander said he passed the killing order to his subordinates, Yokota and Jyo, soon after he received it. With the order went the name lists.

Assisted by his counsel, Kurose, Oishi strongly denied he had ever made a sworn statement to war crimes investigating officers.

Oishi: I was asked to make my statement very clear. But every time I tried to make the statement clear, the interpreter stopped me. I couldn't remember some of the dates and times and they asked me in very strong terms about figures. When I said I could not definitely remember, they held my hand or kicked me, and ordered me to tell the figure.

Counsel: Where were you kicked and how many times?

Oishi: I was kicked with the shoe several times.

Oishi went on to identify the man who had kicked him as Major M. G. A. Watson, leader of the investigating team.

During cross-examination, the assistant prosecutor, Mr Lim, tackled Oishi on his claim of physical coercion. Far from retreating on the issue, Oishi took his charge a step further. He insisted he had not only been kicked by the chief investigator but had been systematically tortured for a number of evenings in a row while in solitary confinement at Changi Jail. His torturers were NCO's and soldiers from the British military guard on duty at the jail. Oishi said those responsible for the torturing had been court martialled and he had been called as a witness. "If you will make an investigation I am sure you will know of this in the records," he added. Oishi's allegations of ill-treatment at the hands of both investigators and jail guards was a damaging point against the prosecution and one that would have to be addressed.

Of all seven Japanese accused, the next witness, Lt. Colonel Yoshitake Yokota, displayed the most outwardly genuine signs of remorse. He told the court how he had been appointed a sector commander by Oishi. He described how he had established his headquarters at the Toyo Hotel in Queen Street, and held responsibility for that part of the city between the Singapore and Kallang rivers. He confirmed he had introduced Shinozaki to Dr Lim Boon Keng and ultimately had facilitated the formation of the Overseas Chinese Association.

"I had heard that Lim Boon Keng was a very prominent citizen and very famous," related Yokota. "And I had received a report from my subordinate saying that he had arrested a person who seemed to be Lim Boon Keng."

Lt. Colonel Masayuki Oishi gave evidence that he had been systematically tortured by British guards while in solitary confinement at Changi Jail.

Yokota said he ordered Dr Lim to be brought to his Toyo Hotel headquarters "so that I could make use of an influential person in my work." Shinozaki was asked to interpret for the meeting between Dr Lim and Yokota.

"The doctor seemed to be very afraid of things and when drinking tea, which I gave him, he trembled," said Yokota. "I told Shinozaki that the doctor seemed to be very much afraid and I thought it was due to my kempeitai uniform. So I told Shinozaki that I would leave the place and it was for him to explain to the doctor to call all the Chinese as the Japanese would like to have the co-operation of the Chinese for future work."

After Shinozaki and Dr Lim had reached agreement over the formation of the Overseas Chinese Association, Yokota secured official consent to the idea from both Kawamura and the Military Administration head, Major General Managi. Yokota told how Shinozaki had personally interceded and secured the release of many influential Chinese and had issued passes to help free many more.

But it was not until Yokota was cross-examined by Major Ward that the kempeitai officer openly displayed the softer side to his nature. The prosecutor attempted to pin Yokota down on the immorality and illegality of the massacre order. He flatly asked Yokota whether he had been a willing party to the course of action that led to the killings.

Yokota: Yes. I was one that obeyed the order.

Prosecutor: Willingly obeyed the order?

Yokota: Not willingly. It was an undesirable order.

Prosecutor: Why do you think it was a wrong order at that time?

Yokota: At that time, I could not judge.

Prosecutor: You say it was an undesirable order. Do you mean an undesirable order from a moral point of view?

Yokota: I said, from a personal standpoint.

Prosecutor: But why undesirable?

Yokota: I am an honest soldier and in the operational forces, to attack a position or any enemy is what a soldier would wish to do.

Prosecutor: Why do you think the order was undesirable?

Yokota: Since this was not a gallant action, I did not like it.

Forty-seven year-old Lt. Colonel Tomotatsu Jyo, the second Kempeitai sector commander for Singapore's downtown area, gave evidence corroborating that given by Oishi and Yokota. The security situation in Singapore immediately following the British surrender had been very grave with widespread looting. The operational order calling for screening and executing Chinese had been received from Oishi and quickly passed down to the two sub-sector commanders, in this case Uezono and Hisamatsu. The kempeitai had carried out the screening. The killing had been done by the hojo kempei.

Jyo's evidence was short. In his cross examination, Major Ward set out to establish clearly the kempeitai line of command down which the massacre order travelled.

Prosecutor: I want to know who at Tanjong Pagar police station would say to the hojo kempei: 'We have collected enough. Take them away and shoot them.?'

Jyo: That is the order. That has already been stated in the order which came from above.

Prosecutor: Major Jyo, somebody at Tanjong Pagar police station must everyday in the evening have said: 'Take these men away from here and shoot them.' An order from the G.H.Q. cannot speak. It is not a gramophone record. Who, at the Tanjong Pagar police station, would give that order?

Jyo: In the order it has been stated that the hojo kempei should execute this order. Therefore there was no need to say every time to take these people away.

Prosecutor: The Tanjong Pagar Police Station was under Hisamatsu's command. Are you suggesting that the hojo kempei, like automatons, just came inside without a word and spirited the bodies away? Or did Hisamatsu say: 'We have collected enough. Take them away and shoot them?'

Jyo: It was stated in the Army order that the execution should be carried out by the hojo kempei and it was not necessary to give orders each time.

Prosecutor: Now, I will give you an illustration. Army H.Q. in Singapore have ordered you to come to this court this morning. Somebody at Changi Jail, whether the warder or guard, got you out of this cell and sent you here. Now, Yamashita's headquarters in Singapore ordered the screening and killing. I want to know who at Tanjong Pagar, having carried out the screening, gave the actual order on the spot: 'Take them away and kill them.?'

Jyo: To pass them on to the hojo kempei is known in the order.

Prosecutor: And who passed them over?

Jyo: It was passed from Hisamatsu and Uezono.

Re-examined by his counsel, Jyo was asked whether he considered he bore any criminal responsibility for his act in passing on the operational order calling for screening and killing.

Jyo replied: "I, as a person in between, passed the order from above to below. I could not add anything to it. And, I don't think I had criminal responsibility."

As Major Satorou Onishi, aged 45 years, and Captain Haruji Hisamatsu, aged 34 years, were the only accused who had functioned at the operational end of the order, what they could tell the court was clearly critical to both prosecution and defence cases. As a result, Onishi's evidence would require him remaining in the witness box for the best part of three days. Hisamatsu would be there for a further two.

Onishi described how he had worked out of the White House Hotel, and how these headquarters had proved conveniently close to the "very large" triangular area enclosed by Jalan Besar, Rochor Canal and Syed Alwi roads which he chose as his overall concentration area. Hisamatsu, on the other hand, told why he chose the Tanjong Pagar police station as his headquarters and how he had established three separate screening areas in the vicinity.

Both men outlined their operational functions in some detail. Onishi admitted to being shocked by the "mopping-up" order when he first saw it and told of his complaints at the time to his immediate superior, Yokota. He informed Yokota that the three-day time limit for completing the work was too short and that it was "difficult to execute any person who is not resisting." Hisamatsu recalled that he had thought the order "very unpleasant" but had obeyed it without question.

Neither man attempted to deny his involvement as a sector

commander. Both insisted their screening functions had been undertaken with considerable care and described how the name lists had been crucial reference documents for the work. Both said they had used members of the volunteer forces, police officers, prominent members of the Chinese community, communists and criminals to identify those to be executed. Onishi claimed he had sent no more that 150 to their deaths from his area. Hisamatsu maintained his total had been around the 250-260 mark. Both these estimates were substantially lower than the death toll figures provided earlier in the trial by witnesses arrested in Jalan Besar.

Onishi and Hisamatsu each made allegations in their evidence about the conduct of Tsuji while the anti-Chinese purge was at its height.

Onishi told of Tsuji's visit to Jalan Besar on February 22 for an on-the-spot review of the numbers screened up to that point. When given a figure of 70, Tsuji had exploded, "Thousands should have been screened — what are you doing?" Onishi claimed he laughed off Tsuji's remarks by retorting, "What are you saying?" But ultimately Onishi took them seriously. He had come to the conclusion that the Army was intending to kill as many people as possible.

Hisamatsu maintained that both Tsuji and Hayashi had visited the Tanjong Pagar concentration areas. He related the story of Hayashi ordering the summary execution of all men detained within the general area of the Singapore Railway Station and Empire Docks. Hisamatsu insisted he had refused to comply with these particular orders.

If continuous recollection of horror had served to numb the minds of those in the court's public gallery by this, the 14th day of the trial, the defence's ninth witness, Lt. General Takajo Numata, was destined to introduce a jolting note of reality. The 55-year-old senior officer was called to substantiate the defence argument that, as orders in the Japanese Army were absolute, the accused had no option but to obey the command to massacre thousands of Chinese civilians. What the general had to say, however, did little more than confirm the chilling brutality of the military system that was on trial.

Numata came with an impressive service background. He joined the Japanese Army in 1905 as a 13-year-old boy recruit. A graduate of the Military Staff College, he was promoted to the rank of Lt. General by the age of 49. During the war, he had, among other appointments, been an infantry regimental commander, a divisional commander, and finally the Southern Expeditionary Forces' Chief-of-Staff. As a Major General and civil servant, he became Director of the Japanese Cabinet's Planning Bureau, and was a military representative at the Tokyo Diet.

Numata produced three Japanese military books as trial exhibits. One was the *Imperial Rescript to Military Forces*. This, he explained, had been issued by the Emperor Meiji in 1902. It was regarded as a sacred document containing fundamental guiding principles for Japanese soldiers. The second was a set of instructions authorized by the Japanese War Ministry to amplify the *Imperial Rescript*. The third was the Japanese Army's *Military Training Regulations.*.

General Numata proceeded to read various extracts.

From the War Ministry's instructions came the passage:

"Even under the circumstances of life and death difficulties, you shall respond immediately to orders of the superiors and yet you shall be glad to sacrifice your lives in the fulfilment of the orders. This is the expression of the spirit of Bushido which is our tradition; it is the glory of the Army.

From the same volume came a further passage:

"The essence of military discipline is in obedience. Therefore, it is necessary that the officers and men of the whole army should form a habit, or a second nature, of sacrificing their lives for their Emperor's country, obeying their superiors with full sincerity and

executing their superior's orders faithfully."

Article 2 of the *Military Training Regulations* said in part:

"The duty of the military is to sacrifice their lives for their country. It is a tradition inherited from the time of the old samurai. A samurai's loyalty to his country has been considered even more important than the worth of his own life. Remember the old saying that life shall be considered as light and negligible as a feather, and loyalty as heavy and lofty as a mountain."

Article 50 of the same document said:

"For the cultivation and maintenance of military discipline, it is necessary, first, to seek absolute obedience and, next, to make officers and men fully understand the significance, particularly the inviolable dignity, of the Supreme Command, so that they will sacrifice their lives willingly for their country at the order of their superiors."

Explaining that any insubordinate member of the Japanese Army risked summary execution in Singapore in February or March, 1942, Numata asserted that none had the power to judge the nature of an order. He read another passage from the War Office documents: *"Subordinates should obey immediately the orders of the superior, irrespective of their nature. Such orders are irresistible."*

When the Japanese Army was founded in 1902, said the general, the Minister of War made it compulsory for all soldiers entering service to take an oath of loyalty and obedience. It was understood that all orders were to be regarded as having come from the Emperor, a living god. Orders were to be obeyed irrespective of their nature. Only the person issuing an order could be held responsible. Those receiving and acting upon it had no responsibility for the outcome whatever.

Asked by defence counsel what steps he would have taken had he been in the positions held by Kawamura or Nishimura in February, 1942, Numata replied quickly: "It is very simple. I would have executed the order. Not only myself, but all the Japanese soldiers would have fulfilled the order."

Major Ward launched into a determined cross-examination of the general in an effort to tear holes in his presentation of the fabric of Japanese Army discipline. But Numata was not easily shaken.

Prosecutor: Your Army Directive No 21 states that life should be considered as 'light and negligible as a feather.' Now whose life is that — a soldier's life?

Numata: It is not only a soldier's life. It is officers' and all service people.

Prosecutor: Yes, but does this entitle Japanese officers to treat the lives of innocent occupants of a country in the occupation of Japan as 'light and negligible as a feather?'

Numata: If they are law abiding citizens, such things would not happen.

Prosecutor: If they are law abiding people such things would not be authorized by Japanese Military Law — is that so?

Numata: Not only is it not allowed, but it is taught in the Japanese Army that you must treat civilians very kindly.

Major Ward asked Numata to imagine himself responsible for ordering the screening of Chinese in Singapore. The general readily agreed it would have been necessary to emphasise the need for extreme care on the part of subordinate officers before deciding those to be killed.

Prosecutor: Would you, under any circumstances, so give your subordinates a free hand that they could indiscriminately, without rhyme or reason, send thousands to their deaths without any proper supervision?

Numata: I believe under some circumstances it is possible that it can happen.

Prosecutor: Would you, as a senior formation commander, by a lack of supervision on your part, allow your subordinates to do such things?

Numata: It is not impossible that I, in the position of General Yamashita, might have taken similar action. I happened to know General Yamashita from my boyhood and I know very well he was not a man of hard or cold heart.

Prosecutor: And would you allow a lack of supervision in the killing of innocent men?

Numata: There is no criminal responsibility but all Japanese leaders in the Army have a conscientious responsibility if such happened.

Prosecutor: I am asking you again, General Numata, would you allow a lack of supervision on your part in the killing by your subordinates of innocent civilians?

Numata: If any legal responsibility is to be imposed upon the commander, in that case I myself would be responsible. In the Japanese law there is no legal criminal responsibility for that of supervision.

Prosecutor: And now my question for the third time — would you have allowed your subordinates, through a lack of supervision on your part, to kill innocent men?

Numata: I shall never, with my own knowledge, let that happen.

Prosecutor: (Pointing towards the accused in the dock) These men did, General Numata.

The bench had a final question before the witness stepped from the box. As he had told the court that obedience to orders in the Japanese Army was absolute, was the bench to assume that officers of general and field rank were not expected to use their own initiative? Numata assured the bench that initiative was not precluded.

With trial regulations enabling the prosecution to query witnesses, through the Court, on matters arising from questions posed by the bench, Major Ward quickly rose to his feet.

Prosecutor: May the witness be asked if he was ordered by his immediate superior to bayonet a small child, would he bayonet that child?

Numata: Me, as a private soldier?

Prosecutor: As an officer.

Numata: I should carry out that order ■

Chapter 14

The trumpable ace

———— ✦ ————

Having come to the end of the defence witnesses, the Japanese lawyers decided it was now time to play their ace card.

Two months before the trial began, the local Chinese Relief Fund Committee had published a book called *The Great War and the Overseas-Chinese*. Printed in Singapore in the Chinese language, the book amounted to a rousing, if somewhat chauvinistic, account of the history, organisation, and wartime exploits of anti-Japanese operations by local Overseas Chinese. In particular, it highlighted in some detail the activities of Singapore's Chinese anti-Japanese Mobilization Committee and the associated Chinese Volunteer Army.

The book's revelations appeared to reinforce strongly the argument the three Tokyo barristers had been making throughout the trial on behalf of the defence. Page after page depicted Singapore in a chaotic state following the British surrender and boasted how the Chinese guerrillas proved a constant menace to the Japanese forces from then onwards. The Japanese resolved to have the book submitted as evidence and accepted as a formal exhibit.

But the Court seemed wary of these tactics. After enquiring as to the title and subject matter of the publication, the court president, Colonel Forsythe, voiced his concern. "The only experience I have of a book being produced to the Court was a book produced in the 'Burma High-Ups' case," he noted. "But that was put in the form of an affidavit and it was signed by the author. So I am not quite sure of the procedure and I think the Court will adjourn to consider whether the book may be admitted as evidence or not, after we have heard what Major Ward has to say."

In his submission, the prosecutor readily admitted that regulations empowered the Court to accept any document purporting to be authentic, provided it could be of assistance in proving or disproving a charge. But he felt there was great danger in admitting a book of this nature.

Major Ward went on to observe: "We do not know the standing or experience of the author, whether he writes from hearsay, repute or his own knowledge. You, gentlemen, must know that a book is liable to journalese — I think that is the term. The press have a certain amount of licence and liberty and even paint pictures according to the readers' tastes."

Still, if rejection of the publication would indicate any sign whatsoever of prejudice, said the prosecutor, he would rather the volume be admitted — though he would dispute whatever it contained.

The Court retired briefly to consider the matter of admissibility and returned to announce: "To avoid prejudice to the defence the Court have decided to accept this book and they will attach the weight to which it is entitled when the proper time comes." The volume was duly marked "Exhibit AK" and relevant passages chosen by the defence were read aloud.

The first extract quoted the authorities in Chungking as having told the British Ambassador there soon after the commencement of hostilities: "The Chinese Government is ready to instruct the Overseas Chinese to stage anti-Japanese movement in co-operation with Britain, if the British Government finds it so necessary." The British ambassador had forwarded this message to Sir Shenton Thomas, Governor of Singapore, who, in turn, had expressed his whole-hearted approval and deep gratitude by telegraph.

"Thereupon, Generalissimo Chiang Kai-shek, chairman of the Military Committee at that time, instructed the Chinese consul-general in Singapore to the effect that the Chinese residents there should be urged to co-operate with the British war effort," said the extract. It went on to describe a meeting on December 28, 1941 between Governor Sir Shenton, the prominent local Chinese businessman, Mr Tan Kah Kee, other leading members of the Chinese community, and a number of newly released communist detainees. This had led to a further gathering two days later at the Chinese Chamber of Commerce and the formation of the Anti-Japanese Mobilization Committee of Singapore with its headquarters in the Shinko Kaikan building on Bukit Panjang Road.

The following day, the committee began organising various departments to facilitate its planned anti-Japanese activities. These included a Workers' Department, a Peace Preservation Department, a Propaganda Department and a People's Armament Department. The latter department was headed by Communist Party of Malaya executive, Mr Lin Chiang-shi who was immediately given the task of raising a Chinese Volunteer Army which on February 1, 1942, when officially commissioned, had a fighting strength of 1,000 men.

Other extracts from the book described how the Chinese Volunteer Army, with its headquarters at the Southsea Chinese Normal School, in Kim Yam Road, arranged training for a total of some "3,000 hot blooded young men". Chief instructor for the volunteers had been Englishman, Lieutenant Colonel John Dalley, from whom the unit derived its name — Dalforce. Although poorly equipped with pre-World War 1 rifles and only 15 cartridges per man, the volunteers had participated in battles at Kranji, in the Bukit Timah area, at Pasir Panjang, and at Jurong. They had suffered very heavy casualties.

On February 13, two days before the final British surrender to the Japanese, the surviving Chinese volunteers had assembled at their Kim Yam Road headquarters to be told by Colonel Dalley that they were to disband. "The army authorities have decided to conclude the battle for Singapore. The British Army Headquarters is still relying heavily on your efforts," Colonel Dalley was reported as telling his men in poor Cantonese. "Your sacrifices will not be in vain., The British forces will return within six months. Then we will ask you again to cooperate with us."

Speaking at the same gathering, another British officer, a lieutenant, said: "If the volunteer force had been organised earlier and if better arms had been supplied by the British, the enemy's invasion and advance would have been checked successfully."

Mr Lin Chiang-shi replied on behalf of the volunteers. "It is now too late for the British authorities to make any new determination for defence and resistance," he said, pointing out that the Caucasian defenders would have no choice but to become prisoners of war. There would, however, be other options open to the Chinese. "Even after this farewell meeting, we Chinese will be able to extend disturbing operations at the rear of the enemy and will strive and struggle, nothing daunted, until we shed the last drop of our blood."

Before this final gathering of the Chinese Volunteer Army dissolved, each surviving member was paid $10.00 for his services.

Other extracts from the book, read to the court, claimed the Chinese Volunteer Army consisted of "communists, nationalists, clerks, labourers, dancers, students and various other different types of people." During the three and a half years of Japanese occupation, the volunteers extended their military activities into Malaya. The Independent Corps embarked on a guerrilla struggle and ultimately emerged as the Malayan People's Anti-Japanese Army (MPAJA). It fought more than 340 battles with the invaders killing or wounding over 5,500 Japanese troops.

Viewed with hindsight, the Japanese efforts to get *The Great*

War and the Overseas Chinese read into the court records on that afternoon of March 28, 1947, was a poignant moment. But the poignancy would be replaced by increasing irony as the years passed.

The Tokyo barristers argued that the Chinese volunteers going underground in the hours prior to the British surrender on February 15, 1942, constituted a major military threat to the conquering Japanese Army. The book, they claimed, judged the Chinese "out of their own mouths."

The prosecutor, for his part, remained adamant that there was no such major threat. Initially he had pledged to dispute the book's contents. But then he changed his mind. On flipping through its pages, he saw a number of photographs depicting Japanese screening activities in various parts of Singapore. He decided to have each caption for these individually read into the trial records.

In the event, even before 1947 was out, the hard-core communist members of the MPAJA — for which the fledgling Chinese Volunteer Army, had been the forerunner — would be back in the Malayan jungles, this time opposing the returning British. And the British would be gearing up for an anti-communist emergency that would demand a huge military commitment by London for the next 12 years.

The truth of the matter was that, in releasing communists from Changi Jail, encouraging their participation in the anti-Japanese Chinese Volunteer Army, and ultimately urging survivors to abandon their uniforms and form guerrilla units, the British had indeed created a serious military threat; not only for the incoming Japanese then, but for themselves five years later. The ramifications of these activities would continue for the British until 1960 and beyond.

Not surprisingly, the revelations of *The Great War and the Overseas Chinese* became the cornerstone of the defence's closing address when, after a four-day break in proceedings, the trial resumed on April 2, 1947. The book was quoted extensively as the Japanese sought to reinforce their first line of defence, namely, that the acts allegedly committed jointly by the seven accused were in the nature of a military operation rendered necessary by the extreme emergency of the hour. Summarizing the arguments for this, Shozaburo Kurose told the court that vindictive punishment had not been the purpose of the 25th Army's "mopping-up" operations in Singapore. These had become "absolutely necessary in order to stabilise, as quickly as possible, a fluid and dangerous situation." Kurose went on to quote a proverb: "The necessity of war overrules the manners of warfare." This applied, he said, to the case of the seven accused

Kurose quoted from numerous military law authorities to support his second line of defence that all Japanese soldiers had a duty to obey military orders, not obviously unlawful. "Incontestably," he said, "the illegality, if any, of the 'mopping-up' operational order applies not to the elimination of subversive espionage elements, but to the slaughter of innocent civilians."

The prosecution, he maintained, had "palpably failed to prove" that the slaughter of innocent civilians had taken place. If the operation had carried with it a risk of illegality, then the risk was by no means obvious, Kurose said. "Indeed, from the legal point of view, a question like this is quite a delicate one on which the pros and cons stand evenly," he added.

The "absolutism" of orders in the Japanese Army, where all commands were considered to have come from the Emperor himself, was the third and final line of defence reviewed by Kurose. Again quoting a variety of legal authorities, and recalling statements made by defence witnesses, he argued that members of the Japanese Army had no option but to obey orders, whether lawful or not. "If we give these points careful consideration, are we just in calling to account men who have carried out the orders of their superiors, when the condition is such that, according to the laws of their own country, they have an absolute legal obligation to do so? Surely, such justice ignores completely the subtler points of human actuality?"

The defence finally went into a point by point discussion of the joint charge as it applied individually to the seven accused.

* **Lt. General Nishimura,** Commanding Officer of the Imperial Guards, had no association with the 25th Army's mopping-up operational order other than formally passing it on for divisional action. This he had done without any enlargement or amplification whatever. He had not personally received the order, nor had he held any conference, discussion or deliberation on its contents. Moreover, he had not even had "one opportunity to confer with Staff Officer Tsuji" on the matter.

* **Lt. General Kawamura,** Singapore Garrison commander at the time of the massacres, acted only as a puppet. He was merely an instrument transmitting the order.

* **Colonel Oishi**, No 2 Kempeitai chief, and **Colonel Yokota,** and **Lt Colonel Jyo**, kempeitai section commanders, had never been connected with any plotting associated with the order. Their positions were those of intermediaries. They had never considered whether the order was lawful or unlawful. All three had merely obeyed an absolute order as was the duty of every Japanese soldier.

* **Major Onishi** and **Captain Hisamatsu**, kempeitai sector commanders, had obeyed, willy-nilly, the operational order. They had no alternative. But they had carried out the order most carefully and along humane lines. No officer in their situation could have behaved in a more "justifiable" manner.

Rising to deliver the prosecution's closing address, Major Ward was quick to attack the defence's claim that military necessity justified the massacres. Under English Criminal Law, he argued, necessity was simply no defence at all and he went ahead to quote a startling case from 1884 to prove his point.

Known as the *Regina vs Dudley and Stevens* case, it arose from the sinking in mid-ocean of a yacht called the *Mignonette* where the sole survivors were three men and a boy.

"After this small party were afloat in an open boat for eight days, the three men resorted to killing the boy and feeding on him for the next four days," explained the prosecutor. "They were then rescued. The court of Queens Bench declared emphatically that there was no general principle of law which entitled a man to take the life of an innocent person to preserve his own."

Major Ward went on to refute defence claims that the Japanese Army, immediately following the British surrender of Singapore, had been battered, exhausted and disorganised and that all this, together with the dispersing guerrillas, had contributed to a major military emergency. "Nor is there any evidence that military necessity was such as to justify any departure from the rules of war. It is difficult to see how any military necessity could justify such a departure as, it is the prosecution's submission, occurred in February, 1942."

Here, of course, was the real counter to all defence arguments based on the contents of *The Great War and The Overseas Chinese*.

Major Ward then came to a very significant — and at the same time highly revealing — segment of his submission. There was, he said, good reason to suppose that the Singapore massacres were pre-arranged. This being the case, any plea of necessity would be defeated. The prosecutor argued that Japan's regime of terror against the non-combatant Chinese population of occupied Singapore had been born of a "definite system", previously planned and encouraged by the Japanese High Command. It had assured full rein be given to the excesses of individual officers and men.

Major Ward continued to expand his theory that the massacres had required considerable pre-planning. "Singapore surrendered on the 15th of February, yet when General Kawamura visited Colonel Oishi's H.Q. on the 18th of February, only three days after the surrender, the lists of people to be screened had already been in the hands of Colonel Oishi for several days."

The prosecutor quoted from the signed statement made by Onishi in Changi Jail on June 1, 1946. Onishi had said: "Before we arrived in Singapore, orders were issued from General HQ which stated that due to the fact that the Army is advancing fast, and in order to preserve the peace behind us, it is essential to massacre many Chinese who appear in any way to have anti-Japanese feelings."

Major Ward observed: "If no mention of the order had been made until after the entry into Singapore, the words 'is advancing fast' would be meaningless. In view of the fact that General Kawamura received his orders on the evening of the 17th February, it is hard to imagine that the operation as subsequently carried out on so large a scale could have been conceived and planned in the space of only two days."

The prosecution had finally come to grips with the critical issue of the extensive preparations that had to have preceded the killing orders. Such extensive preparations, properly pursued by the investigating authorities, should have been proof in themselves that Yamashita was not part of the plot to massacre civilians.

But for Major Ward, all this at the end of the trial represented a dangerous area. The more the prosecution delved, the more it would become clear to the court that a critical component of the overall story was missing. This, of course, was Tsuji.

The way the prosecutor ultimately dealt with the "missing component" evolved as an exercise in skilful deflection. "Now, in considering the execution of this plan," said Major Ward, reading from the eighth page of his 20-page text," we must enquire into the true position of Colonel Tsuji."

There had been an attempt by certain of the accused, he said, to blame Tsuji for the massacres "just as others of the accused have sought to fling the bouncing ball of responsibility at General Yamashita's HQ." But Tsuji had not taken the job out of the hands of the sector commanders, claimed the prosecutor. The colonel might have acted in a supervisory capacity, but he had operated as a liaison officer between the Army HQ and the Keibitai HQ and had no actual power over those doing the work.

It amounted to an extraordinarily inaccurate summary of Tsuji's overall activities.

Interestingly enough, the prosecutor also felt compelled to scotch any suggestion that Tsuji might have been operational in the Imperial Guards' zones of responsibility in the north and east of the island. "It is reasonable to suppose," said Major Ward, "that Colonel Tsuji, as senior staff officer at HQ 25th Army Group, would be so busily employed in his work of co-ordinating and supervising the work of the keibitai and the divisions that he would devote little if any time to directing particularly the work of the Imperial Guards."

In short, Tsuji was being roundly dismissed by the prosecution as insignificant in all massacre areas.

Examining the defence's reliance on the "plea of superior orders", Major Ward observed that had this doctrine been accepted "it would probably have covered most of the Axis War Criminals, except those who actually initiated the orders." He went on to argue that the underlying international principle was that members of armed forces were bound to obey lawful commands only.

Major Ward posed the questions: "Under what

circumstances might the plea of superior orders have been listened to with sympathy? Has any accused come forward and said: 'Yes, we knew that what we were doing was wrong, but we could not help it; we were forced into it, reluctant, unwilling'?"

The answer, he said, was entirely the opposite. They had all agreed that they were willing partners to a course of conduct which they considered justified by military necessity. Yet it was a military necessity of which they now disclaimed having had adequate knowledge at the time. "It is my submission, gentlemen, that they were willing partners in a pre-concerted pattern of aggression, all acquiescing in the common plan, each in turn carrying out his own part with lethal enthusiasm."

Major Ward emphasised that there was no evidence to suggest that the accused had kept within the strict limits of the orders. "Indeed, all the evidence points to the contrary. For batches of teachers, students, and businessmen were carted off and slaughtered, regardless of their past, regardless of their potentiality as hostile. Perhaps it was because they were educated, because some were English-speaking and had absorbed the British way of life and thought. Perhaps they were the ones less likely to remain docile under the yoke of Nippon, less likely to be deluded by the myth of 'co-prosperity'."

Concluding his final address, the prosecutor told the bench that the question before them was clear; and upon their answer to it stood or fell the prosecution case. "Has the conduct of these seven officers — officers of some seniority and experience, every one of them, from the general down to a captain, having had years of experience in the Japanese Army — has their conduct been such as to outrage the laws of humanity and the dictates of the public conscience?"

It was the prosecution's contention that the accused were guilty of conduct which had violated every tenet of humanity, which had imbued their hands with blood, the innocent blood of thousands. "It is on the foregoing arguments that I submit that the evidence fully justifies the conviction of these men, whose harsh brutality and callous indifference stand out on every page of the proceedings of this court."

The trial was over. At exactly midday on April 2, 1947, the hearing adjourned for the president and his four court members to consider the evidence and conclude their findings.

At 2 pm sharp, the five-man bench filed back to their seats and the accused seven were ordered to stand for the verdicts. Solemnly, Colonel Forsythe pronounced each man guilty The prosecution then submitted military record sheets for all seven convicted men. When Colonel Forsythe asked whether any of the seven wished to address the court on matters relating to their record sheets or in mitigation, only Hisamatsu indicated a desire to speak.

On entering the box, he first gazed intently at the public gallery. Then turning to the bench he began to speak softly. An interpreter translated. "The other day, during the prosecutor's cross examination, I mentioned the names of some influential Chinese during the February 1942 operations. These people at the time were influential Chinese of Singapore. They were leading citizens and leading members of the Overseas-Chinese Association and they played a great part in the welfare of the Chinese people."

Hisamatsu continued: "I have heard that these people are now in a very difficult position and I have also heard that some of these people have been killed by guerrilla warfare. On hearing this story I felt very sad. The war has ended and at the time when peace has come back . . . . . . "

Hisamatsu's words trailed away as the court president interrupted, asking whether Kurose had explained to his client the meaning of a plea of mitigation. "The accused, in the box now, can plead for himself — not for influential Chinese. Will you explain that to him, Mr. Kurose?"

Kurose replied: "I beg the pardon of the court, but the

accused wishes to tell the story about his feelings, and if he feels this is a plea of mitigation, let him carry on."

The court acceded to the request and Hisamatsu continued: "Now that peace has come back, I regret very much to know about this. At the time these people co-operated with me there were about 40 to 50 and they didn't do anything but merely comply with the order. Therefore I think they don't have any responsibility. On the same lines, I think my subordinates of the kempeitai do not have any responsibility. What I wish to say is not to have these people charged with responsibilities."

The defence then proceeded to call character witnesses for the seven accused after which a plea of mitigation was entered. Once more the court retired, this time to consider the sentences. On their return Colonel Forsythe read out the punishments deemed to fit the crime:

Lt. General Takuma Nishimura	Imprisonment for life
Lt. General Saburo Kawamura	Death by hanging
Lt Colonel Masayuki Oishi	Death by hanging
Lt Colonel Yoshitaka Yokota	Imprisonment for life
Major Tomotatsu Jyo	Imprisonment for life
Major Satorou Onishi	Imprisonment for life
Captain Haruji Hisamatsu	Imprisonment for life

The following day, all seven convicted Japanese lodged notifications of their intentions to petition the confirming authority against findings and sentences. Their petitions were duly submitted. On May 29, Britain's Singapore-based Commander-in-Chief, South East Asia Land Forces, Sir Neil M. Ritchie, confirmed all seven sentences and, by so doing, signified the petitions had been rejected.

Singapore's colonial government had gone to great lengths to ensure the Chinese Massacre trial became the public spectacle they felt the local Chinese were demanding. From the opening day of the hearing when the Governor, Sir Franklin

Gimson, and his wife were in conspicuous attendance, listening intently to the evidence, the authorities worked hard at conveying the impression that this was the moment of just retribution for which the island, administration and people alike, had been waiting. This would finally lay bear the truth behind the massacres, settle public anxieties and, most important, bury the matter as a political issue once and for all.

But it became very obvious from the reaction of the court's packed public gallery that Singapore's Chinese population would be far from satisfied with the outcome. Within hours of the sentencing, a group of prominent members of the community began organising the Singapore Chinese Appeal Committee and, through it, demanding that all seven Japanese convicted in the massacre trial be sent to their deaths. In addition, the committee insisted the authorities carry out public hangings.

Countering the public outcry, British High Command legal experts were forced to announce that the constitution of the War Crimes Courts prevented retrials with heavier sentences than the original ones.

On June 25, the punishments handed down at the conclusion of the Chinese Massacre trial were formally promulgated as required under the regulations. The executions of General Kawamura and Lt. Colonel Oishi would take place the following day at 9 am. Mr Tay Koh Yat, chairman of the Appeal Committee, told *The Straits Times* of his unhappiness over the "confirmation of the sentences which permits five of the Japanese to live." His committee, he said, would not be satisfied until these Japanese paid for their crimes with their lives. As the authorities had rejected the idea of a public hanging, he demanded ten of his committee members be allowed to witness the executions the next morning.

In the event, eight representatives of the Chinese community — including two women — were given permission to attend. Unbeknown to the 40-odd witnesses, including press, who filed through Changi Jail's grim main gate shortly before the appointed hour, the military authorities had arranged an added, albeit macabre, attraction to the morning's programme. Three Japanese war criminals were to be hanged; not just the expected two.

The third man on the scaffold would be Captain Kosaki Goshi who had been sentenced to death some weeks earlier in Kuala Lumpur for separate atrocities that had taken place there. He had been brought to Singapore and held in Changi Jail after it was decided it would be politically advantageous to delay his execution and, when the time came, combine it with the hangings of Kawamura and Oishi. For it was well appreciated within the Chinese community that Goshi had been the kempeitai officer in charge of the large concentration point at the corner of River Valley Road and Clemenceau Avenue in late February 1942. He would have been a defendant in the Chinese Massacre trial had he not been involved in the earlier Kuala Lumpur proceedings. The trial verdict might have prevented the British from hanging all seven accused. But a bit of convenient manipulation was enabling them to convey the impression locally that at least three of the culprits were going to their deaths that day.

One of the two Chinese women witnesses chosen was 29-year-old Miss Li Poay Keng, chief organiser of the 1,000-strong Singapore Women's Mutual Aid Victims' Association. Two days earlier, she had been quoted in *The Straits Times* as saying that, if the military authorities had agreed, all 1,000 women in her association would have welcomed the opportunity of seeing the Japanese hang. Miss Li, who lost a brother-in-law and an uncle in the massacres, said some of the widows had gone through so much suffering and were so bitter that they had even expressed their willingness to act as the executioners.

As the condemned trio, in prison garb, were led from their cells at 8.45 am, other war criminals and war criminal suspects throughout the jail began singing a Japanese version of "Auld

Governor Sir Franklin Gimson (centre) is conspicuous among the interested spectators on the opening day of the trial; a political gesture aimed at demonstrating to the Singapore Chinese the importance Britain attached to the proceedings.

On April 4, 1947, two days after the Military Court handed down two death sentences and five life imprisonments, surviving relatives of massacre victims meet to discuss the result of the trial. They decide to make representations to the Governor, Sir Franklin Gimson, the Commander in Chief of Britain's South East Asian Land Forces, and the Chinese Consul General. They demand heavier sentences. The meeting is chaired by Mr Tay Koh Yat (standing). Subsequently they demand public executions.

Two women are among the witnesses to the execution of the condemned Japanese. They represent the families of the victims. Here Madam Ong Goh Kee, a widow (left), and Ms Li Poay Keng, head of the Singapore Women's Mutual Aid Victims' Association, enter the main gate of Changi Jail on the morning of June 26, 1947.

The official Return Warrant confirming that the death sentence imposed on Lt. General Saburo Kawamura had been carried out at Changi Jail on June 26, 1947.

RETURN WARRANT

The sentence of death by hanging imposed on J. Gen. KAWAMURA. SABURO.

was put into execution at ..... Changi Jail
(Location)

on ...... 26 June ...194), ... 0940
(Date) (Hour)

Signature of Assistant Provost Marshal

(Counter signature and rank of Identifying Witness)

* This portion will not be detached from the copy which is sent to DJAG SEALF.

On April 19, 1947, The Chinese community in Singapore presents cups to Mr Richard Lim Chuan Hoe (left) and Major Frederick Ward (centre), prosecution lawyers, and Major M.G. Watson, war crimes investigator. The trophies are for work undertaken by the three men on the Singapore massacres case.

Lang Syne." Overhead, a Royal Airforce Meteor jet screamed past in a low dive as military guards manacled the hands of the three Japanese officers behind their backs and placed numbered, black cloth hoods over their heads.

Two minutes before 9 am, the guards ran the three barefooted, hooded figures from the cell block, up a long wooden ramp, to the scaffold's central platform. Positioning them on the elongated trap-door, the guards pinioned their ankles then quickly slipped the nooses over their heads.

Feeling the ropes in place, the condemned men muttered urgently to each other from beneath their hoods then began shouting in Japanese "Long live the Emperor" and "Banzai." Suddenly the trap crashed open. The shouting stopped.

The eight witnesses representing the Singapore Chinese community were ushered to a point where they could view the swinging hooded bodies through a steel grill.

Miss Li told pressmen: "I'm not satisfied. I want to see their faces to make sure they are dead." The other woman witness, Madam Ong Goh Kee, a widow whose son had been a massacre victim, queried: "Are they dead? I'm not so sure." All eight then asked to be allowed to wait for ten minutes after the execution so they could watch the Japanese being taken down from the scaffold and having their hoods removed. The request was refused.

After serving five years of his life sentence in Singapore, Nishimura became part of a repatriation of Japanese war criminals back to Tokyo where, supposedly, they were to serve the remainder of their prison terms. On May 21, 1950, while the ship transporting him was on a stopover in Hong Kong, Nishimura found himself transferred to the *SS Changte* on instructions of the Australian military authorities. From Hong Kong he was taken to Manus Island in the

Admiralty Group. There he faced trial before an Australian military court for ordering the massacre of Australian and Indian prisoners of war at Parit Sulong in Johore in January, 1942. He was found guilty and hanged on June 11, 1951.

Yokota, Jyo, Onishi and Hisamatsu also served five years of their life terms in Singapore before being repatriated back to Japan. From time to time thereafter, war criminals held in Japanese prisons received remissions of sentences. The last remaining war criminals under detention in Japan were released in 1957.

❖ ❖ ❖ ❖

Of the five Kempeitai sector commanders originally detailed to carry out screening activities in Singapore, only two — Onishi and Hisamatsu — had been charged and convicted among the seven defendants in the main "Chinese Massacre" trial. Goshi, one of the five, had been hanged for another crime, but in a manner which, as far as the public at large was concerned, saw him being punished for the massacres. That left two other sector commanders still to be arraigned.

One was Captain Keiji Mizuno, who had been in charge of the densely populated section of the city between Rochor Canal and the Singapore River. He had operated from a concentration centre at the corner of Arab Street and North Bridge Road, beside the Sultan Mosque. The other was a Captain Uezono who had been in charge of a roughly triangular section of the city lying between the Singapore River on one side, Outram and Cantonment Roads on another and the waterfront.

Enquiries listed Uezono as untraceable and probably killed in action in the latter part of the war. From the investigators' point of view, Mizuno represented the only outstanding element of the "Chinese Massacre" affair requiring finalisation.

On March 8, 1948, the then 60-year-old Mizuno was taken before a British Military Court in Singapore. He was charged with having killed "at least 177" Chinese civilian residents between February 18 - 24, 1942. His trial lasted four days and he was ultimately convicted and sentenced to imprisonment for life.

The prosecution's approach to Mizuno's case was identical to that adopted at the main trial the year before. Mizuno was linked directly to the chain of command leading back to Yamashita whom the British military continued to portray as the originating authority for the killing orders.

On March 12, 1948, Britain officially closed the "Chinese Massacre" case. Satisfied that they had appeased local political feelings, struck a blow for international law and demonstrated the power and fairness of British jurisprudence, investigators and prosecuting lawyers alike turned their attentions to other matters. In fact, they remained locked in their race against the calendar. Almost ten thousand suspected Japanese war criminals, for whom there was judged to be sufficient evidence to result in convictions, were still in custody throughout South East Asia. Although the 1947 deadline for wrapping up war crimes trials had come and gone, it now seemed certain a definite halt to investigations would be called before the end of 1948.

No one could dispute that the two Japanese officers, Kawamura and Oishi, who went to their deaths, and the five others who received life sentences, were guilty of involvement in the Singapore massacres. But could it have been a case of some of the right men being convicted for the wrong reasons? Might the unfortunate Kawamura have been spared the hangman's noose had the court possessed evidence on the extent to which he was duped by the real plot? Finally, did the bungling of investigations and prosecutions make it possible for the main culprit — the true perpetrator of the monstrous crime — to escape all blame and all punishment?

These three questions can only be answered in the affirmative.

Highly questionable prosecution tactics during the 1947 trial, then again in early 1948, ensured expediency won over the need to portray an accurate picture of the real "common plan or conspiracy" behind the mass killings. The plot presented by the prosecution as the backbone of their case simply never took place.

It is impossible to accept that both investigating and prosecuting teams were ignorant of the holes in their arguments, or were unaware that their oversimplification of details had amounted to nothing short of gross distortion of the truth.

The fact is that they were confronted on numerous occasions with solid contradictions of their own theories, but always ignored them. In this respect, the prosecution's repeated efforts to brush aside the Tsuji connection throughout the main trial become damning indictments of its entire modus operandi.

What, then, was behind these tactics?

The sudden death of Wild had a major impact. It created a vacuum that proved impossible to fill. Consequently, the overall comprehension of the issues involved, as far as both investigators and prosecution were concerned, suffered significantly. From the outset of the trial, the prosecution decided to down-play Tsuji's involvement, a factor they fully recognised as seriously undermining their case against the seven accused. It was a convenient ruse for it also avoided the humiliation of having to admit in an open court of law that the real culprit had successfully evaded all British attempts at apprehension.

Further complicating these issues were the political pressures of the time. Britain, nursing the shame of her unconditional surrender in February, 1942, felt badly exposed when the Chinese in Singapore began demanding justice for the civilians who had perished during the massacres. Adding to British embarrassment was the clear indication that the Chinese civilian death toll during the two-week massacre period had been substantially higher than the casualties suffered by the white colonial military defenders throughout the 70-day Japanese invasion that preceded it.

A judicial spectacular demonstrating Britain's concern for the demands of her colonial subjects was therefore considered essential if the lid was to be kept on local political emotions. But this introduced an even more alarming prospect. A failure to stage a major Chinese massacre trial would be dangerous enough. To stage one and lose it through acquittals would be disastrous. Only one result would be acceptable: convictions all round.

Pointedly, all this falls short of completely exonerating Yamashita. Certainly he did not order Japanese troops to slaughter Chinese civilians in Singapore. History has been wrongly condemning the 25th Army Commander for the past five decades. But Yamashita still must be held responsible for failing to guard against Tsuji's manipulation of command affairs.

For it was Tsuji, militarist fanatic, who had waited on the sidelines for his opportunity to "determine the destiny of the State." He had decided the glorious Japanese Imperial Army would never become bogged down in Malaya and Singapore as it had on mainland China. He saw the Overseas Chinese as the key to the solution and, to his warped mind, only he fully understood the need to bring them rapidly to heel. His methods: terror and bloodshed.

The plot was ready. The planning had been completed in Taiwan months before.

Tsuji knew exactly how 25th Army officers would react to killing orders ostensibly emanating from Yamashita. The fact that Yamashita's signature would be absent from the formal command would be irrelevant. Tsuji's network was in place.

Both Hayashi and Asaeda, entrusted with full details, were awaiting his directions. He could rely on Sugita's acquiescence.

Tsuji was utterly confident his plot would succeed and the moment to strike came when Yamashita agreed on "mopping up" measures against a perceived military threat from escaping armed Chinese guerrillas.

He arranged for Yamashita, heavily committed to urgent redeployment measures, to issue very general verbal instructions. The written orders, outlining the requirement to target civilians, came directly from Tsuji's office, by-passing the Army Commander.

This was the real plot — a far cry from the prosecution's claims.

The motivations of the prosecution during the Chinese Massacre trial will probably never be fully understood. But what can be verified is the fact that some development around July, 1948, pricked the British military conscience so strongly that senior officers at the Judge Advocate General's chambers in London were sent scurrying for files on the case. By this stage, Major Frederick Ward, the prosecutor at the Singapore trial, had returned to civilian life in Bradford, Yorkshire. On August 10, 1948, Captain S. J. Smith, of the Judge Advocate General's staff, wrote a "confidential" letter to the former military prosecutor. It said:

Dear Mr Ward;

It is a long time since I last heard from you, but the wheels are still continuing to turn in this office and I am writing now in an endeavour officially to enlist your assistance.

Once again the case of the Chinese massacre in Singapore has reared its ugly head and various things relating to this are afoot. As you can probably realise, London was never as fully in the picture in this case as was the Far East and we are rather anxious to run through the original proceedings again as soon as possible. Unfortunately the names of the accused have rather escaped me and everybody else in the office is in the same position. We can, of course, write to Singapore and get details, but you know how laborious are the usual staff channels and it would very much help us all if you could let me have a note of the ranks and names of all the accused. Lest you should be somewhat disturbed by this intelligence, I hasten to say that no question of criticism has arisen in connection with the original trial; this is entirely a new matter which has come to light.

I apologise for troubling you in this matter, but as you prosecuted the case you can probably supply this information quicker than if we wrote direct to Singapore.

I hope life is flourishing for you and that you have settled down into equally flourishing practice.

Yours

Whatever Ward's reply and whatever the precise details of the new matter that had come to light, there quickly followed a series of high level meetings in Singapore involving the Commander-in-Chief, Far East Land Forces (CinC FARELF). These reviewed the previous year's trial and the role Tsuji had played in the massacres. As a result, unprecedented directions were given to re-open the Chinese Massacre case.

In addition, new orders were issued for Tsuji to be tracked down, apprehended and brought to trial in Singapore.

On November 23, 1948, the London-based Director of the Army's Legal Services (DALS) issued a report indicating there would be no further war crimes investigations after December 31, 1948, and no further trials after June 30, 1949. The report noted: "It is understood that the accused Tsuji is still underground in Japan but it is hoped to effect his arrest any time now."

It concluded: "American intelligence is helping."

Therein, as we will discover, lies another fascinating twist to the Tsuji saga.

Meanwhile, the Chinese Massacre case secretly became the sole exception to the general wind-down of British war crimes trials in the Far East. The case remained officially open and orders to arrest Tsuji were kept fully active for more than a year after the last trial concluded.

On July 8, 1949, the legal department of the British High Command in Singapore returned the complete files on the Chinese Massacre case to the Judge Advocate General's office, Spring Gardens, Cockspur Street, London. With them went a note saying: "It is pointed out that these have been retained up to now, in the expectation of the arrest of Colonel Tsuji. Should this man be arrested it will be necessary to ask again for the return of these proceedings." For the remainder of 1949, the British continued actively searching for Tsuji.

So, what *did* happen to Tsuji? ■

Chapter 15

The god cuts a frightful swathe

———— ♦ ————

I n the final days of February, 1942, when Tsuji was at his busiest directing the Singapore massacres, he received orders to return to Imperial Headquarters in Tokyo for re-assignment. He was being recalled by his close friend from Manchurian front days, Takushiro Hattori, by now a full colonel and a most influential figure in Japan's military hierarchy through his position as chief of the Army General Staff's Operations Section.

Hattori, it will be recalled, had been instrumental in arranging War Minister Tojo's personal endorsement of Tsuji as planning director at the Taiwan Army Research Unit. Basking in the reflected glory of the 25th Army's Malayan campaign, Hattori wanted Tsuji back in Tokyo to become the equivalent of the Army's key battlefront trouble-shooter.

On March 18, with the bulk of the Singapore killing over and the emphasis now on subjugation operations against the Chinese in Malaya, Tsuji dispatched a message to Tokyo outlining his plans. "I intend," he said, somewhat grandly, "to take my post there after a late March inspection of battle conditions in the Burmese and Philippine theatres."

Hattori, however, had more urgent plans for his friend and, within a day or two, Tsuji found himself flying directly back to Tokyo via the fastest military schedule.

Soon after his return, he held a press conference in the Japanese capital where he brazenly claimed full credit for the

Malayan campaign's successes. Military censorship ensured newspapers referred to him merely as "Staff Officer X". But very rapidly the identity behind the pseudonym became widely recognised — particularly in military and press circles. Tsuji became popularly tagged the "god of strategy"

Awash in adulation, he wrote a "Summary of the Malaya Campaign" which was published in pamphlet form some weeks later by the prestigious Military Officers Club in Tokyo. The author was listed anonymously as "a Malaya Army Staff Officer," but once again it was public knowledge that Tsuji was the man behind the censored by-line. His account began: "As the official directly responsible for the operation, I was fortunate in being able to tour the various battlefields in the Malaya sector." It continued throughout in similar self-congratulatory vein.

Tsuji certainly had his supporters among the Army top brass. But he also had his detractors who were piqued by his arrogance and unabashed grandstanding. Still, one vital factor worked in the newly returned staff officer's favour. Japan, at this time, was engulfed in a euphoria of militarism following the victories of her Southern Army. She hankered for heroes and the Malaya campaign's chief planner filled the role perfectly. Tsuji played it for all it was worth and none of his critics felt competent to challenge him.

Tsuji's first trouble-shooting assignment saw him dispatched to the Philippines on April 1. His orders were to stiffen the resolve of General Masaharu Homma's 14th Army High Command as it launched a major offensive against American and Filipino forces doggedly defending the Bataan Peninsula and nearby Corregidor Island. Although Tsuji had only been in Tokyo a matter of days, it had been long enough for him to appreciate the level of general dissatisfaction at Imperial Military Headquarters over the performance thus far of the 53-year-old Homma. War Minister Tojo himself was concerned that the battle for the Philippine Islands, about to enter its fourth month, was in danger of becoming bogged down. Original plans called for the 14th Army to capture the Philippines swiftly then press on to the islands directly north of Australia in much the same way as Yamashita's 25th Army was doing in Malaya.

After crippling air raids which all but eliminated America's Philippine-based air and sea power on December 8, 1941, Japanese forces led by Homma began landing on the main island of Luzon two days later. The invasion's first phase was planned to climax with a pincer move to capture Manila. America's commander in the Philippines, General Douglas MacArthur, decided to withdraw to defensive positions on Bataan and Corregidor rather than attempt to hold the capital. Manila was declared an "open city" on December 27. The US tactics unsettled Homma and lured him into a serious strategic error.

Instead of concentrating on smashing the Americans' Bataan redeployment, the Japanese commander chose the politically enticing alternative of seizing Manila first. This he achieved on January 2, 1942. But in the process, he allowed the Americans valuable days to dig in behind a natural defence line straddling the northern end of the Bataan Peninsula. Meanwhile, MacArthur buried his High Command deep in Corregidor's Malinta Tunnel, central feature of the island's 17th Century Spanish fortress, and prepared to sit out a long siege which, he hoped, would ultimately be relieved with reinforcements brought in by the US Navy.

The defending side comprised some 15,000 US and 65,000 Filipino troops. They were well supplied with ammunition. But it soon became obvious that stocks of food and medicines were hopelessly inadequate for any extended action against the invaders. One of MacArthur's first orders was to impose half rations on his Army which quickly proved a starvation diet in the peninsula's heat and rugged terrain

Homma's first major push to dislodge the US defence line

on January 6 was effectively countered by American artillery. The Japanese then attempted outflanking moves but were repulsed, as much by the mountainous jungles as US counter measures. As the struggle for Bataan wore on through February into March, both sides began falling victim to a range of tropical diseases including malaria, dysentery, beri-beri and severe leg ulcers. Treatment of war wounded, particularly injuries from shrapnel among the defenders, became hazardous. Drug supplies were fast dwindling. American and Filipino death tolls mounted and throughout the continuing action the Japanese employed unchallenged airpower.

On March 11, with no relief in sight and US-Filipino morale fast disintegrating, MacArthur, on orders from Washington, was extracted from Corregidor under cover of darkness in a Navy patrol craft. His mission: to move to Australia and from there begin the mammoth task of re-building America's military strength in the Pacific. General Jonathan Wainwright assumed command of the defenders and pledged, "If the Japanese can take the Rock (Corregidor), they'll find me here, no matter what orders I receive." It was a desperate attempt to resuscitate fighting spirits. But in the foxholes of the American frontline more accurate sentiments were expressed when infantrymen cursed:

> *We're the Battling Bastards of Bataan*
> *No mama, no papa, no Uncle Sam,*
> *No aunts, no uncles, no nephews, no nieces*
> *No rifles, no planes or artillery pieces,*
> *And nobody gives a damn!*

Tokyo war planners, for their part, were furious when they learned MacArthur had escaped through the naval blockade and were more determined than ever to deliver a crushing defeat to the Americans. The War Ministry sanctioned the introduction of reinforcements to boost Homma's forces and the commanding general was told in no uncertain terms that the offensive planned to begin in the final days of March must be victorious. On March 31, after several days of directing a relentless aerial and artillery bombardment on the defenders, the Japanese managed to overrun a segment of the American front line. Quickly, they followed this up by thrusting fresh units into battle with the physically exhausted and mentally demoralised US and Filipino troops.

This was the situation into which Tsuji — his Malaya and Singapore reputations preceding him — flew on April 1. The knowledge that such a prominent officer had now been assigned to the Philippines by no less than Imperial Headquarters created for Tsuji an aura of special importance. Immediately he was received with admiration and respect among Japanese Staff Officers in Manila. He could hardly have asked for a situation more conducive to his operational style. Just as he had done when posted to Taiwan, and again when appointed to the 25th Army High Command, Tsuji immediately set about establishing his personal coterie of militarist-minded officers. He alluded to his powerful Tokyo connections, hinted he had access to Tojo himself and insisted he had arrived to speak on behalf of Imperial Headquarters. Most took him at his word.

Tsuji was urging a solution to the problems of Bataan and Corregidor very similar to the one he had devised for the Overseas Chinese in Singapore. Simply put: kill all prisoners.

He repeatedly outlined the idea to his expanding group of High Command supporters as the Japanese offensive against Bataan entered its final stages and an American defeat there became inevitable. Tsuji argued Japan was fighting a racial war in the Philippines. The American prisoners should be executed because they were the white colonialists. The Filipinos should be eliminated because they had betrayed the Asian cause.

Homma, fully occupied directing battle strategy from his forward headquarters, was ignorant of Tsuji's activities at this time; a situation, it should be appreciated, not dissimilar to that in which Yamashita found himself two months earlier in Singapore.

There is yet another strange parallel to the Singapore story. Whereas Yamashita had felt vulnerable to and at odds with top military brass in Tokyo, so, too, did Homma. The 14th Army commander's relations with overall Southern Army supremo, Field Marshal Count Terauchi, in Saigon, were poor. Terauchi's reports on Homma to Imperial Headquarters were becoming increasingly unfavourable.

Homma, like Yamashita, found himself in a no-win situation as far as Tokyo was concerned. Tsuji moved quickly to capitalise on the fall-off in support for Homma and schemed with his clique of staff officers to further undermine the general's control. His scheming went as far as issuing orders in Homma's name without any prior reference to the general himself. They were identical tactics to those he had employed with Yamashita in Singapore when it came to setting the stage for the Singapore massacres.

Tsuji's influence expanded rapidly in Manila and by the end of the first week in April his instructions and advice were being transmitted direct to units engaged on the front line. On April 9, the Bataan defenders surrendered. Tsuji was on hand for the event. Continuing to work through his supporting staff officers, he issued orders to unit commanders to kill prisoners. Some of these found willing acceptance. Others did not. A colonel commanding Japanese troops at Mount Limay on the peninsula was phoned and ordered: "Kill all prisoners and those offering to surrender."

On registering his strong objection, the colonel was told: "The order comes from Imperial Headquarters and has to be obeyed." In this case the outraged colonel slammed down the telephone and promptly commanded that all prisoners his unit had taken, comprising more than 1,000 Filipinos, be immediately released.

The horrendous Bataan Death March got underway as the Japanese sought to move their emaciated captives, primarily on foot, 65 miles north from Mariveles in Bataan to camps in the general San Fernando, Pampanga, area. Corregidor was still holding out and Homma's attentions were then concentrated on actions against this last bastion of American resistance.

Colonel Saburo Watanabe, senior staff officer for the 16th Division which was responsible for the Japanese drive down the west coast of Bataan, would later recall meeting Tsuji near Mariveles on April 9. The Death March had just begun.

After viewing a large group of US prisoners lined up on a road together, Tsuji turned to Watanabe and suggested: "How about we kill them?"

When a shocked Watanabe refused, Tsuji retorted: "You've got no guts."

Dissatisfied with Watanabe's reaction, Tsuji sought out the 16th Division's commanding officer, Lt. General Morioka.

He told Morioka: "Kill the prisoners."

Morioka replied: "Don't be stupid, we can't do that kind of thing."

Tsuji could.

Tsuji himself would recall an incident on the Bataan front when he was with a group of "wild" Takasago tribesmen from Formosa who were volunteers in the Japanese Army. "I made a mistake. When we broke through on the Bataan Peninsula there was a group of white men strung out in the valley. The Takasagos kept on asking if they could attack them. I shouldn't have done it, but I kept quiet."

It was suggested by an interviewer that Tsuji's silence on this occasion might have indicated his tacit approval of the Takasagos' attack.

Tsuji replied: "I tacitly approved. About a hundred of them, screaming "Yaaah!" attacked, cutting off the heads of the Americans who were just at the point of surrender. Three hundred of them had their heads chopped off, and this became known as the Death March. However the Americans never made a big deal of it."

Tsuji went on: "Battlefield mentality is very strange. When you see the blood of a friend or comrade or subordinate, at that moment you just go crazy. If you see your wife or children killed before your eyes, you go off the rails. Afterwards, when you cool down, you understand what you did was wrong."

History records that somewhere between 7,000 and 10,000 US and Filipino prisoners died from starvation, dehydration, malaria, beatings and executions during the Bataan Death March. The same death toll figures would just as accurately apply to the Singapore massacres where Tsuji was undoubtedly the primary culprit.

It is difficult to be precise about the percentage of Death March casualties directly attributable to the activities of Tsuji. But unquestionably his input was highly significant, if not the dominant motivating force. Large numbers of prisoners were certainly executed on verbal instructions originating from this newly arrived celebrity troubleshooter. The massacre by the Takasago tribesmen is a case in point. Tsuji's later suggestion that he "tacitly approved" of the slaughter of 300 surrendering Americans is nonsense. He ordered it.

But Tsuji's manipulations had an even more insidious consequence. They ensured that, at the staff officer echelon, a level of appalling brutality would be accepted during the Death March phase and pass unchallenged. Once such acceptance had been established it opened the flood gates to bestial behaviour by the Japanese throughout the surrender period and in the weeks that followed.

On April 10, Tsuji was back in Manila, staying at the Manila Hotel, but operating from Homma's High Command headquarters. A message came in from Major General Kiyotake Kawaguchi, commander of Japanese forces in the southern Philippine islands group known as the Visayas. It told of the capture of the country's Chief Justice, Mr Jose Abad Santos, and his son, Jose Jnr. The two had been seized the previous evening on Negros Island. Kawaguchi suggested the elder Abad Santos be given a position in the military administration.

Tsuji saw the message and ordered the Chief Justice be executed.

The High Command reply to Kawaguchi read: "His guilt is obvious. Dispose of him immediately."

Kawaguchi, who knew and liked Abad Santos Snr., decided to tap the influence of Major General Yoshide Hayashi, the 14th Army's Military Administrator. Hayashi had been Kawaguchi's former classmate and the two regarded each other as close friends. Kawaguchi sent Hayashi a message emphasising the need to save the Chief Justice. There was no reply. Two weeks later, a command from Manila insisted father and son be transferred to the Japanese garrison in Davao province on Mindanao Island. Both were to be executed.

Kawaguchi resisted further, refusing to send the two away. Tsuji then dispatched a special High Command emissary by the name of Staff Officer Inuzuka to Kawaguchi's headquarters on Cebu. Inuzuka was there to make sure the orders were obeyed. At one point, a livid Kawaguchi threw Inuzuka bodily out of his office.

But Kawaguchi ultimately gave in under pressure. The father was taken to a nearby coconut plantation and shot. The son was spared.

Distraught with remorse, Kawaguchi flew to Manila and confronted Homma. "Why did you authorise the execution of Chief Justice Abad Santos?" he demanded.

Homma flatly denied he had sanctioned the killing. Indeed, he had done quite the opposite. He had approved Kawaguchi's original suggestion that Abad Santos be spared and given an administrative post. Homma claimed he had then passed the matter over to Hayashi for implementation. Kawaguchi tracked down Hayashi who was clearly embarrassed.

Kawaguchi demanded an explanation of his classmate's

"shameful" behaviour. Hayashi pleaded he had no alternative. "Imperial Headquarters insisted on the execution of Abad Santos," he said.

"Imperial Headquarters," thundered Kawaguchi, "What do you mean Imperial Headquarters?"

"Well, it was Tsuji," stammered the shamed Hayashi.

In February, 1946, Homma appeared before a US military court in Manila charged with responsibility for the Bataan Death March. After a trial which will forever remain a black mark on US military justice, the former 14th Army commander was sentenced to death. MacArthur, as he had previously done in the case of Yamashita, rejected Homma's appeal for a review of the sentence. Homma, dressed in civilian clothes, died before a firing squad on April 3, 1946, at Los Baños, south of Manila, where Yamashita had been hanged five weeks earlier.

Soon after the Japanese surrender, the Americans arrested Kawaguchi for the Abad Santos murder. He was convicted and spent a total of seven years and three months in Tokyo's Sugamo Prison and Manila's Muntinlupa Penitentiary. A very bitter Kawaguchi would resurface in Tokyo in the 1950's, hell-bent on exacting revenge for the punishment he claimed he'd suffered for Tsuji's crimes. Kawaguchi's action would have startling repercussions for the Japanese political scene.

In July, 1942, Tsuji was recalled to Tokyo. Now he had victories at Bataan and Corregidor to add to those in Malaya and Singapore already under his belt. For a few days he was feted at Imperial Headquarters in a manner befitting the returning "god of strategy." But it would be a brief respite. Hattori and his staff of operational planners were focusing their attentions on the fast evolving conflict among the islands of the South West Pacific. This would be troubleshooter Tsuji's next assignment on behalf of Imperial Headquarters.

On July 24, he flew to Rabaul on the island of New Britain which had fallen to the Japanese the previous January. Tokyo's key target in the region was Papua New Guinea, particularly the town of Port Moresby on the southern coast of the Papuan Peninsula. Rabaul, 450 miles to the north-east, across the Solomon Sea, was the staging point for the operation to seize Port Moresby.

Four days before Tsuji arrived in Rabaul with broad instructions to help direct tactics throughout the South West Pacific, the Japanese light cruisers *Tenryu* and *Tatsuta*, together with three destroyers, escorted three troop transports out of Rabaul harbour and set course for the northern coast of the Papuan Peninsula. Within 48 hours, Japanese troops were ashore and the northern coastal town of Buna, little more than a mission station and native village, was soon in their hands.

Tsuji quickly transferred to a naval patrol craft and headed towards Buna. Australian warplanes flying interdiction missions spotted the patrol craft, attacked, and Tsuji sustained serious head injuries. The patrol craft limped back to Rabaul and Tsuji was medically evacuated to Tokyo on the first available flight. He arrived in the Japanese capital on August 3 and was immediately hospitalised.

While he was recuperating in hospital, Guadalcanal in the Solomon Islands, first occupied by the Japanese in May, was attacked by the American 1st Marine Division under the command of Major General Alexander A. Vandergrift. The marines landed on August 7 and, after three days of fierce fighting, secured the half completed airstrip the Japanese had been constructing on the flat coastal plains of the Lunga River. Vandergrift immediately set up a defensive perimeter to hold the airstrip. There then began a race against time to transform the re-named Henderson Field into a key US forward fighting airbase.

The Japanese repeatedly moved reinforcements across from Rabaul to wrest control of the airstrip from the Americans. But the marines held their ground and the Japanese failed each time to commit sufficient forces for the job.

Recovered from his head wounds, Tsuji flew into Rabaul in

mid-October. On October 22, he was on Guadalcanal as the senior staff officer responsible for yet another reinforced Japanese lunge against Henderson's marine defenders. This time the plan of attack had been essentially drafted by Tsuji. Japanese anticipation ran high now that the "god" was involved on Guadalcanal. During manoeuvres for position prior to the attack, Tsuji met Kawaguchi, the general he had come to despise six months earlier for his liberal attitudes towards the local population in the Philippines.

Kawaguchi's unit was to be an important element in the attacking force against Henderson. But the general, who had been on Guadalcanal for some weeks, harboured reservations about the frontal assault he was required to make across terrain on which his unit had recently suffered huge casualties. He discussed this with Tsuji who agreed to an adjusted plan of attack, then subsequently abandoned the adjustments without informing Kawaguchi. When the time came to advance on the airfield, Kawaguchi, who was operating on the revised schedule he had agreed with Tsuji, was not in place. Tsuji reported Kawaguchi had refused to advance. As a result, the general was relieved of his command.

As it happened, Tsuji's assault plan proved a disaster. He sent a coded message to Army Headquarters in Tokyo saying: "I must bear full responsibility for the failure of the 2nd Division which fought honourably for days and lost more than half its combat force in desperate attacks. The assault failed because I underestimated the enemy's fighting power and insisted on my own operations plan which was at fault."

Tsuji's message went on to proclaim that he deserved the sentence "of ten thousand deaths" and he asked to be allowed to stay on in Guadalcanal. His request was refused and he was recalled to Tokyo to report on the island's battle situation.

In Tokyo, a decidedly subdued Tsuji now argued that Japan's position on Guadalcanal was desperate. He came out strongly against any proposal to launch further attacks against the American airfield. Indeed, he openly opted for a retreat from the island; a most difficult course of action to propose to Japan's military leaders, who, in December 1942, were still drunk with war euphoria. But, on the last day of the year, Imperial Headquarters ordered the retreat he had recommended.

On January 7, 1943, Tsuji fell ill with malaria that he originally contracted while on Guadalcanal. Complications set in with an attack of pneumonia. He was admitted to hospital where he stayed until February 27. On his discharge from medical care, he became an instructor at the Tokyo Military Academy until August 20, when he was promoted to full colonel and sent to Nanking.

Tsuji remained in China for almost eleven months. In July, 1944, he was transferred to Rangoon, Burma, as a senior staff officer with the 33rd Army under Lt. General Masaki Honda. Japanese forces in Burma were then in a critical position. Their plans to drive across the eastern Indian frontier earlier in the year had crumbled before a series of daring set-piece defence actions by division sized units of the British and British Indian armies, major operations by two Chinese divisions under the controversial US General Joseph "Vinegar Joe" Stilwell, and constant spoiling actions by the legendary Chindits. Japanese battlefield deaths plus those from wounds, jungle diseases and hunger topped 65,000 throughout the Burma theatre between early January and end of June that year. Once again, Tsuji was involved on the planning and tactical side of operations. Rather than orchestrating invasions and assaults, he was now devising strategic withdrawals and outright retreats.

Still, he enjoyed almost mystical status in the Army at this point of his career. If anyone could turn the tide of warfare in Burma back in Tokyo's favour it was the "god of strategy." It was a forlorn hope. The truth was that the brilliant but fanatical Tsuji was being driven more irrational by fears of ultimate defeat. It was a time when he increasingly boasted how he brewed his own special medicine from the livers of executed British airmen and drank this for power and strength. Allied intelligence reports described how he offered this "medicine" to fellow Japanese officers. Kawaguchi would claim that he personally heard Tsuji talking about his "special medicine" techniques at the South Pacific Hotel on the island of Palau as early as July, 1942.

By September, 1944, Tsuji found himself attached to the 33rd Army's forward headquarters at Mangshih in northern Burma, close to the Salween River and the Yunnan province border. His enemy on the ground were the increasingly mobile, US-led, Chinese forces. His enemy in the air were India-based US and British warplanes. At this point, the Japanese had virtually no airpower in Burma. As General Honda and his Chief-of-Staff spent much of their time in rear areas, Tsuji had assumed the acting chief's role and effectively controlled Japanese military action in northern Burma.

At around 8. 00 am on September 26, Lieutenant Benjamin A. Parker of the 14th Airforce's 25th Fighter Squadron, 51st Fighter Group, flying mission no. F1027, began bombing and strafing runs, together with a number of other US aircraft. The target was Tsuji's Mangshi encampment, one and a half miles north-west of the local township. It was a particularly heavy raid based on excellent intelligence data provided by long range scout teams.

During one strafing run at 8. 05 am, other pilots involved in the attack noticed bursts of anti-aircraft fire close behind Parker's plane. Five minutes later, Parker called the mission leader on his radio and said, "I'm hit. I guess I'll have to bail out." The pilots reported Parker was neither seen nor heard from again.

On the afternoon of September 27 a "Radio Tokyo" broadcast announced: "An American pilot was captured on the 26th of September in the Salween River area." Mangshih is, of course, in the Salween River area.

Parker parachuted safely from his crippled aircraft but was soon captured by a Japanese patrol and brought to Tsuji's headquarters. That afternoon, still in his flying suit, the US pilot was taken to the mess hall and interrogated by a Colonel Tanaka using an interpreter by the name of Ota. He refused to divulge any military information and was held overnight under guard.

Three days later, American aircraft returned for a second heavy attack against Mangshih, scoring a number of direct hits with bombs and killing several Japanese troops attached to the High Command. Parker escaped injury in the attack. But as soon as it was over, Tsuji ordered the American be brought outside for public execution. High Command staff officers and other ranks were assembled in a circle, several lines deep, around the airman who stood with his hands bound behind his back.

In front of the gathered troops, Tsuji began questioning Parker using a civilian interpreter by the name of Yoshida. The colonel brandished a bomb fragment, claiming it had come from one of the missiles dropped by the pilot three days earlier. Parker maintained his silence. Tsuji then struck the airman heavily across the face with the piece of jagged steel, causing blood to gush from a deep wound.

Lieutenant Sekimoto, a member of Tsuji's immediate staff, began waving a photograph of Parker's wife in front of the doomed man. The American had been carrying the photograph when captured. Still, Parker refused to cooperate.

An irate Tsuji then decreed the US prisoner would not have the honour of being beheaded by a Japanese sword. He commanded his personal Shan dah (Burmese sword) souvenir be brought from his office. This he gave to Sekimoto, the appointed executioner, telling him: "Get on with it."

A blindfold of dark coloured cloth was tied over Parker's eyes and he was forced to his knees. Sekimoto raised the sword and sliced it down on the back of the airman's neck. But the blade was blunt. The airman fell forward onto his face, blood cascading from a deep neck wound. He was wrenched back onto his knees once more. It would take two further strikes with the dull blade before the head was severed.

Tsuji then ordered a chunk of flesh be carved from the dead airman's thigh and preserved in salt before the body was buried.

Shortly after the execution, the headquarters moved to Mong Yu where Tsuji ordered the flesh to be cooked and served to a group of officers gathered in his hut for a celebration. In addition, Tsuji called Private Soejima, an orderly, and told him to deliver to a nearby hut a section of the flesh measuring some six inches in circumference and about half an inch thick. Some of the Japanese consumed the flesh. Some didn't.

The war moved on. More battles were fought, many more lives were lost, and Tsuji's butchery of the gallant US pilot who refused to talk might well have been reduced to another forgotten statistic. Except that on March 16, 1945, a 27-year-old Japanese called Masao Sasaki surrendered to Allied forces near Mandalay. Under interrogation, he revealed he knew about the fate of Parker. Indeed, he had witnessed the airman's execution and had been there when the cooked flesh was handed around. Sasaki, who also used the Christian name, Michael, had been an interpreter with the 33rd forward headquarters in northern Burma. He was quickly flown to Red Fort, Delhi, for full investigations. In the meantime the South East Asia Translation and Interrogation Centre (SEATIC) issued a special bulletin to Allied commands on May 18, 1945, with a rundown on Sasaki's first interrogation which included graphic details of Parker's beheading and the act of cannibalism that followed.

Michael Sasaki proved to have an interesting background.

Born in Alor Star, Kedah, Malaya, to Japanese parents, he attended elementary school in Singapore and then underwent five years of schooling back in Japan. On his family's return to Singapore he enrolled first at the Anglo-Chinese School then attended another local school for two years. At the conclusion of Sasaki's interrogation in Delhi, the Americans decided Tsuji and Sekimoto should be detained and tried as war criminals once the war was over. A file on the atrocity was formally opened. On July 8, 1946, Captain Albert W. Schneider, chief of the US War Crimes office in Singapore, issued a memorandum which began:

SUBJECT: Re beheading Captain (then Lt) Benjamin A. Parker, O-732336
Japanese Involved: Colonel. Tsuji and Lieutenant Sekimoto

Attached to the file was a report headed "Investigator's Comment." It noted:

"Sasaki was hesitant in answering most questions and appeared to be studying over the questions to keep from involving himself as an active participant in both the beheading and cannibalism."

A year later, another brief report was added to the American file. Stamped "confidential," it explained that as Sasaki had been born and raised in Malaya, he was not involved in any post-war repatriation to Japan but had been released instead in Singapore. The report indicated the Americans had further plans to interrogate him.

In February, 1945, Tsuji, still assigned to Burma, received a special citation of appreciation from Lt. General Heitaro Kimura, Japan's overall Burma theatre commander. The citation was normally awarded posthumously. Tsuji and one other officer were the only soldiers ever to receive it while alive.

Three months later, Imperial Headquarters transferred Tsuji to Bangkok with instructions to strengthen Japan's overall military position in Siam. His new position was chief of operations. With mounting evidence of an imminent Japanese defeat, the Siamese Army, which had tolerated Tokyo's military presence in the kingdom since December 1941, was showing distinct signs of revolt.

Tsuji wrote of his arrival in the Siamese capital:

"The flames of war raging in Burma stretched long tongues of fire towards the Burma-Siamese border. Showers of flaming sparks threatened at any moment to wrap Siam in a mighty conflagration. All the while, the Japanese forces in Bangkok slept on in indolent lethargy. Enemy fifth columnists ran rampant underground and had joined hands with the Free Siam Movement under General Aung Sun, waiting for the moment to strike at the Japanese. It was a clear substantiation of the old Japanese adage: "Only the husband is blind to his wife's infidelities."

Within days of Tsuji's arrival, Japanese forces launched into a programme to fortify all their garrisons in the Bangkok area. Networks of foxholes were dug, pill-boxes constructed, sandbag emplacements positioned and complicated rows of barbed wire laid. Roads linking the various garrison fortifications were patrolled and guarded. Geisha houses were closed down on Tsuji's orders and restaurants placed out of bounds to Japanese military personnel. At the capital's Don Maung airport, huge concrete artillery emplacements were erected against a perceived move by Britain to land airborne troops for a final drive against the city.

Tsuji wrote how, within a period of two months, he had transformed "the Buddhist capital of Bangkok." On July 20, the Japanese High Command, on Tsuji's instigation, opened part of their newly constructed fortifications to a month-long inspection programme for Siam's military leaders, government chiefs, and local and Japanese press.

Tsuji personally greeted the first 200-strong inspection group and explained: "The reason why the Japanese forces in neighbouring Burma lost was because geisha houses prospered while military preparations were neglected. The only way to prevent Bangkok from being thrown into a crucible of war is to complete thorough preparations and to discourage any enemy attacks."

He added: "We are throwing open our secret fortification to you on the basis of the principles of the Japan-Siam Alliance. Please feel free to look around as you see fit. It is our hope that the Siamese forces will prepare fortifications even stronger than these."

But Tsuji's warrior days were fast running out.

Six days after he exhorted the Siamese officers to build bigger and better fortifications, the Allies issued the Potsdam Declaration calling on Japan's immediate and unconditional surrender. If Tokyo failed to comply, she would face the "prompt and utter destruction of the Japanese homeland." The Potsdam Declaration also promised that Japanese war criminals would be punished. Tokyo's leaders chose to ignore the threat.

On August 6, the B-29 bomber 'Enola Gay' from the US 20th Air Force's 393rd Squadron, dropped the 20 kilotonne atomic bomb, nicknamed "Little Boy," over the Japanese city of Hiroshima. At 16 seconds past 8.16 am, local time, the weapon detonated 564 metres above the city wiping out an area of 12 square kilometres, killing some 80,000 people and injuring a similar number. Tokyo remained silent on the demands of the Potsdam Declaration and the Japanese command in Bangkok received only the briefest details about the disaster at Hiroshima.

On August 9, another US B-29 dropped a second 20 kilotonne atomic bomb, this time on Nagasaki, destroying four square kilometres of the city, killing 40,000 and injuring a further 60,000.

That night, Tsuji, who was also in charge of the Army's press operations in Bangkok, was handed a message quoting a San Francisco radio station report that the Soviet Union had declared war on Japan. Film producer Kozaburo Yoshimura, a lieutenant in the press office at the time, later recalled how Tsuji, who had long predicted the USSR would never attack Japan, ranted at the young soldier who brought him the news — news which, as it happened, was accurate.

"At a time like this, how can you be so stupid, being taken in by an enemy announcement?" he asked. Then grasping the handle of his sword he added: "I should cut your stomach open."

On August 11, newspapers in Bangkok reported Tokyo was preparing to accept the Potsdam ultimatum. Tsuji that day flew to Saigon and was soon in meetings with senior officers at the all-powerful Southern Army General Headquarters. Tsuji pleaded to be allowed to fly to Tokyo so he could pressure for rejection of the Potsdam demands. His request was turned down.

That evening, Tsuji and General Hidesumi Hayashi, commanding officer of the 28th Army, met in Tsuji's room at the French-built Continental Hotel in the heart of Saigon. Tsuji said he wanted to go to Manchuria and instruct the Japanese army there on tactics. He was, he said, totally opposed to surrender under the Potsdam arrangements.

The general argued that the only way to avoid another atomic bomb was to accept the ultimatum. Recognising Tsuji had no knowledge of the destructive power of America's latest weapon, Hayashi set about explaining it to his friend. The more he explained, the more irrational Tsuji became.

"The High Command is stupid," Tsuji blurted at one point. "They never said a single thing about this atomic bomb." As the evening wore on, Tsuji began to accept the fact of Japan's defeat.

The conversation drifted to a discussion of likely political trends in East Asia henceforth and from where future regional leadership might come. The two men concluded that the Nationalist Chinese Kuomintang (KMT) movement seemed well positioned to emerge the next leader of the East Asian people.

Hayashi suggested: "Why don't you go back to China and offer your experience to the KMT in its war against the communists?"

Tsuji nodded thoughtfully but refrained from replying. He had been contemplating precisely such measures since the very day he arrived in Bangkok. He feared that if he remained in the Siamese capital for the formal surrender it would be only a matter of time before he was arrested as a war criminal. He was certain the British would want to put him on trial for the Singapore massacres. The Americans would also want him for his role in the Bataan Death March.

Yes, escape to China seemed infinitely preferable to ignominious death by hangman's rope or firing squad bullet. The following day, he would fly back to Bangkok and immediately begin preparing a mysterious disappearance befitting the "god of strategy" ∎

Chapter 16

The god gets away

———— ◆ ————

Tsuji moved swiftly when he returned to Bangkok and his first call was on the Japanese Ambassador to Siam, Kumaichi Yamamoto, in whom he confided his plans. Yamamoto rejected as too dangerous Tsuji's initial idea to hide in the embassy until such time as he had contacted the local Nationalist Chinese underground movement. It was almost certainly Yamamoto who planted in Tsuji's mind the alternative of disguising himself as a monk and hiding in one of the capital's numerous Buddhist temples.

During the three and a half years of Japan's military presence in Siam, there had been considerable interchange at the religious level between Tokyo and Bangkok. Japanese monks attached to local temples had become commonplace. All foreign monks carried identity papers issued by Siam's Department of Religious Education. The ambassador promised to assist Tsuji obtaining these by making private approaches to contacts in the Prime Minister's office and the Ministry of Education. In addition, he agreed to issue Tsuji false passports.

An appointment was made with Kamito Maruyama, a senior Nichiren sect priest attached to the Japanese Hikari Mission in Bangkok. A meeting followed in a private suite at the Japanese-owned Siam Hotel where Tsuji received his saffron robes, learned how to wear them and had his picture taken in full religious garb for the identity documents.

When word spread in the High Command that Tsuji was

about to make his getaway, he was joined by seven fanatical young "special volunteers." They were part of an elite Bangkok-based *kamakazi* soldiers' unit that had been ready for deployment on suicide ground-assault missions. All adopted bogus priestly identities. Tsuji took the name Norinobu Aoki and devised a cover story depicting himself as head of a group of student priests recently arrived from Burma. The group spent hours coordinating their respective backgrounds, studying religious ceremony and rehearsing the mannerisms of monks.

On the night of August 16, 1945, 36 hours after Emperor Hirohito broadcast his unconditional surrender, Tsuji penned a false will together with a phoney death-note indicating he was leaving to commit suicide. Both fake documents would form the basis of pre-arranged messages to Imperial Headquarters in Tokyo reporting Tsuji's demise. Allied investigators were to be given the notes in the hope these would throw them off the trail. Shortly after midnight, Tsuji and his seven "disciples" slipped away from the Japanese military headquarters. They made their way to the Ryab Temple located, as it still is today, near the Royal Palace, in the vicinity of what is now called the Indian Market.

The main temple structure had been heavily damaged in an earlier American air attack. But in one section of the grounds, conveniently secluded behind a high hedge, was a smaller Japanese temple attached to an ossuary. The resident priest was Japanese. Arrangements had been made with him for the eight fugitives to pursue their pious masquerade at the temple while the next phase of the escape was being organised.

Within a matter of days, Tsuji realised his group was too cumbersome and likely to attract attention. His one hope of success, he felt, was to operate alone. Before making his first approach to the Chungking underground network, he arranged for his seven companions to move to the nearby Maharat Temple which had been the venue for numerous joint Japanese-Siamese memorial services during the war.

Immediately after the Japanese surrender, the Chungking "Blue Shirt" society emerged from its wartime clandestine operations throughout Siam to establish numerous overt branch offices of what was called the Kuomintang Party Overseas Section. The main Bangkok office was opened on Suriwong Road in a building formerly occupied by a Japanese trading company. It was here Tsuji made his first contact with Chungking intelligence agents, offering his expertise to help fight communism in China.

Tsuji was desperate to get out of Bangkok before the British occupation forces began arriving in early September. He remained convinced he would be the first they would want to arrest. He was, of course, quite wrong. As we have already learned, for three weeks following Japan's capitulation, the British military lacked any firm directive on war criminals. When, on September 7, London issued the first order on the subject, it merely outlined the broad categories of Japanese personnel to be detained. There was no immediate "wanted" list. This would come weeks later when the South East Asian War Crimes headquarters were properly established in Singapore.

It is at this point that the tall, commanding presence of a 21-year-old Grenadier Guards officer enters the Tsuji story. As the immediate post-war months unfolded, it would prove an uncanny presence and nearly five decades later, Captain Richard O. Crewdson (retired) would be able to provide startling details on the bizarre intrigue that finally decided the outcome of the baffling Tsuji escape.

Crewdson came to South East Asia after military service in Italy where he was twice wounded and ultimately mentioned in dispatches. On VE day, May 9, 1945, he signed up in Siena with Britain's clandestine Special Operations Executive (SOE). Returning briefly to SOE's headquarters in

Mr Richard Crewdson returns to Singapore and his one-time operational headquarters at the Goodwood Park Hotel during research he undertook for this book. A former Grenadier Guards officer, Mr Crewdson, who now lives in London, was the British military's arresting officer in Tokyo from May 1946 to May 1948. He was then personally committed to tracing Tsuji but found his way blocked by powerful influences.

Baker Street, London, he flew to Ceylon (now Sri Lanka) for training in the capital, Colombo, and then at Kandy in the island's central hills. Throughout June and July that year, the young captain's schedule was geared to preparing him for the hazardous task of long range patrol work in China. Suddenly, plans for the China operations were shelved and Crewdson joined the Siam section of SOE's secret South East Asian unit known as Force 136. With Japan's capitulation, he found himself quickly posted to the United Kingdom's military mission in Bangkok where he was involved advising the Siamese on how to disarm the defeated Japanese army in their midst.

Soon after his arrival in Bangkok, Crewdson became aware that friendly rivalry existed between Force 136 members and their US Office of Strategic Services (OSS) counterparts. In particular the two covert operations were involved in an impromptu race to see which would successfully track down and seize the Japanese military's Bangkok gold reserves. There were red faces all round when it was eventually established that a certain lieutenant colonel by the name of Masanobu Tsuji had got to the reserves first and disappeared with vast funds.

Crewdson, at this time unaware of Tsuji's atrocity-ridden past, became fascinated by the seemingly outlandish bravado of the missing thief. He began making his own enquiries and soon established that senior Siamese military circles regarded Tsuji as a "notorious character." Furthermore, they gave little credibility to the Japanese High Command's insistence that its absent operations chief had committed suicide immediately after the surrender.

The inevitable conjecture, from Crewdson's viewpoint, was that Tsuji had taken so much money that he could bribe his way through Asia for months, if not years, and perhaps one day attempt a secret return to Japan.

But Crewdson's activities in Bangkok at this time were unrelated to war crimes investigations. Others had this responsibility and their early reports to Singapore tended to concentrate on the orders they had received to detain Japanese intelligence personnel, kempeitai and POW camp guards. Still, the staff officer's abrupt disappearance was certainly noted by the relevant authorities. In their correspondence with Singapore, they expressed strong scepticism over the claims that Tsuji had killed himself. They speculated he was more probably on the run.

Extraordinarily, none of these communications sparked any correlation back in Singapore between the missing Tsuji in Bangkok and the Japanese officer of the same name wanted for the execution and cannibalism of an American pilot in Burma. The four-month-old SEATIC report, detailing this atrocity and naming Tsuji as the culprit, had become lost in the bureaucratic muddle that accompanied the formation of Britain's South East Asian War Crimes network. Without pressing interest from Singapore, the missing staff officer case became relegated to routine enquiries and ultimately filed away as responsibilities and duties for the occupying army expanded.

Crewdson remained in Bangkok until early March 1946 and throughout his assignment there persevered with his private search for clues to the elusive gold thief. Then he was asked to join the war crimes operation in Singapore. It was a career switch that would shock him to the realisation that his quarry was far from just the brazen, dare-devil bandit who had vanished with a fortune.

The Chinese took their time with Tsuji's application. As the days and weeks passed, the saffron-robed soldier became increasingly paranoid about the incoming British. To his dismay, British officers set up their headquarters within a couple of hundred metres of his temple hideout. Almost daily, British troops would stop outside the temple walls. Each time, the fugitive's heart rate would jump. Tsuji was convinced he, not the shattered temple surrounds, had become the subject of their curiosity. Then the British command installed their officers' club in the building next door to the Kuomintang Party office on Suriwong Road.

Adding to his torment, the Chinese vernacular press began reporting rumours that Japanese army officers were adopting diguises in escape bids. He saw Japanese civilians being herded into concentration camps and learned through his information grapevine that the British soon intended clamping down on all foreign nationals attached to temples.

Tsuji spent 70 cliff-hanging days in the Ryab temple before word came from Chungking that his offer had been accepted. Before departing the temple, he wrote yet another suicide note. This was in the name of the venerable Norinobu Aoki and was addressed jointly to the chief of the government's Religious Education Department and the Bangkok Chief of Police. It told how he intended to throw himself into the waters of the sacred Menam River as he could no longer face life as a defeated Japanese national. It concluded: "Realizing that I would be causing you great trouble if I were to throw myself in the river while still a priest, I am returning my priestly robes and my certificate of priesthood. I shall die as a worldly man."

He left the temple at 9 pm on October 28, 1945, and moved to a safe-house on the outskirts of the Siamese capital provided by the Kuomintang office. Three days later, now disguised as a southern Chinese businessman with pith helmet, white jacket, black trousers and dark glasses, Tsuji and two escorts departed Bangkok by train for neighbouring Laos. Over the next three months he would be taken via a circuitous route through Indo-China to Hanoi from where he flew to Chungking on March 9, 1946. There he was placed in the Anti-Communist Propaganda Department of the so-called Military Control Bureau. It didn't take him long to realise that while, on the one hand, he had escaped capture by the British, he had, on the other, become a virtual prisoner of the Chinese.

In Chungking, Tsuji worked feverishly to make personal contact with Nationalist leader, Generalissimo and President Chiang Kai-shek. He needed to be able to exert influence, drop names and generally wheel and deal as he had done within the Japanese military heirarchy. Going to the top, he felt, was the route most likely to produce quick results. On March 31, 1946, he wrote a long obsequious letter to Chiang setting out his views on the need to forge special post-war ties between Japan and China. In it he assumed the self-appointed role of intermediary between the Chinese leader and the Japanese Emperor.

Tsuji later claimed that at one point in the letter he told Chiang: "I know I am being presumptuous, but I believe that I have not been able to come here by my virtue alone, but by the guidance of the gods and that I have been entrusted with the mission of meeting Your Excellency directly, to report His Majesty's Imperial will and to take the first step in establishing eternal Japan-China friendship and collaboration."

Chiang did not take the bait and Tsuji never got to meet the Chinese leader. Still, it remains an historical fact that the KMT's intelligence activity in Japan, from that period onwards, became directed primarily towards effecting Sino-Japanese collaboration. The American assessment saw the Nationalists' long range objective as the realisation of a Sino-Japanese bloc or Asiatic union comparable to the former Japanese idea of a Greater East Asia Co-Prosperity Sphere. Only this time, predicted US intelligence reports, China was planning to be the sponsor and leading power.

The trend worried some Americans. Recognising that sound economic cooperation between Japan and China was "necessary and desirable for both countries," one US intelligence history of the period went on to argue that there remained an inherent subversive potential in such a relationship. The idea of "Asia for the Asiatics" could be propagated among susceptible Japanese to the detriment of

United States prestige and interests.

It is not that Tsuji was instrumental in influencing China's foreign affairs thinking at this juncture. Rather, his views were uncannily close to the official Chungking line and his letter to Chiang seems to have helped him establish his bona fides in very senior Chinese circles.

On June 30, the Nationalists transferred Tsuji to Nanking where he was first given a position in the Defence Department's information section located on the second floor of the old Central Military Academy building on Wangpoo Road. There Tsuji came into contact with other Japanese military escapees in situations similar to his own. The Nationalist Chinese were tapping Japanese military expertise for their burgeoning struggle against the communists. Furthermore, they were clearly willing to overlook past misdeeds providing the prospective employee's special talents were considered valuable enough. In Tsuji's case, the Chinese were under no illusions about his background and had complete reports of his activities in Singapore, as well.

Through fellow Japanese advisers, Tsuji learned that his old friend Hattori, who had been captured in China, was now back in Tokyo. He had been sent back in May, 1946. Tsuji at first thought, not unreasonably, that Hattori had been designated a war criminal. Had it been so, he would later write, "I could not stay idle like this in China. I should present myself and take over the whole responsibility for any of the crimes attributed to him." This is a particularly interesting reaction raising a string of questions as to the extent to which Imperial Headquarters were directly involved in both the Singapore massacres and the Bataan Death March.

Tsuji eventually established that Hattori was back in Tokyo, not as a war criminal, but as an employee of the Americans. He was working as chief of the Repatriation Agency's investigation department but was also on the payroll of American military intelligence. Part of his official job was to identify home-coming

Japanese wanted by the Allies. Tsuji could hardly believe his good fortune. Within weeks he had contacted Hattori and set up a private channel of communications the two could use whenever they wanted to make contact.

While working for the information section, Tsuji compiled a comprehensive reference manual for military operations in extreme winter conditions. As a result of the manual's enthusiastic reception by senior Nationalist Army officers, he was moved to a sensitive intelligence unit known as the Third Research Group, located on Nanking's Chien-yeh road. The unit was headed by Lt. General Cheng Chieh-min and functioned under the code cover of "The Bamboo Shelter." After several months, "The Bamboo Shelter" moved to Kiangsu road and as the Chinese became more appreciative of the work undertaken by Tsuji, his restrictions were gradually relaxed. He was even granted limited access to some of the Japanese war criminals undergoing sentences in the Nanking Jail.

In mid-1947, "The Bamboo Shelter" operation was dissolved and Tsuji's three Japanese companions there returned quietly to Tokyo. Tsuji asked them to sound out the climate in Japan to see if it was safe for him to return.

By now, the "god of strategy" was homesick, depressed and lonely. What was more, he was growing increasingly disillusioned with the Nationalist Chinese whom he regarded as unconscionably corrupt. He also saw them becoming increasingly inept from a military standpoint and personally doubted whether they would still control China in a further two years. In the midst of his depression, Tsuji received a message from Hattori. His friend was advising him to remain in China for another six months. Tsuji would later write: "In all my 20 years of army life I never felt as grateful for a trustworthy senior as Hattori. If any other man had given me such a warning I might not have listened. However, I felt that I should follow Hattori's advice unconditionally."

During the next six months, Tsuji worked on translating and

reorganising a massive Japanese military report entitled "The Industrial and Military Potentials of the Soviet Union." The report had taken the intelligence section of the Japanese Kwantung Army over five years to compile and was completed shortly before the war ended. The Japanese study had been buried at Mukden, Manchuria, by the unit responsible for its production. Discovering its existence, the Americans dug it up and crated it ready for transportation to Washington. But a Nationalist Chinese intelligence operation spirited the crates away before shipment could be effected.

Once again, Tsuji's KMT employers were grateful for his labours. So much so, that, when he finally approached them for permission to return to Japan, they acceded to his wishes, creating none of the severance problems he had anticipated.

Again, he resorted to his passion for disguise. On May 16, 1948, Tsuji boarded a ship in the port of Shanghai with the identification papers of Professor Kenshin Aoki, from the Classical History Department at the University of Peking. He had, of course, notified Hattori in advance of his travel arrangements and his intended masquerade. When the ship arrived at the port of Sasebo, Kyushu, on May 26, the slightly stooped, eccentric-looking academic in round, rimless glasses aroused no suspicion ∎

Chapter 17

Confusing the chase

————— ◆ —————

I n order to examine the effectiveness of Allied efforts to trace Tsuji during this period, we must roll back the calendar to the immediate post-war weeks.

The chronology of events associated with early British attempts to come to grips with the Tsuji case now becomes critical to our investigations.

It will be recalled that Major Cyril Wild emerged from incarceration as a prisoner of war and joined the War Crimes Section in Singapore in early September, 1945.

It was on September 7 that the War Office in London finally issued its first directives on the procedures for handling war criminals and war crimes trials. The clear indication was that Britain had failed to make any early preparations for establishing the necessary administrative framework for such work and was thus caught badly lagging when the Japanese capitulated.

On September 18, Wild, fired with enthusiasm for his new job, submitted to Admiral Lord Louis Mountbatten's SACSEA High Command his first "wanted" list of Japanese suspects. The name of Staff Officer Ichiji Sugita, intelligence chief for General Yamashita's 25th Army, was No 2 on this list. But we now know it took Wild almost a year to have Sugita arrested. Japanese delaying tactics in Tokyo were partly to blame. But British military bureaucracy was also a factor.

In February, 1946, the uniquely qualified Wild was

appointed head of war crimes investigations in Malaya and Singapore. He received an immediate promotion to full colonel, an elevation which provided him a rank commensurate with the position and responsibilities he had assumed. .

Once again, the figure of Grenadier Guards officer, Captain Richard Crewdson, enters the picture. A brief assignment to Singapore in March, 1946, was aimed at providing him personal experience in dealing with Japanese war criminals before being dispatched to a sensitive posting in Tokyo. He was attached to the War Crimes South East Asian headquarters located in the distinctive old tower block of the Goodwood Park Hotel, and for several weeks assisted on the defence side of a number of trials.

In April, 1946, the United Kingdom War Crimes Liaison Mission opened in Tokyo. Late the following month, Crewdson flew in to join the mission as its official arresting officer. His task was to identify, track down and arrest suspects believed to have returned to Japan. The basic information on which he operated was fed to Tokyo, via the Singapore headquarters, by the 17 British investigating teams operating throughout the South East Asian region.

Crewdson and his fellow UK Liaison Mission colleagues functioned from offices within the Legal Section of General Douglas MacArthur's Supreme Commander Allied Powers (SCAP) organisation. The Legal Section, comprising a powerful US investigations department, an apprehension department, numerous attorneys and a big administration unit, was on the seventh and eighth floors of the Meiji Building. SCAP headquarters were in the Dai-Ichi Building, two blocks away.

Within a week of arriving in the Japanese capital, Crewdson had received from Singapore his first "wanted" list. It had been prepared through the facilities of the war crimes registry which, by then, was well established at the Goodwood Park and functioning from an area occupied today by the hotel's Tudor Ballroom.

On the initial list were a total of 12 names. Two of them, though wrongly spelt, had a familiar ring to the newly posted arresting officer. Later that week, a further two names were cabled from Singapore to be added to the original 12. One of these, again wrongly spelt, also seemed familiar to Crewdson.

The British officer hurried to SCAP headquarters to enlist the assistance of experts in the department headed by MacArthur's Assistant Chief of Staff, Intelligence, Major General Charles Willoughby. There, with the aid of a detailed card index of senior Japanese officers, Crewdson confirmed his suspicions. Three of the first 14 names he had been given were, in fact, misspelt variations of the same wanted man — his old Bangkok quarry, Colonel Masanobu Tsuji. Crewdson corrected the spelling, obtained accurate identification information via the American network and submitted, as required under the regulations, what he believes to have been the first formal British request to SCAP for Tsuji's arrest. It was now the final week of May, 1946.

Crewdson began developing his own card index system where, among other details, he noted the crimes for which the various suspects were wanted. His card index would expand from 14 to over 2,000 names within the next 18 months. Today he can clearly recall that Tsuji was initially wanted for three separate atrocities. Two in Singapore —the Alexandra Hospital Massacre and the Chinese Massacre — and the third in Burma involving an internment camp case. Pointedly, the latter case was unrelated to the Parker execution.

By this stage Wild had personally taken control of investigations into both the Alexandra Hospital and Chinese massacres. Thus, he was almost certainly the source of the two original Singapore requests to Tokyo for the apprehension of Tsuji. Crewdson speculates that the confused garbling of names probably occurred within War Crimes' headquarters. He makes the point that similar inefficiencies within the system relating to improper identification of suspects undermined the effective functioning of the UK War Crimes mission in Tokyo for months.

But the clear indication is that Wild, at least by the end of May, 1946, had indeed grasped the significance of Tsuji's role in the Chinese Massacre affair. That Wild was also after the missing staff officer in connection with the inexplicably brutal killing of over 200 patients and staff at Alexandra Hospital, only hours before the British surrender, provides another fascinating aspect that we will examine later.

Mid-1946 was approaching. In Singapore, the British had already begun prosecuting those Japanese suspects who had been relatively easy to identify and locate. One of the earliest arrests was a 35-year-old kempeitai warrant officer called Tadamori Monai.

He had been apprehended in October 1945 at Bangkok, flown back to Singapore and charged in the infamous "Double Tenth" case. The case took its name from the date — October 10, 1943 — when the kempeitai authorised the round up of suspected spies among Changi Jail's civilian inmates. There followed numerous associated raids against local civilians living in different parts of Singapore. The kempeitai were endeavouring to identify an espionage network they believed had assisted a successful Australian commando raid against Japanese shipping in Singapore Harbour.

Among those seized for interrogation was Mrs Elizabeth Choy, to whom we have already referred in Chapter 5. Also arrested was her husband, Koon Heng. Wife and husband were incarcerated separately at the kempeitai headquarters in the old YMCA building on Orchard Road. Both were subjected to torture and at one point were instructed to bid their final farewells as, according to their interrogators, they were to be executed. As War Crimes gathered evidence in the case it was not long before investigators were taking statements from the Choys. The couple subsequently went on to swear formal affidavits telling of their experiences as captives

Kempeitai Warrant Officer Tadamori Monai, sentenced to death for torturing prisoners at Singapore's YMCA building on Orchard Road. During a death cell interrogation, he provided the British with startling information about Lt. Colonel Masanobu Tsuji's October, 1945, disappearance from Bangkok.

The old YMCA on Orchard Road, now demolished and replaced by a new building, was the main kempeitai interrogation and detention centre. This is where Warrant Officer Monai tortured Mrs Elizabeth Choy and her husband.

of the Japanese.

Mrs Choy was able to identify Monai as the man who had tortured her in front of her husband. Monai had made her kneel, stripped to the waist, holding chains above her head. He had finally tied her to a frame and administered electrical shocks. Her evidence helped convict Monai who, on April 15, 1946, was sentenced to death.

Changi Jail authorities scheduled Monai's execution for July 11. A fortnight before the condemned warrant officer was to die, he was visited by a member of British military intelligence. As a result of this death row meeting, the intelligence unit in Singapore issued a lengthy secret report. Furthermore, urgent messages were dispatched to Bangkok for renewed efforts to track down the elusive Tsuji. Monai, in his final days, had provided the British with their most comprehensive rundown, thus far, on Tsuji's escape. More important still, he had furnished alarming information as to possible reasons why the colonel had chosen to make his getaway.

The report explained the unusual circumstances under which the information had been gathered. It began:

Source (Monai) *is condemned to die within two weeks. He has been in gaol at Outram Rd and Changi since October last year awaiting trial. Now that his trial is over and his fate decided, he has volunteered all the information he has concerning a stay-behind organisation in Bangkok with possible ramifications in French Indo-China and other parts of South East Asia, an organisation which has as its goal the rebirth of Japan as a military nation and another war within 30 years to wipe out the shame of the 1945 surrender.*

Source explains his reasons for revealing this information as follows:

(a) He is condemned to death. For him, it is all over. He is receiving the just punishment for his crimes in Singapore and is quite prepared to die. However, before he dies, out of love for his

country, he considers it his duty to reveal the intentions of a few proud militarists, who, regardless of the misery they and their class have brought upon the Japanese people by their ambition and their fanaticism, firmly intend once more to plunge the nation even into worse trouble as soon as they get the opportunity.

(b) These fanatics represent the Military Clique (Gunbatsu); the Gunbatsu which was responsible for starting the war; the Gunbatsu which refused to accept any responsibility for the many crimes committed by individuals who had been working in accordance with the doctrines and policy laid down by the Gunbatsu.

Monai went on to identify Tsuji as a *Gunbatsu* member and leader of the stay-behind organisation. According to Monai, the Japanese military had falsely reported Tsuji killed in action. The truth, he said, was that Tsuji and some young probationary officers had gone into hiding in one of the many Bangkok temples, disguised as Buddhist monks. The report continued:

"Source also heard that Colonel Tsuji was shortly to link up with the stay-behind organisation in French Indo-China of which he will assume command, probably leaving Lt. Colonel Ishida in command of the Bangkok organisation.

In concluding comments, the intelligence officer who conducted the interrogation noted:

"It is felt that in the meantime, there is not much more information that can be obtained from Warrant Officer Monai on this subject. He does not even pretend to have anything more to say which might justify a delay in his execution.

There was no delay. Monai was sent to the gallows, as scheduled, at dawn on July 11.

The Monai report provided an entirely new emphasis to the Tsuji case. It focused on Tsuji, the hard-core desperado, now pledged to reverse the shame of Japan's defeat through yet another massive military showdown within three decades. The spectre of Japan rising from the ashes of defeat, led essentially by the same Gunbatsu fanatics the Allies had been battling for three and a half years, was obviously a matter of grave concern.

But did the suddenly threatening image of the committed warmonger who conveniently had sizable financial resources at his disposal, eclipse that of the wanted mass killer? Were Wild's requirements superseded by misdirected High Command agitation over the implications of the Monai report?

Indications certainly are that the British military authorities in Singapore took the Monai report very seriously; passing it on to the Americans with high ratings for its credibility. Moreover, it seems the report indeed jolted the Americans into action.

Here we must return to the July 8, 1946, special memorandum, prepared by Captain Schneider, chief of the US War Crimes Office in Singapore, and mentioned in chapter 15. This discussed details of the beheading of Lieutenant Parker in Burma and identified Colonel Tsuji and Lieutenant Sekimoto as the Japanese involved in the atrocity. The date of the memorandum, July 8, is significant. It indicates the report was written exactly ten days after Monai's death row interrogation.

The final paragraph of the memorandum states that investigations had failed to disclose the whereabouts of both Tsuji and Sekimoto.

"Colonel Tsuji is listed by the Japanese Army Headquarters as missing, but he is believed by British Intelligence to be operating close to the Siamese-French Indo-China border. Lt. Sekimoto was transferred shortly after V-J Day from Bangkok to French Indo-China and was attached to Hqs Imperial Japanese Army of the Southern Regions until about 20 January, 1946, at which

time he is alleged to have deserted. Subsequently, after being pressed on the matter, the Japanese headquarters submitted proof of his suicide. However, it is believed that this report is false and that Lt. Sekimoto escaped into the country and has joined Colonel Tsuji and are (sic) *operating a renegade group near the Siam-French Indo-China border."*

Captain Schneider interestingly concluded his memorandum with the statement:

"This matter has been discussed with British Intelligence, Singapore, and they have agreed to co-operate in locating Colonel Tsuji and Lt. Sekimoto, and to keep American authorities informed as to any progress."

Thus, in late May the UK Military Liaison Mission in Tokyo was formally requesting the Americans to help track down Tsuji in Japan. Five weeks later, British intelligence in Singapore was promising to assist the Americans trace the same man in South East Asia.

Bureaucratic blinkers and lack of departmental coordination aside, Tsuji had clearly been the subject of detailed discussions between the American and British intelligence teams in Singapore during the first week of July. But Captain Schneider's memorandum reveals that the British military in Singapore, perhaps blinded by the apparent threat of Tsuji's continuing pro-war activities, were now somehow decidedly less interested in linking him to the Singapore massacres. Neither were the Americans associating him in any way with the Bataan Death March. The US wanted the runaway staff officer solely for the execution of Lieutenant Parker in Mangshih.

In short, it was as late as mid-1946 before British and American military intelligence operations began jointly recognising the fact that Tsuji indeed had a background worth investigating. It was only then that they established a working liaison in the field aimed at tracking the man down. The problem was, when they finally initiated follow-up measures, these seemed to ignore completely the work of Wild, the one man who probably best understood the case. Instead, they focused on areas of Tsuji's wartime past which, though serious, were deceptively unrelated to the truly monstrous crimes he had perpetrated. Then, of course, it was too late. By this time the "god of strategy" was safely ensconced in China, working for Generalissimo Chiang Kai-shek ■

Chapter 18

Saved . . . by British bureaucracy and American intelligence!

————— ✦ —————

A s the Tokyo summer of 1946 gave way to autumn, Captain Richard Crewdson and his UK Liaison Mission colleagues became increasingly convinced that the fugitive Tsuji was the most important of all Japanese war criminal suspects wanted by the Allies.

Acting on his recollections of Bangkok, the British arresting officer, with the assistance of SCAP's investigations section, identified members of Tsuji's family and arranged for secret monitoring of their individual bank accounts. If the missing staff officer attempted transferring some of the funds he had taken for his escape from Siam, there was a good chance of tracing him through the remittance details; whether these originated in Japan or somewhere in South East Asia.

The Liaison Mission staff also collected as many photographs of Tsuji as they could. These were dispatched to the Singapore registry with requests that copies be distributed to all Allied commands and investigation teams in the Asian area. As the months passed, Allied intelligence reports, relevant to the South East Asian theatre, flowed across Crewdson's desk. From time to time there would be mention of Tsuji. When this occurred the information would be extracted and placed on file.

Crewdson recalls Colonel Wild's arrival in Tokyo in August, 1946. The two men discussed the need to improve interrogation techniques in the field and coordination of information handling between the Singapore registry and Tokyo. Wild promised to take remedial measures, requested his Tokyo arresting officer fly back to Singapore later in the year for consultations, flew off and was killed in the Hong Kong air crash. Crewdson remembers the loss of Wild had an immediate and lasting impact on Britain's South East Asian war crimes operation. Particularly noticeable thereafter was Singapore's rapidly declining interest in the Tsuji case.

In early April, 1947, the two death penalties and five terms of life imprisonment were handed down at the end of the Chinese Massacre trial. Later that same month, an American report on the interrogation of Lt. General Kiyoo Yamamoto, a 54-year-old father of seven who had been Chief-of-Staff of the Japanese 33rd Army in Burma, landed on Crewdson's desk. In it Yamamoto testified that Tsuji had personally told him about executing the American airman in Mangshih and eating his flesh.

In a subsequent interrogation, Yamamoto revealed he had punished his subordinate officer by, four months later, reducing his pay. Here, finally, was firm evidence of Tsuji admitting the atrocity. Perhaps this would prod Singapore from its apparent lethargy on the subject. Perhaps now the Americans would act with more determination.

Crewdson brought the reports to the attention of Lt. Colonel Nicholas Reid-Collins, head of the UK War Crimes Mission in Tokyo, who was equally convinced of the need to track down and seize Tsuji. Together, the two officers did their best to generate heightened interest in the case.

Crewdson's file had, from the outset, identified Hayashi and Asaeda as Tsuji's two "disciples" in Singapore. In the meantime, painstaking enquiries had confirmed Hayashi's death in a wartime air crash. Asaeda, on the other hand, had been traced to a Russian prison camp in Siberia.

On April 3, 1947, Reid-Collins wrote to the British Embassy in Tokyo forwarding the names of five Japanese war crimes suspects required for trial in South East Asia. All five had been confirmed by the Soviet authorities as in Soviet custody.

Major Shigeharu Asaeda was the third name on the list. The details showed he was wanted on two charges. The second one read:

That he aided and abetted, while an executive staff officer HQ 25 Army, the massacre of 5,000 Chinese by troops of the 25 Army at Singapore, February, 1942.

Reid-Collins' letter went on:

It would be much appreciated if the Soviet Mission could be requested to deliver these suspects to British custody at the British Consulate, Shanghai, British Minor War Crimes Liaison Section, Tokyo, War Crimes Investigation Unit, Hong Kong, or to any other convenient American or British Agency.

His letter concluded:

Please may this be treated as urgent.

Two weeks later, the British Chancery in Tokyo forwarded a copy of Reid-Collins' request to the Foreign Office War Crimes Section in London.

The Chancery officer noted that, from past experience, it was considered difficult getting results in matters of this sort by dealing with the Russian Mission in Tokyo.

In a piece of classic diplomatic buck-passing he suggested that if a determined effort was to be made to get the Russians to hand over the suspects, it would best be done on a government level through the British Embassy in Moscow. Reinforcing his decision to do nothing, he added:

On the other hand, it is for consideration whether it would not be better to say nothing at all to the Russians and simply wait until the wanted persons are returned to Japan in the normal course of repatriation. We ourselves feel that once the names of the suspects are divulged, it will afford the authorities in the USSR an extra hold over the individuals who may choose to remain "voluntarily" in Russian territory.

Predictably, the Foreign Office concurred with their man in Tokyo and wrote to the Judge Advocate General's Department on May 13, 1947, agreeing that the best approach was certainly to do nothing. Two weeks later, back came confirmation to the Foreign Office from the Judge Advocate General's department:

It is agreed that it is useless to approach the Russians about those people and that the only course is to wait in the hope that some of them may turn up in Japan.

This perfunctory exercise in international paper shuffling would have been amusing were it not for the fact that one of the war criminal suspects, Asaeda, was wanted for aiding and abetting a crime involving the slaughter of 5,000 civilians! Tragically, this was not an isolated example of the bureaucracy encountered by Allied investigators trying to track down Japanese war criminals. Similar intellectual indolence allowed literally hundreds of suspects to escape prosecution.

The more Crewdson worked on the Tsuji case, the more frustrating it became for him. In June, 1947, he flew to Hong Kong and Singapore in an effort to upgrade the general processing of information through the War Crimes communications system. He returned via Bangkok were he was disappointed to learn that British investigators there had all but forgotten the case of the missing Japanese staff officer.

Shigaharu Asaeda, now living in retirement in Tokyo, ponders his Pacific War memorabilia. Originally chosen by Tsuji because of his fearlessness and knowledge of intelligence gathering, Asaeda became a close associate of his mentor both in Malaya and Singapore and in Japan after the war.

An official certificate of gratitude awarded to Shigaharu Asaeda on September 20, 1988. It expresses "heartfelt appreciation" for Asaeda's suffering during his "enforced detention" in Siberia after World War 11. The certificate is signed by the then Japanese Prime Minister Toshiki Kaifu.

Back in Tokyo, he confided in Reid-Collins his fear that Britain's drive to bring Japanese war criminals to justice in South East Asia was slowing down.

One morning in early November, a knock on the door of Crewdson's eighth floor office, overlooking the Imperial Palace, announced the arrival of an assistant to the head of SCAP's Legal Section. Colonel Alva C. Carpenter was extending his compliments and wanted to see Crewdson in his office immediately.

Crewdson hurried down to Colonel Carpenter's room on the seventh floor. There he was introduced to a Major who had come specially for the meeting from the office of General Charles A. Willoughby, the SCAP's controversial intelligence overlord.

"We have some important information to pass on to you, " Colonel Carpenter told his British visitor.

The American officer continued: "It appears that our friend, Colonel Tsuji, has joined General Chiang Kai-shek in the fight against the communists in China. In the circumstances, General Willoughby asks that the United Kingdom drops her efforts to trace this officer and, in addition, all plans to prosecute him."

Concealing his astonishment, Crewdson replied: "This is an interesting development, sir. I'm sure Colonel Reid-Collins would wish to consult Singapore before making any comment."

Taking his leave, the British officer headed straight for Reid-Collins' eighth floor office to report his conversation with Carpenter. Reid-Collins was flabbergasted. "They can't do this," he stormed. "I'll send a cable to Singapore immediately. I'm sure they won't agree."

Reid-Collins began working on the cable, choosing his words carefully. His aim was to phrase the message in such a way that Singapore would understand the Liaison Mission in Tokyo was clearly eager for a rejection of Willoughby's approach. In the body of the cable was the suggestion that the added weight of Britain's Tokyo Embassy might be helpful in countering the American proposal.

Both Crewdson and Reid-Collins were under the impression — wrongly as we will soon establish — that the request to drop the Tsuji case had originated from Chiang Kai-shek himself. Singapore, they felt, would arrive at the same conclusion. They therefore worried whether a desk officer, sitting in the Goodwood Park Hotel, would be prepared to take a firm stand, given the possible political implications involved.

They had their answer in a little over 24 hours. Singapore, to their disgust, acquiesced. An angry Crewdson returned to Colonel Carpenter's office to report: "You can have your man, Tsuji, sir."

Four months later — on an afternoon in March, 1948 — Crewdson was in his office interrogating a Japanese soldier. The prisoner, a private who had been a farmer in civilian life, was in the process of making a full confession to the torture and murder of several civilians at the Cold Storage premises on Singapore's Orchard Road. It was a particularly brutal case. The victims had been strung up by rope and beaten to death. Assisting Crewdson during the interrogation were an interpreter, a US Nisei sergeant and a Japanese policeman.

At a tense point in the questioning, the door opened and Reid-Collins strode into the room clutching a cable which he handed to Crewdson without comment. The arresting officer read the brief message from Singapore headquarters. It informed that Britain's South East Asian war crimes work was to be wound down. The Tokyo team was ordered to drop all cases, release all Japanese suspects being held in Sugamo Prison — some 50 men — and prepare to close down the office.

A cable was quickly sent back to the Goodwood Park headquarters informing of the Japanese private's complete confession to charges of multiple murder and emphasising that reactions of this nature were rare. It explained how months of exhausting police work had gone into locating the suspect, and sought permission to proceed with the prosecution of this one last case.

The interrogation continued the following day while Crewdson awaited Singapore's final reply. When it came, it said, quite simply, that the prisoner must be set free immediately. All war crimes trials were to cease.

The UK War Crimes Liaison Mission in Tokyo wrapped up its operations within eight weeks. Crewdson flew out in late May. On May 26, perhaps two or three days after the British arresting officer's departure, Tsuji, in his Peking University professor disguise, returned to Japan through the port of Sasebo ∎

Chapter 19

The god's homecoming

———— ✦ ————

Tsuji's disguise and a lot of help from his friends saw him safely through Sasebo's customs and immigration formalities. Once home he became quickly and secretly cocooned in a network of old military cronies headed by the ever loyal Hattori.

Hattori, by this time, had transferred from the murky investigative side of the Repatriation Agency to the even murkier world of the US Civil Intelligence Section (CIS) under the leadership of MacArthur's controversial intelligence chief, Major General Charles Willoughby.

In order to understand this phase of Tsuji's escape, we must look briefly at the impact Willoughby's octopus-like activities were having on occupied Japan.

When the CIS began operations in October 1945, one of its primary functions was the apprehension of war criminals and the purging of irresponsible militarists and ultranationalists who had led Japan to war in the first place. This conformed with the overall grand objective of America's military occupation which was essentially the smooth democratization of the defeated nation and its eventual emergence as a pro-American, North East Asian buffer against the spread of communism. But as the months passed, the CIS gradually changed its focus of attention. By early 1948 the Section's operational interests had dramatically swung from "rightwing extremists" to "leftwing subversives."

As Japan struggled with the psychological and economic traumas of the early occupation, it was not surprising that the country's overwhelmingly socialist trade unions simmered with dissent; much of it expressed in Marxist phraseology. Communist infiltration of the labour movement was taking place. To what extent these developments posed a direct threat to America's long term ambitions in Japan was a matter of continuing debate. For his part, the arrogant and autocratic Willoughby seized the communist bogey and ran with it. His right wing militarist views began dictating entirely new policy directions in the sensitive intelligence gathering and counter-intelligence fields. Similarly, the delicate Japanese demobilisation and disarmament programmes, which so many faceless American civilian officials were working quietly to complete, became instant targets for operational intriguing by the man they variously referred to as "Baron von Willoughby," "Sir Charles," and "Charles the Terrible."

Born the son of a baron in Heidelberg, Germany, on March 8, 1892, Karl von Tscheppe-Weidenbach changed his name to Charles Andrew Willoughby soon after arriving in the United States in 1910. He became a naturalised citizen and enlisted in the US Army as a Second Lieutenant in 1916. As a member of the American Expeditionary Force, he saw action on the Mexican border chasing the renegade Pancho Villa. After graduating from Infantry School in 1919 and the Fort Leavenworth Command and Staff School in 1930, Willoughby was eventually assigned to the Philippines. In 1941 he became General MacArthur's assistant Chief of Staff, Intelligence, and served in this capacity throughout the Pacific War and in occupied Japan until his retirement in 1951. During this latter period, senior Tokyo-based UK officials, both military and civilian, recognised the US intelligence chief as positively anti-British, a characteristic they attributed to his

Germanic background.

As Willoughby's preoccupation with communism intensified into outright obsession, his extremist views began paralleling those of the old guard Japanese militarists.

A close working relationship had developed between Willoughby and the head of Japanese military intelligence, General Seizo Arisue. Theirs was a bond sealed by mutual anti-communist goals. Through Arisue, Willoughby employed a large number of senior Japanese officers under the general cover of assistants attached to an historical research project. They were given the nominal task of recording Pacific war developments from the Japanese viewpoint.

In fact, the historical research operation was primarily a camouflage for Willoughby's extraordinary personal plot to retain, in an accessible situation, the ready-made core of a Japanese anti-communist army. It was to this core that Willoughby, in mid-1947, transferred the able and ambitious Colonel Takushiro Hattori as leader after his year-long stint in the Repatriation Agency. Hattori now enjoyed the prestige of a private office, a Tokyo staff, and a network of some 60 officers fully paid and positioned throughout the country. He soon became one of Willoughby's closest and most trusted advisors and, before long, the historical research project was being referred to as "Hattori's Agency."

So, when the time came, Hattori was admirably placed to assist in the return of the old warrior Tsuji to the bosom of his homeland; albeit a return somewhat marred by the historical complications of two major massacres, a few individual murders, and a spot of cannibalism.

Hattori's initial objective, from the time Tsuji first made contact in Nanking, was to confirm he could open the right doors in Tokyo and at the same time guarantee his friend's safety from arrest. Playing it cautiously, Hattori resolved to tackle the problem from two separate angles.

The first was to use his influence to persuade the Americans

US Military Intelligence Chief in occupied Japan, Major General Charles. A. Willoughby. Referred to by detractors as "Baron von Willoughby," his politics, aggressive style and frequently outlandish plots made him the scourge of many an American official trying to heal the war-ravaged land. His intervention in the Tsuji case proved critical. After retirement from the US army, Willoughby spent much of his time editing, writing and publicising anti-communist Cold War themes. He also worked as a consultant to Spanish dictator Generalissimo Franco.

that Tsuji's anti-communist bona fides, together with his renowned planning skills, made him a valuable property for post-war Japan; and one thus worth protecting. The second was to get the Americans committed to rescinding Tsuji's war criminal status so that ultimately he would be in the clear.

Both angles demanded the active participation of Willoughby.

Willoughby, as it happened, needed little persuasion. He regarded Tsuji's talents, as outlined by Hattori, as just what Japan needed at that critical stage of her re-birth as a nation. But there was one sticking point. Both British and American war crimes investigators had been pressing for the fugitive staff officer's apprehension. Willoughby knew he could handle the American side with little difficulty. He would need time to convince the British to call off the hounds.

It was then that Hattori advised his friend in Nanking, via their private communications channel, that he should resolve to remain where he was for another six months. In fact it would be closer to eight months before Willoughby gave Hattori the nod that Tsuji could return to Japan. The understanding was that he should remain incognito until such time as his war criminal status was formally wiped clean.

Willoughby's decision to seek the UK War Crimes Section's agreement to dropping the Tsuji hunt, was greatly influenced by classified information he was receiving from Washington. Britain, he was told, could be expected to close down her Tokyo Liaison Mission by mid-1948 and wrap-up all South East Asian war criminal trials by the end of the same year.

Chiang Kai-shek made no representations whatever on Tsuji's behalf, although there were obvious advantages for Willoughby if the British thought he had. Indeed, Tsuji first signalled to the Chinese his wish to return to Japan some weeks before Willoughby's approach to the UK Tokyo Liaison Mission. In short, Willoughby's actions were purely directed at preparing the grounds for the mass killer's safe and secret return to Japan.

Clearly, Willoughby and Hattori had hoped their beneficiary's clandestine lifestyle would be short-lived and that he would soon be enjoying the full protection provided to all employees of the historical research project. But then came a serious hiccough. The British, having closed down their Military Liaison Office in Tokyo, suddenly reversed their decision to drop the Tsuji case. The Americans were told that the fugitive was now to be vigorously pursued and, if apprehended, brought to trial.

This occurred round August, 1948, at a time when Tsuji was shuttling between safe houses in Yoshinoyama, Tajima, Asama, Kyushu-Omura and Okutama and working on his first book, the memoirs of his escape. Britain's change of heart closely followed the high level military meetings in Singapore, referred to in chapter 13, and the formal re-opening the "Chinese Massacre" case. It was an unprecedented turn of events that amounted to official acceptance that a serious error had been made with the "Chinese Massacre" trial the previous year.

Apparently oblivious to Willoughby's real motives in the Tsuji case, the British once again sought the assistance of US military intelligence. Reliable reports reaching Singapore were placing Tsuji back in his homeland and "underground." Could the Americans assist? The answer from the Willoughby network was in the affirmative and inter-departmental British communications reassuringly reported, "American intelligence is helping."

Reality was quite the opposite. American intelligence was positively hindering; although in fairness, officials in Washington probably had no indication whatever that the British were being purposefully hoodwinked by the Willoughby operation.

It is inconceivable that MacArthur's assistant Chief-of-Staff was ignorant of the wanted man's background. His own intelligence reports had finally begun piecing together the truth of the Bataan Death March, two years after the pathetic Homma had been subjected to nothing less than a US kangaroo court and executed for crimes against American and Filipino forces largely perpetrated by Tsuji. In Willoughby's own intelligence files was a thick dossier on how Tsuji had beheaded the US airman in Burma. By then there was also the report confirming that the culprit had admitted his crime to a senior fellow officer. All this had been accumulating since the very first report of the incident filed on May 18, 1945. In addition, there was Britain's on-again off-again insistence that Tsuji be arrested and charged with the Singapore massacres.

By all accounts, Tsuji was the most insidious, calculating, coldly brutal and singularly successful mass killer in the entire Japanese war criminal line up. Fully recognising this, Willoughby and Hattori went right ahead and conspired to doublecross the British, thereby ensuring Tsuji would remain untraced, would never face trial, and would escape all punishment.

In essence, the Willoughby/Hattori plan was to keep the British misinformed and at the same time ensure their protege remained safely concealed until the crisis had subsided. At a chosen time, his war criminal status would be lifted and employment quietly arranged.

Towards late 1949, when Hattori felt the main threat had subsided, he organised a small reunion at his home. Tsuji was there. Also in attendance was Asaeda, Tsuji's assistant in Singapore. Asaeda had recently returned to Japan from detention under the Russians in Siberia; just as the British Embassy in Tokyo had predicted he would. Only Asaeda, like Tsuji, returned after the UK Liaison Mission closed shop. Asaeda, too, was hiding from the Allied war crimes authorities. He, too, was seeking a job within Willoughby's intelligence empire. He, too, had Hattori as his mentor.

The following account of a statement made by Tsuji at this reunion has been verified for us by Asaeda.

Overcome with emotion at seeing his Singapore side-kick, Tsuji, with tears running down his cheeks, told Asaeda: "I see you managed to get back safely. Your return has become news, even in the papers. The British also know. They'll ask MacArthur to hand you over. This is terrible. I must do what I can."

The three friends were soon dining on *sukiyaki*. Tsuji, speaking briefly in the third person, continued: "As for the Singapore Chinese affair, that was Staff Officer Tsuji's campaign, an arbitrary action done without the permission of General Yamashita or Chief-of-Staff Suzuki."

Turning to Asaeda, Tsuji went on: "I'll admit everything. You're still young and must live on to fight for Japan's recovery. As for me, it doesn't matter if I die now."

This was clearly an astonishing offer. That the quotation has been confirmed as accurate by Asaeda amounts to final proof of Tsuji's true Singapore role.

Sensing that Tsuji was irritated at the lack of resolution of his status, Hattori interrupted: "Tsuji, leave it to me. Don't go that far. Even if you step forward and confess now, you'll just be sent back to Singapore and hanged. That would be a mistake. It would be a waste. You're needed for the future of Japan. I'll also speak to MacArthur about you."

Before the trio parted, Hattori urged both Asaeda and Tsuji to be patient. The administrative wheels were turning. It would be just a matter of time before their separate problems were resolved.

Asaeda's problems, as it happened, were solved within a matter a days. He was employed not only by Hattori's group, but also drew a salary from the fledgling US Central Intelligence Agency (CIA). He was attached to the CIA's Japanese network which then operated largely under the Willoughby umbrella, dispatching spies and moles to the Soviet Union and communist movements throughout Asia.

Tsuji's case, on the other hand, proved more difficult. The

British determination to bring him to trial at this point seemed unshakeable. Still, Hattori stayed in close touch and, as December 1949 approached, he was able to advise Tsuji that dramatic developments were about to take place. These came on December 4 when America revealed she was ready to sign a US-Japan Friendship Treaty.

Three days later, the US suffered an enormous blow to its prestige in the region. Chiang Kai-shek, the Chinese leader Washington had been stoutly backing for two decades, buckled under communist military pressure and retreated to Taiwan.

On New Year's Day, 1950, Tsuji's war criminal status was officially lifted by the Americans. Henceforth he could no longer be charged with any crime committed in pursuance of his country's dream of that East Asian Co-Prosperity Sphere. He was a free man. At the time he was hiding out in a large two-storey wooden house in Okutama-cho, Tokyo, still writing the memoirs of his escape.

He immediately left his hiding place and joined his wife and family in Setagaya, another section of Tokyo.

Tsuji completed his manuscript, deciding on the title "Praying for Asia." But the novelist, Eiji Yoshikawa, suggested instead "Underground Escape."

Tsuji agreed. Serialisation rights were sold to the Mainichi Magazine and, once again, he was at the centre of public attention.

Fearful that Tsuji's memoirs could prove a publishing hot potato, the magazine editor chose to play his serialisation carefully.

He wrote an introductory piece which said:

"We realise that the readers of this book *will be left with various impressions. The two or three pieces previously written by Tsuji have received a lot of criticism. Many people consider his writing presumptuous , coming from one who has returned to Japan in her present situation.*

"We fully expect further criticism of the writer and his publisher. That is fine. But we hope Japan will derive some future benefit from the public airing of these matters. If that happens, we will be very satisfied."

The magazine editor needn't have worried. *Underground Escape* proved highly popular as a magazine series and, when published in book form in August, 1950, became a run-away best seller. Overnight, Tsuji was transformed into one of the most recognised names in Japan.

The "god of strategy" had discovered that there truly was life after defeat. Literary success provided him a degree of wealth he had not enjoyed since lifting the military funds in Bangkok. It returned him the public adulation which he had missed and in which he revelled. But, above all, it once more provided him with that taste of power which he truly craved.

Regular employment in the Hattori agency added a sense of security and there was the added attraction that he was now engaged recording episodes of the Pacific War's history that would, in time, become basic reference documents. Indeed, defeat for the colonel was beginning to provide most agreeable compensations. Very soon, the heady world of politics would beckon and, being Tsuji, the temptation would be simply irresistible ■

Chapter 20

A new career

———— ✦ ————

Masanobu Tsuji, despite his megalomania, recognised that a man with his past and reputation would be compelled to make drastic readjustments in order to live as a prominent figure in immediate post-war Japan. His first book propelled him into the public arena, gave him instant celebrity status and indicated a likely grassroots political following, ready and waiting for exploitation.

At the same time, Tsuji was under no illusions about the strong feelings of animosity towards him within influential ex-servicemen's circles. Former middle ranking officers, over whom he had ridden roughshod throughout the Pacific War, were waiting to extract their revenge. There were also a number of senior officers who had suffered personal humiliation, even punishment, for crimes he had perpetrated. Tsuji knew they, too, would be just as eager to settle scores.

If he was to have any chance in politics, he would somehow have to make his peace with former senior military figures who could otherwise prove potent enemies. He decided on a most un-Japanese approach to the problem: personal confrontation.

One of the first comrades-in-arms tracked down by Tsuji was former 25th Army intelligence chief, Ichiji Sugita, the man who had been transferred to Singapore as a prime suspect in the Chinese Massacre affair, attempted suicide in custody, and was forced to give prosecution evidence at the trial. Now aged 88 and living in retirement in Tokyo, Sugita, who in the early

Sixties, went on to become Chief-of-Staff of Japan's Ground Self Defence Force, recalled for our researcher the day in 1950 when Tsuji paid him a visit.

"He came to apologise for the fact that he had run away, despite his responsibility, and this action had caused trouble for me, " Sugita explained.

"He was very humble. He chose his words for his apology very carefully. The apology really seemed to be from his heart."

Asked whether Tsuji was expressing his true emotions, Sugita replied: "Well, really I got the feeling he was doing it as a matter of form."

Had Tsuji offered any excuse for his behaviour?

"Nothing. He just apologised. We didn't sit down and chat or anything. I sat down here and he was way over there," said Sugita, indicating a position at the far end of the room.in which he was speaking. Sugita then demonstrated how Tsuji had bowed his head in a show of deep atonement.

During the same interview with our researcher, Sugita made plain his firm belief that Tsuji and Hayashi had been the ones responsible for the massacres in Singapore. Yamashita had given a general verbal order which, in Sugita's view, was never intended to kill large numbers of Chinese. Tsuji and Hayashi had conspired to exploit that order, he said.

Sugita went on to explain that Tsuji's motives for disappearing into China immediately after the Japanese surrender in August, 1945, had nothing to do with assisting the re-emergence of Japan. "He was escaping. Everyone believed he was responsible for various atrocities."

And the Chinese?

"From the Chinese point of view," said Sugita, "they saw Tsuji as someone they could use for their own benefit.

"He knew a lot about the situation in Japan. The Chinese would have asked him: 'Didn't you kill a lot of Chinese in Singapore?' Then they would have taken advantage of this threat and used him."

Tsuji's first book, *Underground Escape,* was published in June, 1950. Quickly following up this success, his second book, *Guadalcanal,* was in the bookshops before the end of the same year. By early 1952, his highly controversial account of the Malaya campaign, *Singapore: The Hinge of Fate,* was being avidly read by millions throughout Japan. In under two years he had emerged as one of his country's most widely recognised figures.

As the months passed and elections loomed, Tsuji arranged to give a public address on the evening of August 15, 1952, in Kanazawa, the capital of Ishikawa prefecture, some 200 miles north-west of Tokyo. The venue was to have been a small hall with an audience capacity of 500. When local police reported that the communist party was threatening to disrupt the event, Tsuji switched the time of his talk to 3 pm and the venue outside to the centrally located Kenroku Park. It was a shrewd decision. Some ten thousand people flocked to hear their favourite author and war hero deliver a two-hour lecture entitled "The Dawn of Asia."

Tsuji recounted and embellished episodes from his four and a half years on the run — a period he colourfully termed his "underground years." He spoke out strongly against both communism and the United States, declaring Soviet dictator Joseph Stalin and US President Harry S. Truman the world's two worst war criminals. He called for Japan to adopt a general policy of neutrality, but at the same time urged Asian economic co-prosperity based on close co-operation among the peoples of the region. .

Tsuji's speech was met with rapturous applause from the huge crowd which later hysterically mobbed him. On August 28, Prime Minister Seiichi Yoshida's cabinet was dissolved. Four days later, Tsuji called a press conference in Kanazawa to announce he would be standing as an independent candidate for Ishikawa's first district in the October 1 national polls He would be one of eight hopefuls in his home prefecture contesting three seats in the nation's House of Representatives.

Without the financial backing of a large party machine, Tsuji was forced to rely on an army of volunteers, many of them former rank and file soldiers. He met campaign expenses from the 500,000 yen advance he had received for film rights to *Underground Escape*. Wherever he went on the campaign trail, the mass-killer-turned-politician drew wildly enthusiastic crowds. On polling day, Tsuji won 64,913 votes in his district, 20,000 votes more than the next candidate.

Taking his seat in the Diet, Tsuji held on stoically to his independence, shunning any form of alignment to either the Yoshida government or the conservative anti-Yoshida faction. He made his maiden parliamentary speech exactly four weeks after the elections and spoke as a representative of the Diet's 20-strong grouping of non-aligned politicians.

He told the house that even though the government had assured Japan's National Security Forces would never be introduced to Korea, there were still widespread public fears over the dangers imposed by the nearby conflict. If the United States and the Soviet Union were drawn into open warfare, he postulated, the US Army would probably just abandon Japan.

"We should prepare our own defence forces and demand the withdrawal of all American troops from Japanese soil," he declared.

Attacking the government for failing to take adequate measures against the communists, he pointed contemptuously at left-wing seats in the house and proclaimed: "There are some Japanese who, under the pretext of Macarthur's constitution, are opposed even to military preparations for our own self-defence.

"But if the nation is ruined, can there be a peace constitution?"

Tsuji went on to demand concrete government plans for bolstering Japan's defence capability. He then wrapped up his remarks by directing a broadside at the establishment; tactics guaranteed to gain him nationwide publicity, if somewhat diminished contacts among fellow politicians. Why, he asked, at a time of financial suffering for the population at large, were Diet members seeking increases in their allowances? This was, he said, unforgivable!

For ex-officers who had known him on the battlefield, the speech was vintage Tsuji: glory-seeking, grandstanding and belligerently self-righteous. He glared, he remonstrated and above all, he talked down to everyone in the House. All that was missing was the "violence akin to madness."

It was too much for the gathered members. The house erupted and his closing passages became lost in the uproar. But Tsuji had made his mark on national politics, dealing with the Diet's Lower House in much the same way as he had steamrollered his way through Pacific theatre staff commands.

His speech set the pattern for his political career and observers soon began predicting a dynamic future for the new representative from Ishikawa Prefecture. He became widely recognised as a leading proponent of Japanese armed neutrality. He was also seen as anti-communist, anti-American, and strongly opposed to his country's Security Treaty with the US. To the delight of the masses, and particularly the Japanese press of the day, he remained an habitual critic of the costs of government, the country's renowned money politics, and corruption in high places.

By January, 1953, however, the backlash from former military officers feared by Tsuji since the day he emerged from hiding, had begun taking shape. Especially bitter in his public swipes before old Army colleagues was retired Major General Kiyotake Kawaguchi who had not long returned from six years incarceration as a war criminal in Manila's Muntinlupa Prison. That was his punishment for the murder of Philippine Chief Justice Jose Abad Santos Snr., a killing ordered by Tsuji.

The March 4 edition of the Japanese daily newspaper,

Four weeks after his first election victory, Masanobu Tsuji, member of the Japanese House of Representatives, delivers his maiden speech in the Diet. It is vintage Tsuji.

Yomiuri Shimbun, carried a startling story by Kawaguchi headed: "I was innocent but punished for Staff Officer Tsuji's crime." The account described how Tsuji had ordered Abad Santos' execution. It went on to berate Tsuji's conduct during the fighting on Guadalcanal which had resulted in Kawaguchi's withdrawal from the island in disgrace and his ultimate early retirement from the military.

The controversy generated by Kawaguchi's accusations, amazingly enough, had only modest impact on Tsuji's political support. In elections held the following month, he was safely returned. However, he fell from first to second place in the three-seat prefectual line-up and his votes dropped to a total of 50,090.

Soon after the 1953 polls, he was asked by a reporter to outline his political directions for the up-coming parliamentary term. Tsuji said he intended pressing for the abandoning of Japan's pro-American policies and a revision of the constitution imposed on the country by US Supremo, MacArthur. In addition, he would work hard to prevent the nation's security forces becoming Washington's hired troops. These forces, he maintained, must be allowed to evolve into an effective self-defence system, ready to defend the motherland from both internal and external threats.

But eight months as a Diet member had been enough to convince the power-hungry Tsuji that the role of an independent representative carried with it strict limitations. If he was to forge a career in big-time politics, he would have to become identified with one of the country's main power groupings. So it was he began spreading word of his willingness to join any party supporting his armed neutrality stand.

Tsuji's timing was impeccable. The recent elections had provided clear evidence that Japan's left-wing parties were expanding their influence. Worried conservatives concluded there was an urgent need to unite right-wing elements, in particular the Liberal and Progressive parties. One of the prime movers behind this consolidation was Bukichi Miki, secretary general of the Liberal party and one of its founders. Miki was at this time one of his country's most powerful behind-scenes politicians.

As a means of canvassing nation-wide support for the idea of a united right, Miki dispatched four separate political teams around the country. He chose Tsuji to lead one of these. Thus the mass killer became a key player in one of the most important episodes of political manoeuvring in post-war Japan. As a direct result, the Japanese Democratic Party was inaugurated in 1954 with Tsuji as one of its founder members. Enshrined in the party's platform were pledges covering two of Tsuji's key political goals: improved Japanese relations with China and the USSR and reform of the national constitution. By the end of that year, the Democratic Party was in government. Twelve months later the Liberal and Democratic parties had merged to become the Liberal Democratic Party (LDP) which has ruled Japan ever since. Significantly, in the LDP's original platform was a call for the review and voluntary revision of Japan's postwar constitution.

Obviously emboldened by his growing importance in the run-up to the Democratic Party's formation, Tsuji characteristically began perceiving an even loftier political roll for himself; this time on the international stage. A visit to Japan in late 1953 by the then Vice President of the United States, Mr Richard M. Nixon, inspired an extraordinary personal approach by the Japanese politician.

On his return to Washington, Nixon received a rambling six-page letter from Tsuji, written from the Diet building in Tokyo. Dated December 10, 1953, it offered the writer's services as a virtual personal adviser to the Vice President on a whole range of Asian subjects, but particularly on the highly controversial matter of Japanese re-armament.

Tsuji told Nixon that the country's self defence budget

should be "appropriate" to Japan's "national power." The main force should consist of a kernel of several well-equipped divisions "to act against specific and direct aggression." There should also be air and naval forces for passive self-defence, together with civil forces, or auxiliaries, "to meet domestic violence or revolution."

His letter went on: "I do not propose to go into details of my plan here, but I will always be willing, if you wish, to give you concrete data concerning it. I should like to have your opinion on the foregoing matter."

In the opening paragraphs, Tsuji at first praised Nixon for admitting in a speech that the United States' policy towards Japan in 1946 had been a mistake and that re-arming the defeated nation should now be encouraged. But then he bluntly chided the Vice President for failing to take his criticism of America one step further and condemn US policy decisions that had engineered the trial of "major" Japanese war criminals by the International Military Tribunal for the Far East (IMTFE).

"Is it really reasonable, " he asked, "that the victor, as one of the participants in a war, should try the vanquished, the other participant?"

Tsuji then turned to one of his original political hobbyhorses: "According to my opinion — if God, from his impartial position, tried all of those who participated in the late World War — Mr Truman, the former President of the United States, should be the first war criminal for his supreme responsibility for the atomic-bomb attacks on Hiroshima and Nagasaki, killing more than 200,000 non-combatants, and for the planned indiscriminate bombing of Japanese cities and towns, killing thousands of unarmed residents thereof."

Joseph Stalin, said Tsuji, would be pronounced the No 2 war criminal by the Almighty because the USSR leader was responsible "for such atrocities in Manchuria and Korea as the history of mankind has never before produced . . ."

One particularly interesting segment of the letter spoke of

the need for the United States to correct the status of Sino-Japanese relations. Tsuji urged that America allow Tokyo to establish immediate "economic and diplomatic communications" with the communist government in Peking. Given the politics of the day, this was a decidedly curious request from a supposedly staunch anti-communist, actively involved at the time consolidating his country's conservative elements against a perceived expanding left-wing threat.

Tsuji took the issue further. He asked Nixon to consider the possibility of the United States using Japan as a conduit through which to demonstrate "more good-will and support for the economic construction of China than the USSR . . . . ." This way, Tsuji said, Nixon could induce Communist China to move from behind the Iron Curtain into the Asian camp — a neutral camp with good will towards the United States.

Some two decades later, the then President Nixon secretly dispatched his Secretary of State, Mr Henry Kissinger, to Peking and startled the world with a daring switch in US policy towards Communist China. Ironically, Washington's radical new approach to Peking bore striking similarities to those original proposals outlined by Masanobu Tsuji, Japanese parliamentarian and war criminal extraordinaire.

Before concluding his December 1953 letter, Tsuji, not one to miss a promotional opportunity, told Nixon he was posting, by separate mail, a copy of *Underground Escape* which he described as "the record of my humble experiences." He expressed the hope that the Vice President would read the book and find it "useful to your Asian policy."

With the coming of the new year, Tsuji sensed he was on the threshold of important public office. He felt confident he would soon be offered at least the position of Vice-Minister for Defence. Only one issue threatened his ambitions. It was that persistent war criminal stigma, kept alive through continuing public denunciations by a livid Kawaguchi. Tsuji resolved to crush the threat once and for all.

He knew the next elections, though yet unannounced, were only weeks away. Determined to clear his name before the campaigning began, he agreed to engage Kawaguchi in a public showdown debate. Tsuji set the date: January 18. He also chose the venue: His hometown, Kanazawa.

The crowd jammed the hall and spilled onto the streets outside. An angry, aging, partially deaf general was simply no match for the ostentatious orator performing in the very heartland of his following. Long before a formal winner could be declared the debate disintegrated in uproar. Tsuji had cunningly devised the occasion as a spectacular springboard for his electoral campaign which he fought, this time, with the support of the Democratic Party. His tactics proved outstandingly successful.

Forty days later, on February 27, 1955, he was resoundingly re-elected to represent Ishikawa's first district. He won the support of over 83,000 voters, a record for the prefecture, and returned to top position on the candidates' list. As one Japanese commentator would write: "It was as if Kawaguchi had never made his accusations."

T suji's political star had never been brighter. The Democratic Party had emerged the major political grouping in the Diet and the "god of strategy" returned to Tokyo fully expecting to be rewarded with a ministerial position. But it was not to be. Tsuji was by-passed when Prime Minister Ichirou Hatoyama came to choose his second cabinet. The rumours of Tsuji's war criminal past were seemingly regarded by party power brokers as still too heavy a risk. Then, of course, there was the matter of his temperament.

In reality, there was little common ground between Tsuji and the majority of his supposed conservative allies. His relentless public statements on corruption and vigorous opposition to salary increases for Diet members became regular catalysts for intra-party friction. His overbearing, dogmatic style grated. Personality conflicts erupted and it was not long before he found himself banished from the party inner circle.

In November, 1956, he was linked to an ugly local scandal. Tsuji's eldest son, Toru, widely recognised as his father's political secretary, was charged with physically attacking his estranged wife. The incident attracted lurid press reports which, in turn, prompted numerous calls for Tsuji's resignation.

At the time, the Middle East was embroiled in the Suez Crisis. Ever the strategist, Tsuji decided to divert Japanese public attention from the scandal at home by embarking on a globe-trotting mission. It would, he hoped, gain him decidedly more responsible headlines. Along with him, interestingly enough, went his trusted assistant during the Malaya campaign and initial Singapore occupation period, Shigeharu Asaeda. According to Asaeda, he travelled as Tsuji's English language interpreter. Tsuji could speak both Chinese and Russian but not English.

By late January, 1957, the two former staff officers, both once wanted by the British for their roles in the Singapore massacres, had flown to Cairo and were about to embark on an amazing six-week trek through international corridors of power. They were surely the oddest of emissaries, yet at no time during the journey did ghosts from the past come to block, or even haunt, their progress. Indeed, wherever they went, they were received with warmth and admiration.

Egyptian strongman, President Gamal Abdel Nasser, willingly posed for photographs with the two Japanese visitors before, during and after their lengthy conference. Nasser offered his views on the Suez Crisis and, in turn, listened to Tsuji expound his ideas for an independent, non-aligned, neutral Japan.

By the first week in February, Tsuji and Asaeda were in Belgrade as official guests of the Yugoslav Government. On February 4 they were immersed in discussions with one of the

I was ashamed when I learned that upon your departure from Japan the speaker of the House of Representatives of the Japanese Diet presented you a set of Japanese armor which was a national treasure. If you had declined to receive this present, saying that it was the Japanese themselves who should defend their mother-country as did their ancesters clad in this armor, and put it on Premier Yoshida, your visit to Japan would have gained vastly.

In closing this letter, I sincerely hope that, with your young passion, your boldness to correct mistakes and your good sense, you will achieve your great mission of assisting President Eisenhower, whom I heartily respect, in the saving of mankind from the crisis of utter destruction. I offer my best wishes for your good health.

Respectfully yours,

Masanobu Tsuji

The concluding lines of Tsuji's December 10, 1953 letter to Vice President Richard M. Nixon.

Masanobu Tsuji, parliamentarian, walks from the Diet Building in Tokyo. Both photographs, taken in 1957, show Tsuji as a Liberal Democratic Party member before his ouster from the ruling party.

314

founders of the world Non-Aligned Movement, President Josip Tito. It was while in Belgrade that the duo finalised the most audacious segment of their itinerary. While enroute back home, they would make a side-trip to Communist China. As Japan had no diplomatic relations with Peking, the issuing of visas alone called for delicate organisation.

For almost two weeks nothing was heard of the two Japanese travellers. Then, suddenly, they emerged in Peking where, on February 27, they held a wide ranging, three-hour meeting with Chinese Premier Chou En-lai. As always, photographs were an important requirement from Tsuji's point of view and the Chinese leader seemed more than happy to oblige. He posed separately with Tsuji and in a group shot where Asaeda stood on his right and Tsuji on his left. Throughout their stay, the Chinese government received the two unofficial emissaries from Tokyo with what was described as "exceptional hospitality." When it came time for them to leave, government officials were at the airport to bid farewell in a formal display of respect.

Back in Japan, Tsuji's career found direction once more. But the roller coaster of political fortune would carry him into a particularly steep dive in time for the next general elections on May 22, 1958. Although he won a seat, it was obvious his public appeal had plummeted since the previous polls. A dejected Tsuji wanted to retire and only reluctantly agreed to remain in politics after pressure from close advisers, prominent among them being Asaeda.

The reluctant representative from Ishikawa soon fell foul of the new Prime Minister, Nobusuke Kishi, whom he had known during his military days in Manchuria. Tsuji had been a young staff officer in the Kwantung Army when Kishi was director of the Department for Manchurian National Industries. Relationships between them had been amicable enough in the old days, but the back-biting world of politics quickly changed all that. Tsuji became hostile immediately Kishi was appointed the Democratic Party's Secretary General. His animosity reached a climax in December, 1958, when, during a session of the House of Representatives, he openly accused the Prime Minister of buying votes in the course of the previous electoral campaign. Once again, Tsuji was at the centre of turmoil in the House. This time, however, he had gone too far and he was formally ejected.

Resorting to his favourite steamroller tactics, Tsuji maintained a barrage of criticism aimed at Kishi until he achieved his objective. In April, 1959, the ruling Liberal Democratic Party (LDP) expelled him. Revelling in the publicity, Tsuji swiftly announced his candidacy for the House of Councillors' elections scheduled for June 2. He ran an independent campaign on an anti-Kishi platform, struck a responsive chord with the electorate and spectacularly won a seat in the Upper House, totalling over 683,000 votes. He had gained the third highest following in the National Constituency.

Retired Major General Kiyotake Kawaguchi could stand it no longer. Working from home, he spent several days and nights preparing a lengthy written exposé of Tsuji's wartime activities, enumerating the atrocities for which the "god of strategy" had been responsible. In addition, Kawaguchi drafted an open letter to the newly elected Councillor, summarizing the atrocities and demanding he resign from the House of Councillors and apologise to the world.

Kawaguchi personally travelled to Tokyo on June 22 and circulated copies of both damning documents among members of the Upper and Lower Houses. It was a political bombshell for which Tsuji appeared to have no immediate counter. Yet another public scandal was swirling around his name and once again the Japanese newspapers were having a field day.

"You, Mr Tsuji," challenged Kawaguchi in his open letter, "were the planner, instigator, and executor of the Massacre of

Cairo, late January, 1957. Egyptian President Gamal Abdel Nasser is flanked by two self-satisfied globetrotting Japanese emissaries: Shigaharu Asaeda (left) and parliamentarian Masanobu Tsuji.

Cementing friendship with a handshake; Egyptian President Nasser (left) and Tsuji.

Belgrade, February 4, 1957. Masanobu Tsuji (facing camera second from left) in conference with Yugoslav President Josip Tito (facing camera second from right).

317

Peking, February 27, 1957. Chinese Premier Chou En-lai (fourth from left) poses for photographs after a three-hour meeting in the Chinese capital with Japanese guests Asaeda (on his right) and Tsuji (on his left).

Tsuji (left) in separate conversation with Chou En-lai.

Once a soldier, always a soldier. Tsuji, now a politician, goes on manoeuvres with Japan's National Security forces.

Singapore Chinese merchants, the Bataan Death March, the massacre of doctors and nurses at Alexandra Military Hospital in Singapore, and the atrocious murder of the leading Philippine government official, Jose Abad Santos, and many other terrible acts."

The Major General continued: "For these acts, many of our superiors, colleagues and men were branded war criminals following the end of hostilities, and were confined to prison for many years and, in extreme cases, they were put to death."

Kawaguchi claimed Tsuji had misrepresented and insulted him in his book, *Guadalcanal*, and that this was inexcusable behaviour for a military man.

"Your actions and statements as a politician in recent years are either playing up to the people or publicity-seeking. There can be found no constructive opinions in what you have said or done. They run counter to our nation's traditional political morality and they are to be despised. You are absolutely without qualifications to be a member of the National Diet."

If this was tough language, the accompanying document, an expanded explanation of the accusations contained in the letter, was tougher still.

Dealing first with the Singapore massacres, Kawaguchi maintained that Tsuji had drawn up an order for the purge of "two million" Chinese merchants in the Malayan Peninsula and Singapore. He placed the minimum death toll in Singapore at 2,000 and the maximum at 10,000.

Kawaguchi explained that Singapore had been divided into six separate military police districts for the purpose of the massacres.

"Staff Officer Tsuji made the rounds of the six military police stations, stepped up the liquidations and witnessed the executions. If there were some who tried to escape, he admonished and egged on the military police and made them carry out the execution."

Turning to the subject of the Bataan Death March,

Kawaguchi said:

"Some time after the fall of Singapore, Mr Tsuji was reassigned as Staff Officer of the Imperial General Headquarters (chief of operations group). Around the time of the fall of Bataan, he arrived in the Philippines to direct the operations. On April 9, he arrived at the 16th Army General Headquarters which was stationed near Mariveles in Bataan. His arrival coincided with the surrender of Major General King and many other officers of the US Philippine Army, who came down from the mountains to surrender. Mr Tsuji demanded that the Senior Staff Officer of the 16th Army, Colonel Saburo Watanabe, kill all prisoners of war of the US Philippine Army surrendering at the time. Senior Staff Officer Watanabe naturally refused. When the Commanding General of the 16th Army, Lt General Morioka, heard about this, he was extremely angered, and immediately sent Mr Tsuji packing. Staff Officer Tsuji, who regarded this treatment with great dissatisfaction, sent an order to the commanding officer of supplies, who was in charge of the treatment of prisoners of war, demanding their harsh treatment in the name of the Staff of the Imperial General Headquarters."

Expanding on his charges that Tsuji was directly responsible for the Alexandra Hospital Massacre, Kawaguchi said the colonel had arranged the mass killing of medical staff and patients in retribution for the heavy casualties British artillery had inflicted on Japanese forces in the area. Tsuji accused the hospital of giving protection to British gunners.

Kawaguchi's allegations on the Alexandra Hospital massacre are particularly interesting in the light of Richard Crewdson's recollections that Tsuji was initially wanted by the British for this crime as well as the massacre of Singapore Chinese. Pointedly, it can be proved conclusively that Tsuji was at the forward headquarters of the Japanese unit responsible for the attack on the hospital, and just three hundred yards from the massacre scene, when the killing began.

On the murder of Philippine Chief Chief Justice Jose Abad Santos, Kawaguchi said: "This incident involves me personally, and as it is a complicated and mysterious affair, I will leave out the details.

"It happened that Staff Officer Tsuji, after completing his tour of inspection of Bataan mentioned above, came to the Military Headquarters at Manila on April 10. I recommended by telegram that a high government official of the Philippines, Jose Abad Santos, whom my men had captured, be used for military administration. Staff Officer Tsuji's reaction to the cable I had dispatched was to issue a strong demand to the Military Headquarters in Manila to 'kill Santos immediately,' and force them to issue the order."

Kawaguchi went on: "I tried two more times to save Santos and to take steps to get him to cooperate with our country, but I was unable to oppose the three successive orders from the Military Headquarters and was forced to carry out this execution.

"This Santos was an extremely fine gentleman, and if he had been alive, he would very likely have become president. No words can express the loss the execution of such a man means. Because of this, I was sentenced to a six-year imprisonment, and spent seven years and three months in Sugamo Prison and the prison in Muntinlupa in the Philippines."

Kawaguchi then summarised a number of other atrocities with which he connected Tsuji and observed: "In short, Mr Tsuji's atrocities rival those of the Jewish manhunt by the Nazis and the Soviet Union's Katyn Forest, where a number of Polish citizens were killed. German and Soviet atrocities were carried out by organisations, but in the case of Mr Tsuji, he did it on his own initiative."

The Germans had confined their atrocities to their own territory. But, insisted the old general, Tsuji had resorted to such acts in every part of Asia. Nero in the West, and Chieh and Chou of China had long been regarded symbolically cruel rulers. Japan, however, had not witnessed such men in her history until Tsuji. The staff officer had been regarded as a "god of strategy". But he had not been a god, rather a satan, maintained Kawaguchi.

Concluding his diatribe, Kawaguchi said his conscience and sense of justice could not tolerate Tsuji, who had deceived 683,000 good people with his "insufferable words", being elected to the House of Councillors.

Tsuji should resign "in the name of my past friend, Lt General Kawamura, who lost his life because of Mr Tsuji, in the name of the souls of those people who were executed, in the name of the ghosts of my former men, who gave up their lives on the southern islands, and in the name of their bereaved families."

The US Embassy in Tokyo duly reported to the State Department on the furore and dispatched to Washington full translations of both documents distributed by Kawaguchi.

Dated June 10, 1959, and signed on behalf of the ambassador by the counselor, Mr Harlan B. Clark, the report provided a thumbnail sketch of the feud between Kawaguchi and Tsuji and made the following comments:

"Tsuji's propensity for gaining headlines has kept him in the public eye, both during the war when journalists bestowed on him the title of "god of strategy" and in the postwar era when his independent, outspoken views have often brought him into conflict with the government party of which he was a member.

"One recent article in the *Shukan Bungei* mentioned recurrent rumours that Tsuji was engaged in espionage activities for the Soviet Union and Communist China which he visited in recent years. It is a well known fact, however, that Tsuji's inability to get along with others has earned him wide-spread enmity of which Kawaguchi's represents only a small portion."

The Embassy's report concluded with a curious final paragraph. "While it is not possible to determine the validity of

Kawaguchi's allegations against Tsuji, it appears likely that they contain more than a kernel of truth. More important, perhaps, is the fact that these charges are currently receiving considerable publicity."

So, was the Embassy privy to the protection afforded Tsuji by Willoughby a decade earlier and just fudging the embarrassment? Or was it really in the dark? Either way, it is difficult to ignore the report's somewhat casual indifference towards the accusations that had been made about the deaths of thousands of US servicemen in the Bataan Death March. After all, this was the worst collective atrocity inflicted on US fighting men in World War 11 ∎

Chapter 21

Chasing past glories

———— ◆ ————

While, in 1959, Japan's political world reeled from the latest Tsuji wartime scandal, earnest Australian admirers of the Japanese staff officer turned politician worked diligently to publish his Singapore book in the English language.

Mr Hedley Vicars Howe, who had been Military Secretary to the Australian Minister for the Army from 1940 to 1946, was in the final stages of editing the translated manuscript. A more than happy to oblige Lt. General H. Gordon Bennett, Commander, Australian Imperial Force in Malaya, 1941-2, was busy at his home in Turramurra, New South Wales, writing the requested introduction.

The Australians decided to call their English language edition: *Singapore, the Japanese version.*

The original text, part of Tsuji's massive hoax to conceal the truth of his monstrous wartime activities and portray himself as a rational, learned authority on the conflict, conveniently concludes with the fall of Singapore. No reference is made to the massacres which began immediately thereafter and for which he was directly responsible. Indeed, in none of Tsuji's books is there reference to any of the atrocities that can be directly linked to him.

The late Mr Louis Allen, a former Royal Army Intelligence Corps officer and, until his death in early 1992, Britain's foremost expert on Japanese war criminals, dismissed Tsuji's

Singapore book as a "megalomaniac account." If you relied on it, he said, you would have to believe the author waged the campaign almost single-handedly.

Mr Allen, who was Honorary Fellow at the East Asian Studies Centre, Durham University for many years, regarded Tsuji as one of the most "interesting and preposterous figures of the entire Japanese war."

But far from considering Tsuji preposterous or monstrous, the Australians took the mass killer very seriously indeed.

In his editorial notes to the English language edition, Mr Howe described writing to Tsuji in 1953 and telling him:

"It is, I think, of the utmost importance that history should be fully and accurately recorded, and this cannot be done unless Allied historians are able to read the Japanese account of the campaign in Malaya written by the officer principally responsible for its planning and execution. In order that the operations of the Japanese Army may be correctly presented to the English-speaking peoples of the world, I strongly urge upon you the desirability of publishing an English translation of your book."

The publication finally came onto the Australian market in 1960 with all footnotes supplied by the editor. On the subject of Tsuji's sudden disappearance from Bangkok after Japan's capitulation, Mr Howe noted: *"When the war ended, Colonel Tsuji was ordered by the Japanese High Command to disappear and preserve himself for the reconstruction of Japan. In disguise, he spent some years wandering through Siam, Indo-China and China before returning to Japan."*

Even more outlandish were the book's introductory remarks by General Bennett who controversially fled Singapore hours after the British surrender, leaving orders forbidding all surrendered Australian servicemen from attempting similar action.

Said Bennett: *"Every soldier worthy of the name pays ungrudging tribute to the military capacity of his outstanding opponents. I have no hesitation in recognizing Colonel Masanobu Tsuji as one of the ablest of mine."*

Briefly reviewing Japan's Malayan campaign, Bennett went on to lavish further praise: *"Colonel Tsuji's career proves him a master planner and an outstanding field officer. He now appears an excellent writer and is to be congratulated upon his book, and also upon the motives which led to his escape from the Allied forces after the national surrender, of which he tells in another book, Underground Escape.*

As if this were not enough, Bennett then made the mind-boggling observation that Tsuji, like many soldiers in all countries, seemed subject to strong religious influences. He had pondered the consequences of defeat in the light of his Buddhist faith and determined that a paramount obligation had been imposed upon him to work for the regeneration of his country.

The former Australian commanding officer concluded: *"With the approval of higher Army authority he thereupon evaded arrest by Allied forces, disappeared, and for three years wandered through Asia, until, cleared of all charges against him, he was able to return to Japan, which he now serves as a Member of the House of Councillors in the National Diet."*

Australian newspapers in their book reviews heaped further kudos on Tsuji and it wasn't long before the British press were following suit with one defence expert describing him as a "military strategist and planner of the highest calibre."

The Australian publishing house, Ure Smith Pty. Ltd., in Sydney, brought out the original English language edition of Tsuji's Malaya-Singapore book. It proved a most successful venture and several reprints followed. In 1988, the prestigious Oxford University Press issued a paperback edition authoritatively titled: *Singapore 1941-1942 — The Japanese Version of the Malayan Campaign of World War 11.*

In the three decades since first appearing in the English language, the book has become recognised among Western military authorities, historians and academics as the definitive Japanese word on what Oxford University Press editors chose to call *Japan's Greatest Victory — Britain's Worst Defeat*. Countless newspaper and magazine articles have been angled on its boasts, claims and assessments. Similarly, Tsuji is a repeatedly quoted authority in contemporary historical studies. As such, this book must rank unchallenged as the most calculatingly deceptive and cunningly distortive of all Pacific War accounts.

If Tsuji's grand deception was pulling the wool over the eyes of the world at large by 1960, at least the Japanese in their homeland were beginning to have serious second thoughts about their publicity-hogging Upper House member. He had made too many political enemies during the previous decade and there were just too many unanswered questions about his wartime past. Despite championing free text books for students and demanding that educational publications become more directly involved stirring up nationalist feelings, Tsuji's popularity dived to an all time low by the end of 1960. Worse still, the Japanese press had become bored with him.

It is difficult to pin down exactly when the "god" devised his last piece of desperate strategy aimed at preserving both his hoax and his career. But it seems likely this occurred in the first few weeks of 1961. He was now 58 years of age. Looking back on his incredible life, the fading Tsuji must have been convinced, more than ever, that the real high points had all occurred overseas. The stuff of the Tsuji myth was international adventurism. If he was to retrieve lost glory and rekindle public fascination with the phoney aura that once surrounded him, he would have to leave Japan and embark on one final, dramatic foray.

Perhaps not surprisingly, he chose to return to Indo-China through which he had spent time travelling after fleeing

Bangkok in October 1945. The two Vietnams, Cambodia and Laos were simmering with intrigue and already erupting in renewed violence. The 1954 Geneva accords which allowed the defeated French to withdraw, albeit ignominiously, from the morass of the first Indo-China conflict, were proving ineffectual against Hanoi's determination to impose communism on the entire region.

America under President John F. Kennedy supported the South Vietnamese administration headed by President Ngo Dinh Diem and his influential brother, Ngo Dinh Nghu. Furthermore, Washington had begun to assign civilian and military advisors to the country, the first step to inevitable major commitment.

Hanoi, for her part, was busily expanding the communist guerrilla network she had been reviving in South Vietnam throughout the late 1950's. In addition, she was heavily involved training, supplying and advising the Pathet Lao insurgency in Laos and the Khmer Rouge in Cambodia. Communist China was ranged staunchly behind Hanoi. Moscow's support was more ambivalent, but showing signs of solidifying.

From Tsuji's viewpoint in early 1961, if ever there was an international military showdown in the making, Indo-China was it. Here was the ideal conflict for both his expertise and requirements. Family members and those close to Tsuji insist he was convinced he could make a major contribution to peace in Indo-China. If true, it is a fair measure of the delusion under which he lived for most of his adult life.

Before departing Tokyo, Tsuji informed those closest to him he was embarking on a 40-day personal inspection of South East Asia. He would, he said, be returning home in mid-May. Airline records revealed he flew into Saigon's Ton Son Nhut airport on April 4, 1961. During the next 10 days he visited Phnom Penh in neighbouring Cambodia. He made a brief stop-over in Bangkok, probably to obtain a Lao visa. Eventually he turned up at Vientiane, the administrative capital of Laos, where he openly enquired about tourist travel north to the royal capital of Luang Prabang.

Lao government officials subsequently found that Tsuji's announced plans for sightseeing in Luang Prabang were a cover. His real intention was to cross military lines and visit communist Pathet Lao rebels in Xieng Khouang, south-east of the royal capital. There he expected an interview with the Pathet Lao leader, Prince Souphanouvong.

On April 16, Tsuji is known to have boarded a local bus travelling north. But, at a regular checkpoint on the outskirts of Vientiane, he was removed from the vehicle by police and sent back. Undeterred by the government's intervention in his schemes, he decided on a characteristic ruse. Resorting to his penchant for disguise, he once more donned the robes of a Buddhist monk. Sallying forth in saffron splendour on April 21, he was this time able to bluff his way to a point 70 km north of Vientiane.

Here, his luck ran out when suspicious government forces seized and detained him.

The Tsuji trail now blurs. One report suggests the government side released him on May 5 whereupon he was promptly captured by Pathet Lao troops who held him for a further two weeks. There is certainly no indication that he succeeded in meeting Prince Souphanouvong. Back in Vientiane after being set free by the communists, Tsuji decided to abandon the Buddhist robes and return to the role of travelling Japanese politician.

He then ventured to the southern panhandle region of the kingdom travelling sometimes by road and sometimes by boat along the Mekong River. During this time he is believed to have moved in the company of communist groups.

On the morning of July 10, he was seen at Vientiane's airport boarding a Russian aircraft bound for Hanoi. At this point, the Tsuji trail blots out completely.

His term as a member of the House of Councillors lapsed on June 1, 1965.

He was officially pronounced dead on July 7, 1968.

But the Tsuji mystery persists to this day. Over the years, there have been numerous reports of him living in various parts of South East Asia. During the second Vietnam war, for instance, conflicting stories had him residing in both Hanoi and Saigon. As late as 1989-90, he was supposed to have been spotted in Bangkok and even in Singapore. Other information has placed him as far afield as Havana, Cuba. Japanese intelligence agents have pursued many leads. They insist all have led nowhere.

In 1978, war historian Hidehiko Ushijima claimed to have unearthed a treasure map revealing where Tsuji had secretly buried 23 gold bars. This was the loot the escaping staff officer had originally lifted from the Japanese Army's Bangkok reserves. (See page 266). The map came with a letter, supposedly written by Tsuji in 1954, asking a friend to retrieve the gold from its hiding place in central Hanoi. A Mainichi Shimbun account of the find failed to identify the historian's source for the map and letter.

Tsuji's family roundly rejected the newspaper story, claiming it was unthinkable money had motivated him in this way. Tsuji's wife, Chitose, was especially vocal. "There were a lot of groundless rumours floating around after the war about hidden gold. It was stupid," she said. "Some people even went to Hanoi looking for the treasure. This, too, was stupid. Someone forged the document to make my husband look bad. The kanji inside the map in particular don't look like his," she added.

But our research in Japan has revealed that the letter and map are indeed authentic. Both were handed personally by Tsuji to his friend and wartime associate, Shigeharu Asaeda.

Vientiane, Laos, April 21, 1961. One for the album. Japanese parliamentarian, Masanobu Tsuji, has his photograph taken in the saffron robes he used to disguise himself as a Buddhist monk for a trip to contested territory north of the Lao administrative capital.

The statue erected in January 1979 at Aratanimachi to commemorate Tsuji. This ten million yen gesture by a political following still loyal to his memory.is close to Imadachimachi, the town where the young Tsuji grew up.

Tsuji's childhood home at Imadachimachi in Ishikawa prefecture. The house is now uninhabited but the notice outside proudly names its former occupants.

This was verified for us by Asaeda himself who confirmed he gave copies of the map and letter to the historian in 1978. Asaeda further revealed he had travelled to Vietnam in 1954 on Tsuji's behalf in quest of the illicit gold hoard. But the sudden fall of Dien Bien Phu prevented him from going beyond Saigon.

The 1978 Mainichi Shimbun article claimed Tsuji was unable to go to Hanoi and retrieve his treasure because "he was a member of the Diet." However, Asaeda told our researcher, Cameron Hay, that Tsuji was scared to return to South East Asia in 1954 as he still feared British reaction.

Tsuji needed the gold to fund his political career. He instructed Asaeda to carry the bars to Hong Kong, if this was possible. Once in the British colony, Asaeda was to convert the bullion into American currency.

He advised Asaeda to approach American military intelligence in Vietnam for assistance and identified a "Colonel Blake" as the proper contact. The Americans were to be told that the gold represented the personal savings of various Japanese officers and war criminals. Tsuji advised his friend to offer the Americans a portion of the gold in exchange for their help.

Asaeda said he had never heard of anyone discovering Tsuji's gold stash in Hanoi. But he assumed it was no longer where Tsuji buried it and suspected "some Chinese in Vietnam" had learned about it and dug it up.

Then, was Tsuji after the gold when he left Vientiane for Hanoi? Asaeda denies this, offering as a more plausible explanation the likelihood that his wartime crony was on an intelligence gathering mission. Still, there are many who would take issue with Asaeda on this matter.

By the late 1970's, the 3,000 or so members of Tsuji's electoral group appeared to have accepted, finally, the news of his death. Together with a movement called the Self Defence Alliance, they raised ten million yen to erect a monument at

Aratanimachi, in Ishikawa prefecture, just outside Tsuji's boyhood hometown of Imadachimachi. The tribute, depicting a bespectacled Tsuji in civilian clothes, was unveiled in January 1979.

In the months following the mysterious flight from Vientiane, the Japanese Foreign Office became convinced that Tsuji, after arriving in Hanoi, had ultimately crossed the North Vietnamese frontier into Communist China.

Several Japanese newspapers revealed in 1967 that there existed intelligence reports indicating Tsuji had been a "quintruplicate spy" working for Communist China.

A Japanese source, identified as having held high office in one of the government security agencies, was quoted as saying Tsuji had intelligence links to five countries. He identified these as the United States, Britain, the Soviet Union, Communist China and Nationalist China. Tsuji, according to the source, had made his contacts with all five foreign intelligence networks during his World War 11 period in Yunnan, southern China. Chinese intelligence agents who fled from the mainland had testified receiving information from Tsuji during the war years.

The intelligence expert elaborated: "In our view he was, in principle, working in line with Communist Chinese policies.

"Peking aimed at dividing the (Japanese) conservative party during the uproar over the revised Security Treaty. The Communist Chinese expected Tsuji to play a roll in toppling the Kishi cabinet and manoeuvring to have Ichiro Kono, take over."

Peking's manipulations were prompted by the belief that Kono would prove more accommodating towards Communist China than Hayato Ikeda who, in the event, replaced Kishi.

This would certainly explain Tsuji's vehement anti-Kishi stand. Moreover, the possibility of Tsuji being an agent of the communist regime in Peking adds an intriguing dimension to his December, 1953, letter to US Vice President Nixon.

Why, then, would the Communist Chinese wish to eliminate

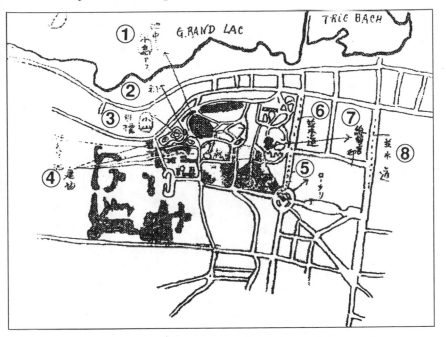

Tsuji appears to have hand-traced the basic outlines of this map from a published Hanoi road guide of the day. On the tracing he noted a total of eight distinguishing reference features within a section of the city immediately south of the large lake the French colonialists called Grand Lac and the Vietnamese renamed Ho Tay. For the purposes of identification we have numbered these 1 to 8.

No 1 has an arrow originating from what is described as "a pond with a small island." No 2 identifies the point where the 23 gold bars are buried. Here Tsuji has written the word "casket" — presumably a reference to the container in which he concealed the treasure.

No 3 indicates what Tsuji called "a small hill." This phrase has been encircled and alongside is written the word: "target."

It would appear that notations 1 to 3 were Tsuji's primary reference points for locating the gold which he buried at the eastern foot of the small hill at a point overlooking the pond. The remaining features apply more generally to approach routes. No 4 identifies three groups of buildings, No 5, a road roundabout, Nos 6 and 8, tree-lined streets, and No 7, a specific building.

Superimposed on a present-day Hanoi road map, the Tsuji drawing places the treasure trove in the city's Ba Dinh district, just south of Hoang Hoa Tham Street, and a few hundred metres north-west of the Ho Chi Minh Mausoleum site. The area was a French-built parkland and is retained as such today.

Tsuji's letter to Asaeda

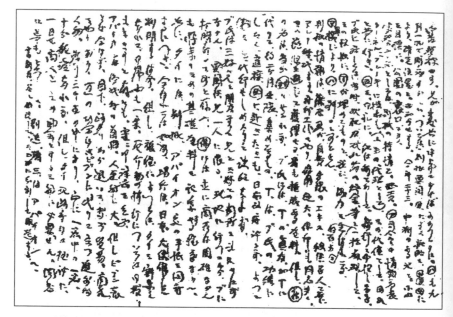

While Tsuji's wife, Chitose, questioned whether her husband had penned the the kanji characters on the map, she pointedly made no reference to the legitimacy of the accompanying letter. Asaeda is emphatic that Tsuji gave him both the map and letter. As a result, Asaeda travelled to Vietnam in the hopes of retrieving the treasure on his friend's behalf.

their man?

As the retired intelligence officer explained it, Peking had changed its mind about Tsuji. "At first, the Chinese apparently believed Tsuji kept contact with the other four nations to collect intelligence for Peking. But later they came to think the opposite was the case."

So, was it a matter of the Communist Chinese finally snuffing out the man whose rampant opportunism had grown insufferable? As an agent, had the Japanese Councillor become a distinct liability? These assertions were ridiculed at the time by Asaeda who maintained the execution theory was "unthinkable." He speculated that Tsuji was far more likely to have been held under detention "somewhere in China."

In 1983, Kinosuke Imai, a Japanese national born in China who had been imprisoned in a Chinese jail as a "counter-revolutionary," claimed he had evidence Tsuji was being held by the Peking authorities. In a Mainichi Shimbun story, Imai recalled meeting a former prison guard, then himself a prisoner. The guard had spoken of having known a Japanese man called "Suji" who fitted the description of the missing parliamentarian.

The man called "Suji" maintained he had been "a staff officer in the 18th Army" and had given the guard a Pilot clutch pencil. The pencil fitted the description of the one Tsuji had taken with him to Indo-China in 1961. The pencil was not among Tsuji's belongings left in Vientiane and finally returned to his family.

Imai's account immediately rekindled speculation of Tsuji's espionage activities. Years earlier, however, Tsuji's wife had also laughed off the spy theory.

"He's really a simple-minded man," Chitose Tsuji said. "Spy? Nonsense. I still wonder how he could have been a staff officer. He is, so to speak, a Don Quixote."

On November 28, 1986, the respected Japanese author and historian, Eitarou Tatamiya, writing in the *Asahi Shimbun,* painted a very different picture of Tsuji. Discussing means by which the Pacific War might have been avoided in the first place, he said one way would have been to throw out of the Staff Headquarters' Operations Department the combination that had pushed for Japan's "advance to the south." He identified the critical pair in this department as Hattori and Tsuji.

"It was this combination," wrote the historian, "that pressed the military leaders to break off US-Japan negotiations and open up hostilities."

Masanobu Tsuji; "god of strategy," perpetrator of massacres, cannibal, gold thief, master of disguise, best-selling author, haranguing politician, "quintruplicate spy," publicity-seeking moralist, unbridled opportunist and sometime Don Quixote. Here, surely, is the most bizarre character to emerge from the annals of the Pacific War.

But the Tsuji saga is far more than just a string of baffling tales. Its impact has been monstrously profound. The man and his grotesque machinations have been allowed to warp and mangle history. What is more, the Japanese, the British and the Americans must all share the onus for letting him get away with it ■

The grave that isn't.
Tsuji's official grave at the Kannon Jigan Temple in
Nozaki, Osaka Prefecture.

Index